IMAGES
of America

SCOTIA AND RIO DELL

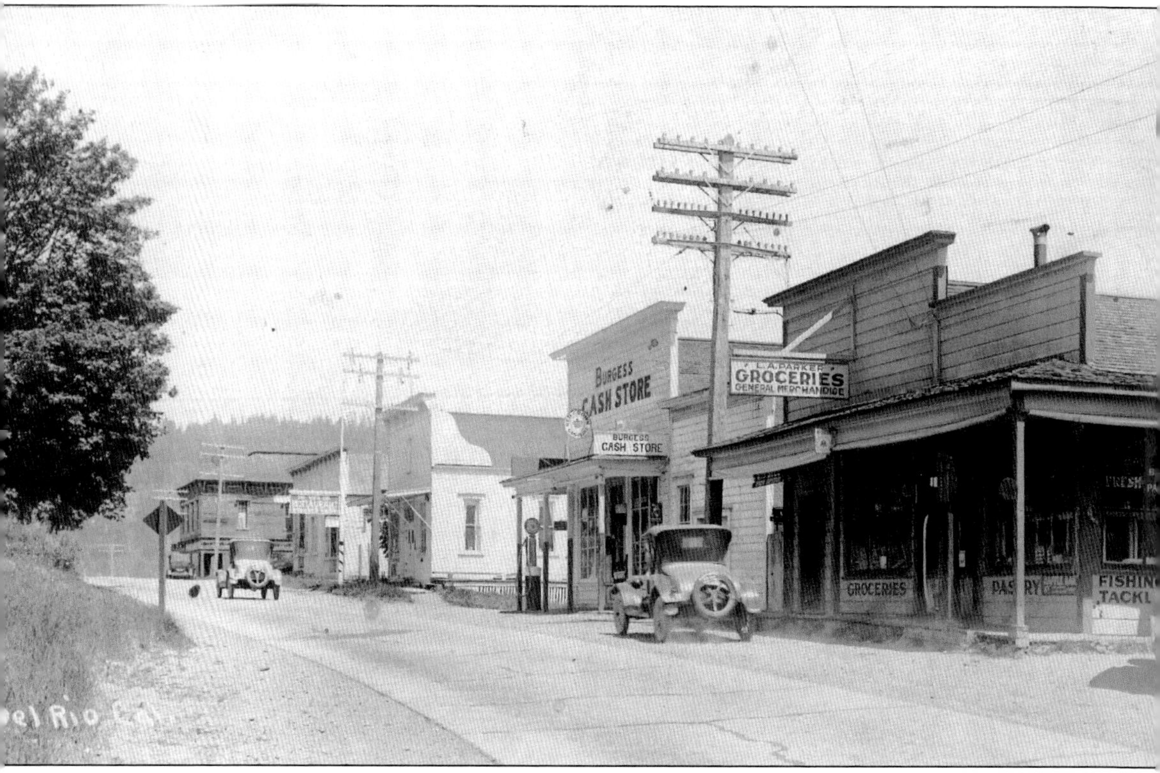

Rio Dell's Main Street, now Pacific Avenue, was the center of activity on Eagle Prairie from the 1880s until the 1920s. Stores, restaurants, and other businesses once thrived on this now quiet street. By the 1940s, most businesses on the prairie were located along present-day Wildwood Avenue. (Courtesy of the Humboldt County Historical Society.)

On the Cover: A handsome couple makes their way up the county road on Eagle Prairie past the Davis ranch in Rio Dell during the early 1900s. In the background, one can see that the Bayside Lumber Company has been busy logging the hillside above Nanning Creek on the Scotia Bluffs. (Courtesy of the Todd-Schuler/Bartleson family.)

IMAGES
of America

SCOTIA AND RIO DELL

James R. Garrison

ARCADIA
PUBLISHING

ISBN 978-1-4671-3316-6

Published by Arcadia Publishing
Charleston, South Carolina

Printed in the United States of America

Library of Congress Control Number: 2014950525

For all general information, please contact Arcadia Publishing:
Telephone 843-853-2070
Fax 843-853-0044
E-mail sales@arcadiapublishing.com
For customer service and orders:
Toll-Free 1-888-313-2665

Visit us on the Internet at www.arcadiapublishing.com

This book is dedicated to my loving wife, Lara Garrison. Without her strength and continuous support, I would not be who I am today.

CONTENTS

Acknowledgments

It has been said that any worthy endeavor is one percent inspiration and 99 percent perspiration. It is also said that nothing worth doing is easy, and without the help of librarians, museum curators, local historians, collectors, enthusiasts, and supporters, this book would not have become a reality. I would like to extend special thanks to all of those who were supportive in my research for this book. Thank you to Joan Berman, Kathryn Lasala, and Carly Moreno of Humboldt State University Library's Humboldt Room for your information, pictures, and allowing me to continuously bug you for more. Thanks also to Dr. Alex Service at the Fortuna Depot Museum, Eldon Whitehead, Barry Jeffers, the staff at the Ferndale Museum, the staff at the Humboldt County Historical Society, Don Tuttle at the Humboldt County Office of Public Works, the Mercer Frasier Company, Greg Rumney, Jerry Rohde, Frank Bacik at the Town of Scotia Company, Karen Bartleson, and the Myers family at Chapman's Gem and Mineral Museum for your pictures, stories, and assistance. Thanks also go to Lynette Mullen for putting me in touch with Arcadia Publishing.

I would also like to extend my gratitude to Paul Geck, Dr. Tom Mays, Dr. Gayle Olsen-Raymer, Dr. Robert Cliver, Dr. Dakota Hamilton, and the rest of the Humboldt State University History Department for starting me on this path and encouraging me every step of the way.

I would like to extend a very special thank-you to my good friend and fellow local history enthusiast Sean Mitchell. His writing skills, vast knowledge of local railroads, and tireless support and encouragement were instrumental in the making of this book.

Finally, I would like to thank my family for their unending patience and understanding as I labored through the challenging process of this book's creation. I could not have finished without them to cheer me on.

INTRODUCTION

Eagle Prairie's first non-native visitors were members of the Gregg-Wood party, whose historic and adventurous rediscovery of Humboldt Bay in 1849 opened the area to shipping, facilitating easier access to the goldfields to the east and to the Humboldt region for settlement. Following its discovery, the group split up, unable to reach a consensus over the route it should take south to San Francisco. Josiah Gregg led half the group along the coast, while Lewis K. Wood took the other half south along the Eel River, which the party named for the abundant Pacific lamprey the party had seen harvested from it by the local Wiyot people. Wood and his companions visited Eagle Prairie on their way through in January 1850. In June 1851, US Indian agent Redick McKee visited the still-unsettled and nameless valley, describing it in his reports to Washington, DC, as "an area of humid atmosphere bounded by the Eel River on the north, south, and east, and only by Indian trails to the west."

The lush river terraces of California's Eel River Valley, located in the heart of Humboldt County's majestic redwood forest, had since time immemorial been inhabited by the indigenous people. Eagle Prairie was home to a village belonging to the Bear River tribe. Some Wiyot people lived on the prairie as well and reportedly called the place Tokemuk. Another village sat on the riverside flat across the Eel River to the south called Tokenewolok, near the present-day site of Scotia. The people who lived here relied on the area's abundant resources for their subsistence. Salmon and lamprey were taken from the river, and game, wild berries, and seeds were harvested from the prairie and forests. Life for Northern California's native people was irrevocably changed after the discovery of gold in the Trinity Mountains in 1849. As settlers and fortune-seekers flocked to the area, native people were displaced from their traditional homes, resulting in conflicts and hostility between the indigenous people and the newcomers. Settlers and their livestock competed with the local Indians and game animals for food sources, and irresponsible mining practices wreaked havoc on Humboldt's once-pristine streams and rivers, causing serious damage to the local fisheries. To make matters worse, in 1850, the California legislature passed the Act for the Governance and Protection of Indians, which legalized the indenture of Indian children despite California having entered the Union as a free state. This essentially legalized Indian slavery and created opportunities for unscrupulous men to profit from the sale of Indian children. These factors worsened the already tense relations between the settlers and the indigenous people, leading to attacks on cattle and outlying homesteads. Hostilities between the native people and the new settlers continued in the area for nearly two decades.

With news of the discovery of Humboldt Bay came a flood of newcomers to the region. While many of these new arrivals came to strike it rich in the goldfields, others sought to settle in the area. It wasn't long before Eagle Prairie attracted the attention of settlers like William B. Shively, originally from Ohio, who filed a preemption claim in 1853 and began farming. The Shivelys were eventually joined on the prairie by other farming families, and as these newcomers transformed the once-wild prairie into orchards, farm plots, and grazing land, they increasingly came into conflict with the native people. During the early 1860s, these conflicts boiled to a head. Some indigenous people began to push back against white incursions, attacking homesteads and livestock. These attacks prompted violent reprisals from some members of the white population, and several horrific massacres against the local tribes were committed. Shively's farm was burned in 1864, prompting him to help out with rounding up and removing Humboldt's native people to reservations. In 1865, the Indian War came to an end with the removal of most local natives to the reservation established in Hoopa.

The late 1860s and 1870s saw significant growth in the fledgling community of Eagle Prairie, particularly with the arrival of another Ohio native, Lorenzo Dow Painter, in 1870. A shrewd businessman known to be somewhat eccentric, Painter played an important role in the building and development of the village of Rio Dell. He opened up a resort, the Rio Dell Hotel, which became a popular vacation spot in addition to hosting community celebrations and serving as a meeting place for conducting town business. Painter built a town meeting hall and arranged for a school to be built on his property. He also laid out the first streets in town, subdividing his property and selling lots for homes and businesses. He built the first waterworks and served as the town's first postmaster. Painter was instrumental in shaping the blossoming community that would become Rio Dell. While Rio Dell residents would remain focused on farming and dairying, the township also hosted a small but flourishing business district. By the 1880s, Main Street (Pacific Avenue today) featured a blacksmith, livery, millinery, mercantile store, grocery store, wine and liquor store, and saloon.

Soon, however, the primary occupation in the area became the timber industry, reaping the "red gold" of Northern California's ancient redwood forests. The sheer size of these giants made this job an imposing task. The men who took up this pursuit were first-rate innovators, often inventing the tools of the trade as required and adapting existing technologies where feasible to make the job of harvesting the giant trees possible. At first water and animal power were used to transport logs to the mills, but soon these methods were replaced by steam engines and railroads. The history of the Pacific Lumber Company (PL) began with the purchase of a 6,500 acre belt of some of the richest timberland in the county by Henry Weatherbee and A.W. McPherson of Mendocino County's Albion Lumber. In 1868, San Francisco banker William Ralston convinced McPherson that the "Humboldt tract" of Albion Lumber should be its own company with its own backing. With the purchase of another 4,000 acres, the new company was incorporated as the Pacific Lumber Company in 1869. When Ralston died in 1875, his holdings in PL were signed over to his friend Allen A. Curtis and his associates John A. Paxton, W.S. Gage, and John C. Hampton, known as the Nevada Big Four.

By 1882, the company was ready to begin timber operations in the county. Allegedly thwarted in its efforts to build its sawmill on Eagle Prairie, the company set up its operations across the river in a place known at the time as Forestville. By 1885, Pacific Lumber's railroad was complete, connecting its operations in Forestville with the Eel River & Eureka Railroad line at Alton. PL's railroad, built around the slide-prone Scotia Bluffs, was essential to its redwood timber enterprise, enabling it to get its lumber to the docks in Fields Landing.

In 1887, Pacific Lumber completed its sawmill, and timber fellers began clearing the area that would one day become the heart of the company-owned town of Scotia. The company set to work in earnest and produced a tremendous amount of timber products for California's housing booms. As the mill prospered and expanded, so did Scotia. By the middle of the 1890s, the town had grown to include a sawmill, shingle mill, railroad, and shop buildings, as well as a hotel, a cookhouse, a saloon, and 48 dwellings, all equipped with running water. There was also a company store, a creamery, and a meat market to supply the needs of the workforce. A fire in 1895 destroyed the sawmill and much of the town, forcing PL to rebuild, but this gave it an opportunity to upgrade its equipment and expand its operations. By the beginning of the 20th century, the company was one of the area's largest employers and lumber producers.

By 1905, the Pacific Lumber Company had control of a tremendous amount of the county's vast timberland. Simon J. Murphy, partnered with the Santa Fe Land Development Company, had gained control of PL's stock, in addition to the Eel River & Eureka Railroad, the Eureka & Freshwater Railroad, the Humboldt Logging Company, and the Excelsior Redwood Company. By 1905, Murphy had purchased all assets of the company outright, forming a new corporation separate from Santa Fe interests and incorporating as the Pacific Lumber Company of Maine. The family of Simon J. Murphy played a big role in the development of the Pacific Lumber Company and its town of Scotia, and the Murphy family are known in Humboldt County not only for their benevolent management and good forestry practices but also for their continued service and commitment to the community.

The Pacific Lumber Company adapted and changed with the times, both with regard to the company and to its town. Company-owned towns in America were very common, particularly in remote areas like Scotia, and many earned a reputation for exploiting their workers. These charges were often well founded, and in many company towns, serious abuses of power occurred regularly, leading to unrest and conflicts between labor and management. Scotia avoided many of these problems by adopting policies to address the welfare and happiness of the workforce and the community. PL's goal of creating not just a profitable and sustainable business but also a prosperous and contented community enabled Scotia to thrive for well over a century as a company-owned town.

By 1910, PL had finished construction of its second mill and the expansion of its log pond. As Scotia prospered and grew, so too did PL's workforce, soon outstripping the company's ability to house them. The jobs created with the construction of PL's new mill attracted many Italian immigrants to the area, many of whom found homes across the river near Rio Dell.

The south end of the prairie grew into a small community and came to be known as Wildwood or "Little Italy." Wildwood expanded as more homes and businesses were built, particularly after the construction of a bridge between Scotia and Wildwood in 1914. Wildwood soon gained a reputation for rowdy lumbermen, bootleg whiskey, and bordellos. By the time Prohibition went into effect in the United States in 1920, the Pacific Lumber Company management had closed down the bars in its town of Scotia but was powerless to curtail these sorts of activities across the river. Wildwood officially became part of Rio Dell with the opening of a new post office in the 1940s but retained its distinctiveness and reputation for many years to come.

The Pacific Lumber Company saw many changes over the years, both in management and in logging practices. The technology changed along with the company, as animals and manpower were gradually replaced by machinery. From teams of oxen and locomotives to crawler tractors and logging trucks, the company continued to work its holdings for generations, through good times and bad. Pacific Lumber is remembered fondly as a great place to work, and the communities that grew up around the mills as good places to live and raise families. What really made the Pacific Lumber Company special, however, was that it truly wanted to be a part of the communities it helped build.

Scotia and Rio Dell grew into towns together, separated by the Eel River but joined in the common purpose of seeing to the needs of the local workforce. They were like two halves of the same coin, one shaped by the vision of the paternalistic Pacific Lumber Company management into a well-ordered and prosperous community, the other formed in response to the needs of the local workforce that were not provided by Scotia, namely wine, women, and song. Today Northern California's timber industry, the primary economic engine for the region for well over a century, is a pale shadow of its former self, following in the steps of the county's once-thriving agriculture industry. The construction of sawmills and railroads helped shape our communities, creating jobs and opportunities and bringing long-term prosperity to the region. While the railroads, waste burners, and one-log loads are now a part of history, they live on in the collective memories of the families who have called this area home and who continue to make it a great place to live.

This book is not intended to be a complete or definitive history of Rio Dell, Scotia, or Humboldt County. Restricted to the confines of the cover, this is but a glimpse into a near-forgotten time through the photographic artifacts collected over the history of these places. It is the author's hope that this work will be enjoyed for what it is, namely a pictorial exhibit highlighting the past events of these communities and the towns they have grown into.

One

From Eagle Prairie to Rio Dell

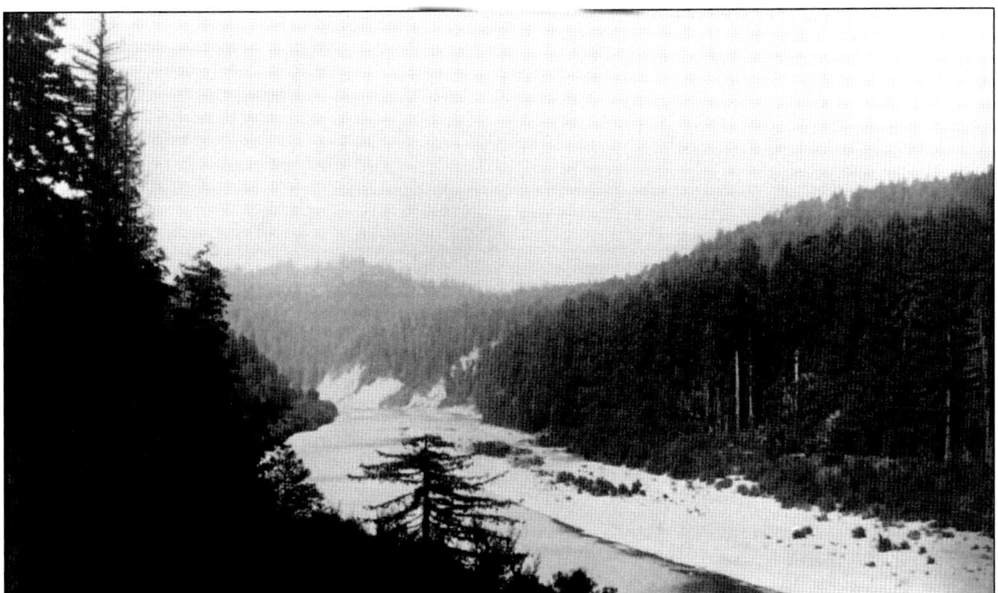

Situated on a wide bend of the Eel River and surrounded by the towering Scotia Bluffs, the river plateau that would become Rio Dell was once the southern boundary of lands inhabited by the Wiyot people. The warm valley—rich in game, covered in ferns, and dotted sporadically with redwoods—soon drew the attention of new settlers. (Courtesy of the Humboldt County Office of Public Works, Tuttle Collection.)

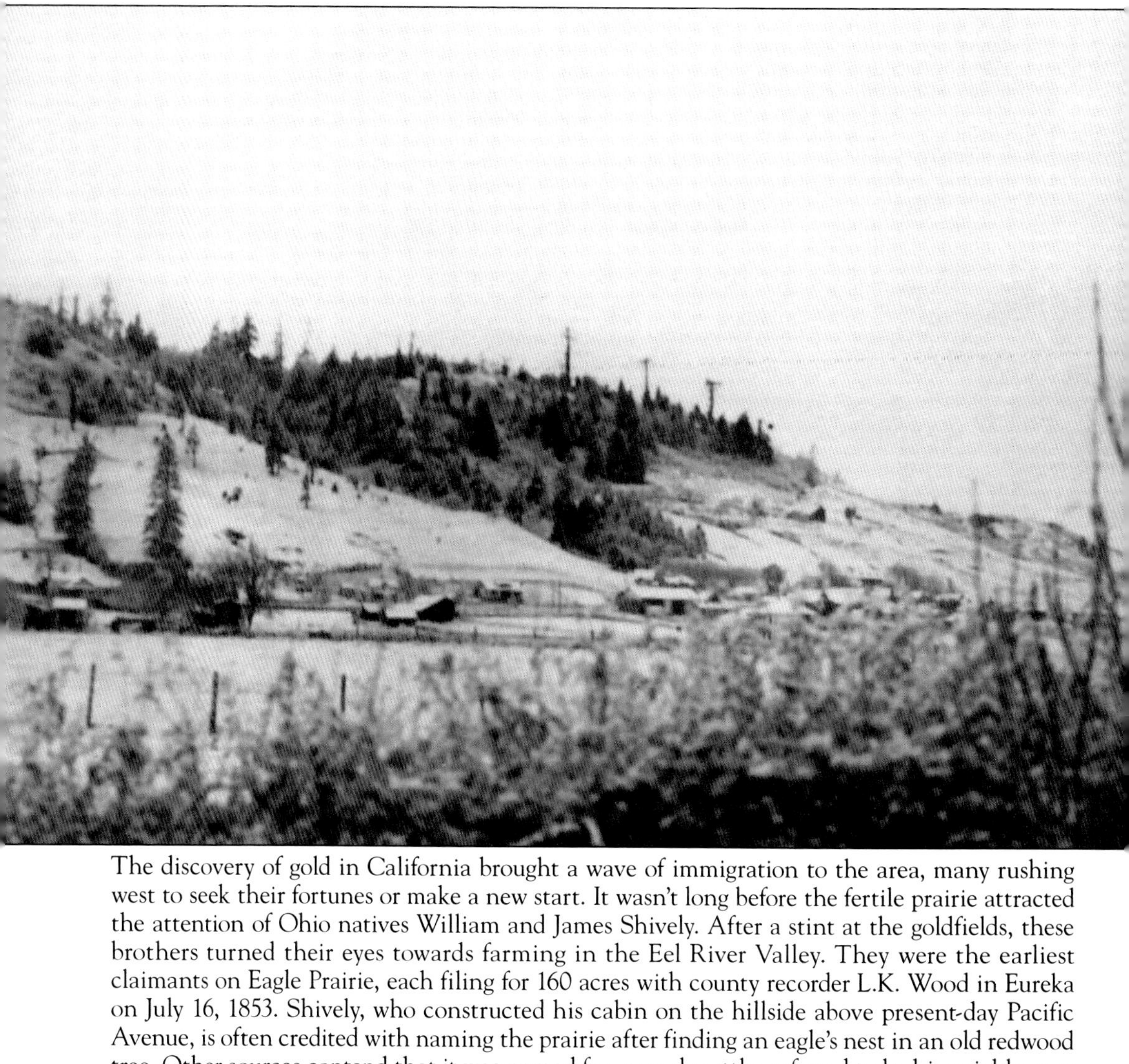

The discovery of gold in California brought a wave of immigration to the area, many rushing west to seek their fortunes or make a new start. It wasn't long before the fertile prairie attracted the attention of Ohio natives William and James Shively. After a stint at the goldfields, these brothers turned their eyes towards farming in the Eel River Valley. They were the earliest claimants on Eagle Prairie, each filing for 160 acres with county recorder L.K. Wood in Eureka on July 16, 1853. Shively, who constructed his cabin on the hillside above present-day Pacific Avenue, is often credited with naming the prairie after finding an eagle's nest in an old redwood tree. Other sources contend that it was named for an early settler referred to by his neighbors as "Old Eagle Beak." In 1874, the Shivelys moved upriver to Bluff Prairie, renamed Shively in later years in the family's honor. Eagle Prairie's population continued to grow, and it became home to many hard-working and industrious people in the coming years. (Courtesy of the Todd-Schuler/Bartleson family.)

The prairie and the country around it teemed with wildlife, drawing the attention of hunters and trappers like Seth Kinman, an eccentric frontiersman and an early pioneer to the Humboldt region. Kinman owned ranches on Table Bluff and on Bear River Ridge in the hills above Rio Dell to the southwest. He made much of his living by hunting, providing elk and deer meat for the citizens of Eureka and the soldiers at Fort Humboldt. He gained national fame for his gift of handmade elk-horn chairs to several US presidents, including Buchanan, Lincoln, Johnson, and Hayes. Kinman claimed to have been in Ford's Theater the night President Lincoln was shot and received nationwide press when he served in the president's funeral procession wearing buckskins and carrying his rifle, "Old Cotton-Blossom." Kinman toured the country with his elk-horn chairs and Indian artifacts, entertaining people with his outrageous frontier tales and his eccentric dress and personality. (Courtesy of the Ferndale Museum.)

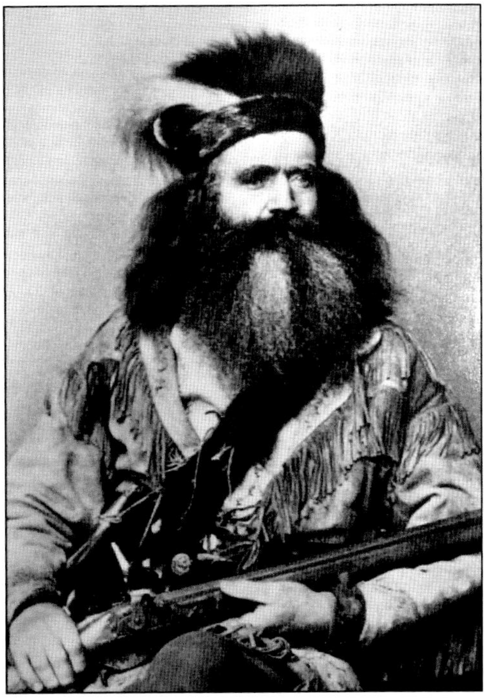

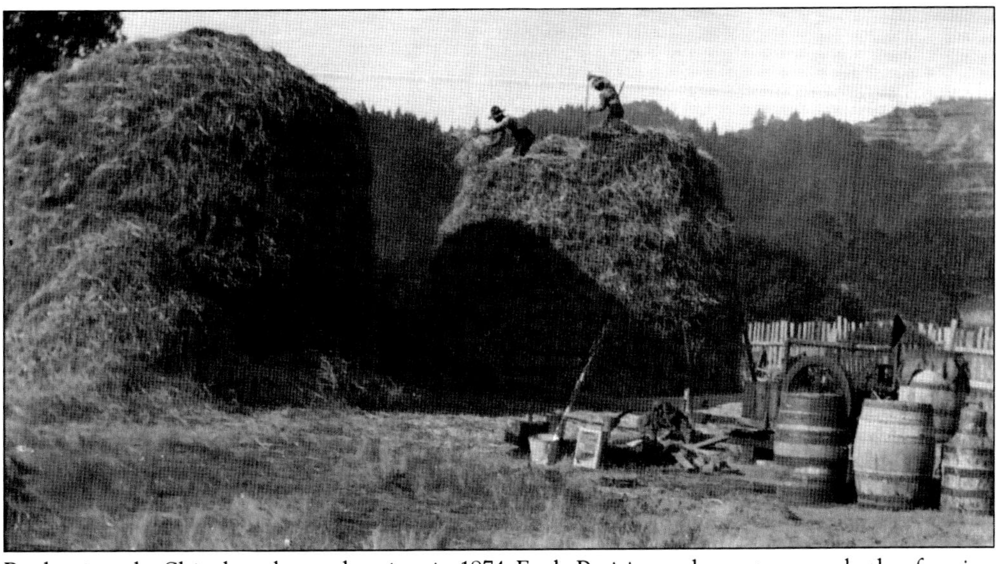

By the time the Shivelys relocated upriver in 1874, Eagle Prairie was home to several other farming and ranching families. Azel Fuller, Archibald Crisman, Hiram Dean, and others filed claims on the prairie in the 1860s and 1870s. These men made their living primarily by farming and ranching but kept their eyes open for other opportunities. A vein of coal was discovered by Crisman in the Scotia Bluffs, but it proved to be of insufficient quantity to make it worth mining. Another early settler to the area was Lorenzo Dow Painter, a carpenter by trade, who came to Humboldt County in the summer of 1870 and by 1874 had acquired nearly 500 acres on Eagle Prairie. The years between his arrival and his death in 1892 have been called the era of Lorenzo Painter in Rio Dell in honor of his tireless determination to convert the isolated prairie into a cohesive town. (Courtesy of the Humboldt County Historical Society.)

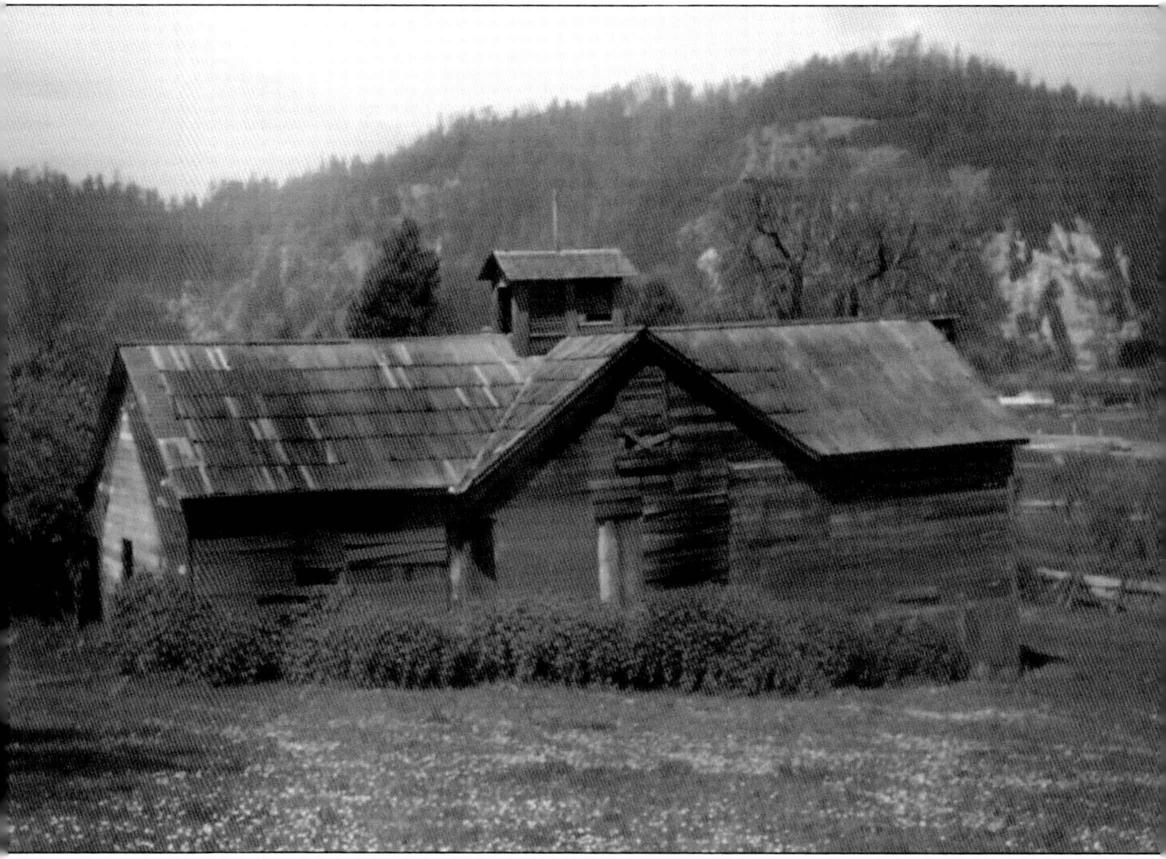

Few early settlers did as much to transform Eagle Prairie from a small collection of farms into a community as Lorenzo Painter. Well respected in the community, Painter was known for his generosity and leadership in founding Rio Dell as a legitimate township in the county. He took the initiative in building and maintaining public roads and schools and in establishing voting precincts, post offices, and other public improvements. Eagle Prairie's original schoolhouse was the first building erected on Painter's land, built in February 1874. Painter's wife, A.P. Painter, was elected as the new district's school trustee, making her the first female in the county to be elected to public office. Painter built the community's first waterworks, constructing a storage tank on the hill above his house from which water was delivered to residents in pipes made from redwood. A very public-spirited man, he later built a town "amusement hall" for community events and gatherings that he eventually deeded to the Rio Dell Liberal and Spiritual Society for one dollar. (Courtesy of Greg Rumney.)

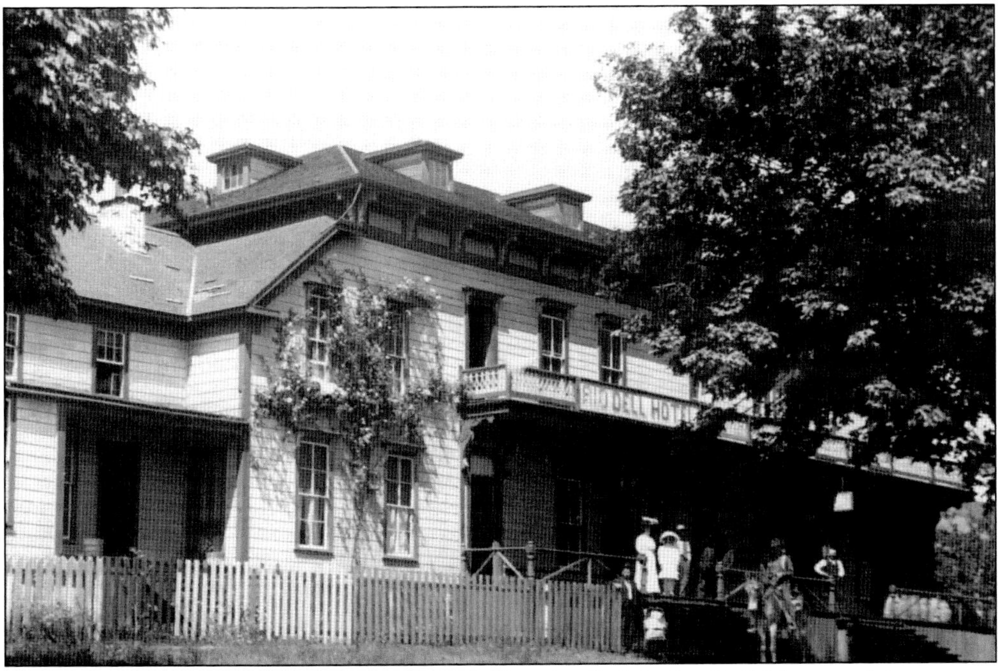

In August 1875, Lorenzo Painter opened a resort hotel called the Rio Dell House on his property, which became a popular destination for summer vacationers throughout the county. Painter advertised his place as "a summer and pleasure resort" located in the "Florida of Humboldt County." Orchards were planted to increase the productiveness and appeal of his property, and livestock grazed the hills above. The resort offered mineral springs that were believed to improve health, and a saloon that was popular with vacationers and residents alike. Painter can just barely be seen standing in the doorway of his hotel below, surrounded by unidentified family members, hotel employees, and guests. (Above, courtesy of the Todd-Schuler/Bartleson family; below, courtesy of the Humboldt County Historical Society.)

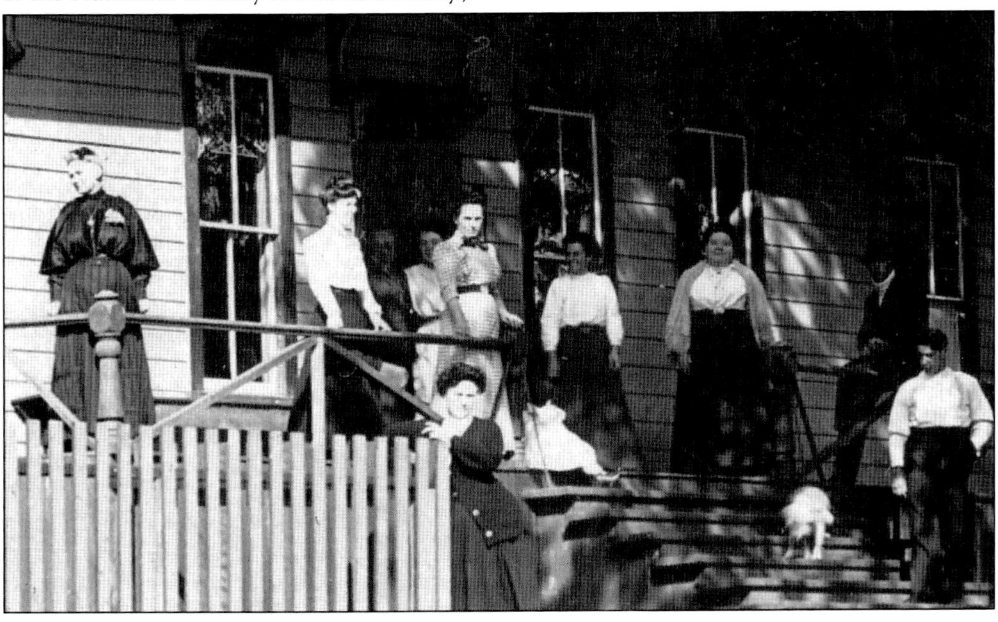

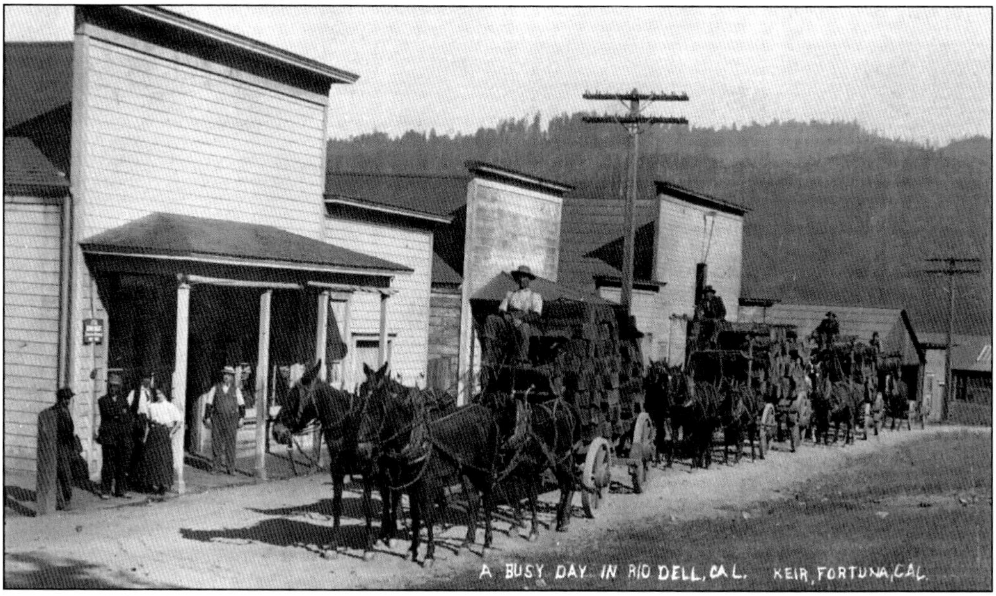

Painter subdivided 320 acres of his land into 13 blocks and put lots for businesses and homes up for sale. He laid out Main Street (now Pacific Avenue), Rigby Avenue, Painter Street, and Center Street, forming a town center that would become the heart of old Rio Dell. Lots across the street from Painter's hotel were sold or leased to business owners. (Courtesy of Greg Rumney.)

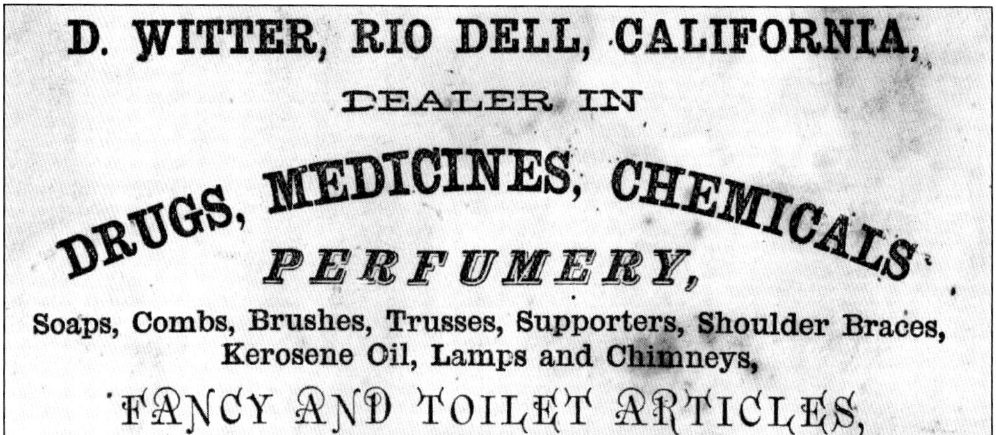
D. WITTER, RIO DELL, CALIFORNIA,

DEALER IN

DRUGS, MEDICINES, CHEMICALS,

PERFUMERY,

Soaps, Combs, Brushes, Trusses, Supporters, Shoulder Braces,
Kerosene Oil, Lamps and Chimneys,

FANCY AND TOILET ARTICLES,

Glass, Putty, Paints, Oils, Varnishes, Dye-Stuffs,

PATENT MEDICINES,

AND ALL OTHER GOODS USUALLY KEPT BY RETAIL DRUGGISTS.

Family Medicines and Physicians' Prescriptions accurately compounded at all hours.

Goods selected with care and warranted as represented.

It did not take long before storefronts lined the street opposite Painter's hotel, including Pedrotti's Mercantile, Sutherland's Grocery, Mrs. Roller's Millinery and Varieties, and Dr. Witter's drugstore. Dr. Dexter Witter served as the town's doctor, dentist, and druggist in the 1880s and 1890s. Residents of remote Eagle Prairie who were seriously ill or injured faced a long trip to the hospital in Eureka. (Courtesy of the Todd-Schuler/Bartleson family.)

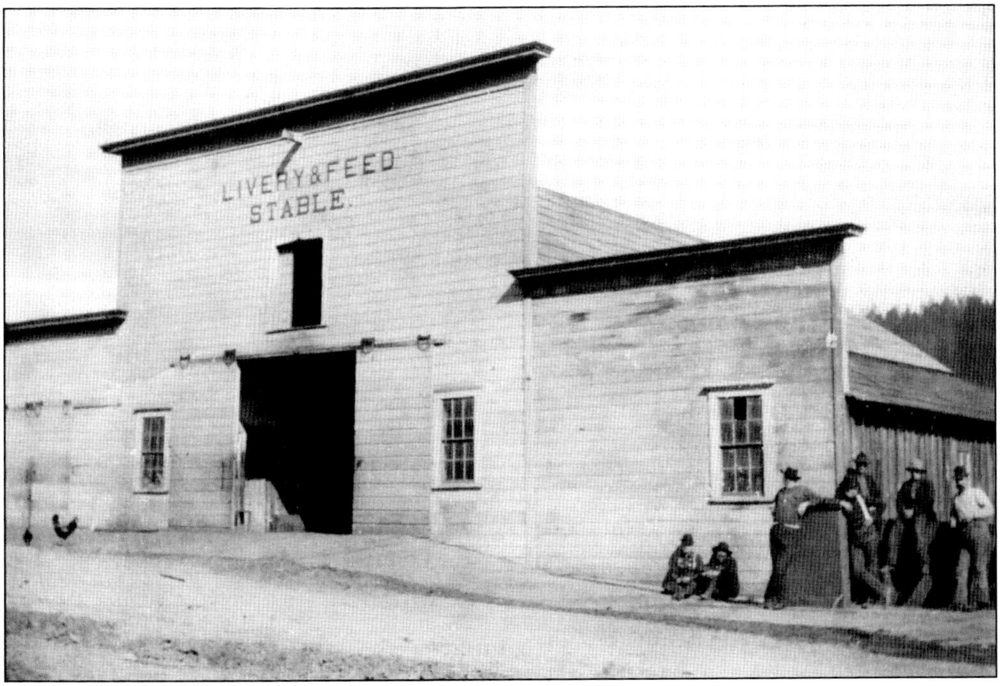

South of these businesses was a livery stable owned by H. Mills and Edwin Meller. This was a stable where horses, teams, and wagons could be rented or hired or where privately owned horses could be boarded for a short time. Conveniently located across from Painter's hotel, the livery also served as the offices for the stage line. (Courtesy of the Todd-Schuler/Bartleson family.)

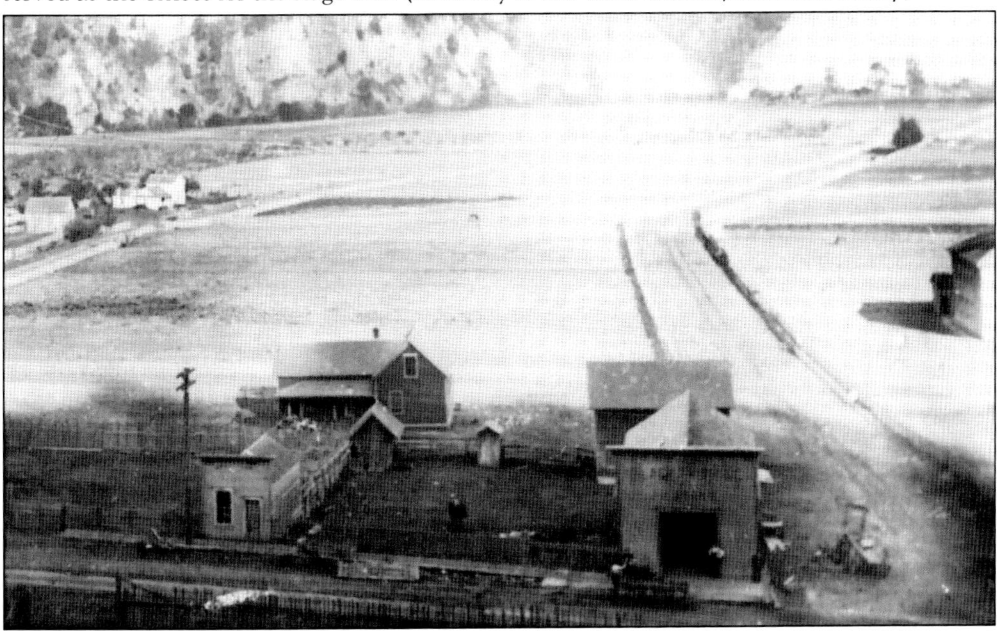

The town's blacksmith shop (lower right) was owned and operated by John Henderson Brown. Born in Grizzly Bluff in 1856, Brown learned the blacksmithing trade as an apprentice in Rohnerville before opening his shop in Rio Dell in 1885. Known for his quality work, Brown ran his shop until 1908, when ill health forced him to retire. (Courtesy of the Humboldt County Historical Society.)

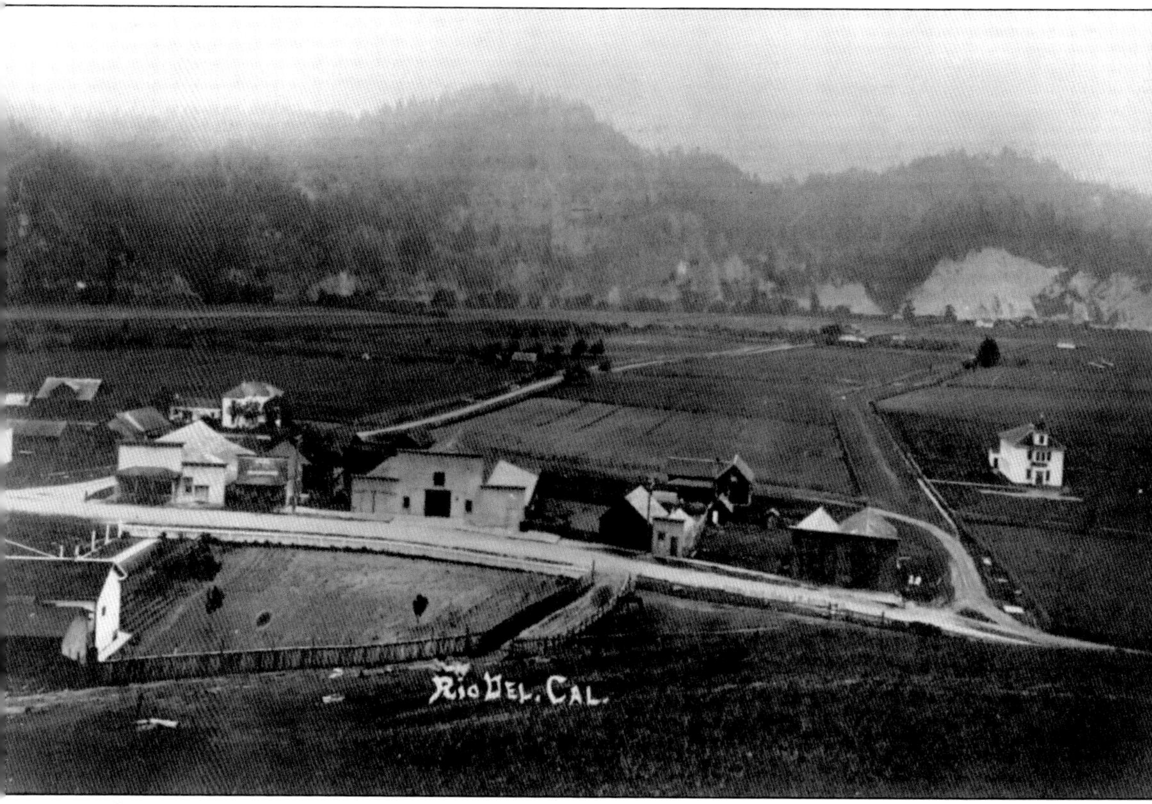

Painter's investments, hard work, and careful planning paid off, and before the 1880s, Rio Dell was on its way to becoming a popular resort destination and an established community. The popularity of the Rio Dell Hotel contributed to the success of the town's small businesses, and the small village prospered. In 1876, the US Postal Department established the first post office on the prairie, naming it the Rio Dell Post Office. Lorenzo Painter was appointed the town's first postmaster by Pres. U.S. Grant, himself an early Humboldt resident who served briefly as quartermaster at Fort Humboldt in Eureka in 1853. Painter held the position of postmaster for the next 11 years, after which the position was held by William Egan. (Courtesy of the Todd-Schuler/Bartleson family.)

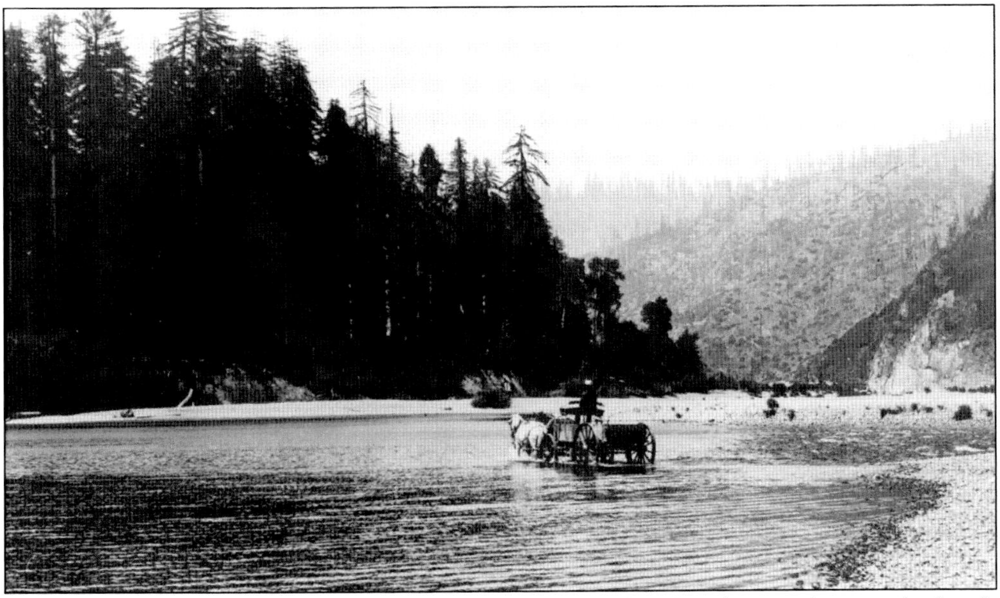

Getting to and from the remote Eagle Prairie was more difficult before the introduction of railroads and automobiles. Travelers heading south by wagon had to ford two rivers, the Van Duzen and the Eel, to reach the prairie. This was possible only during times when the river was low, making this route unusable for much of the year. (Courtesy of the Fortuna Depot Museum.)

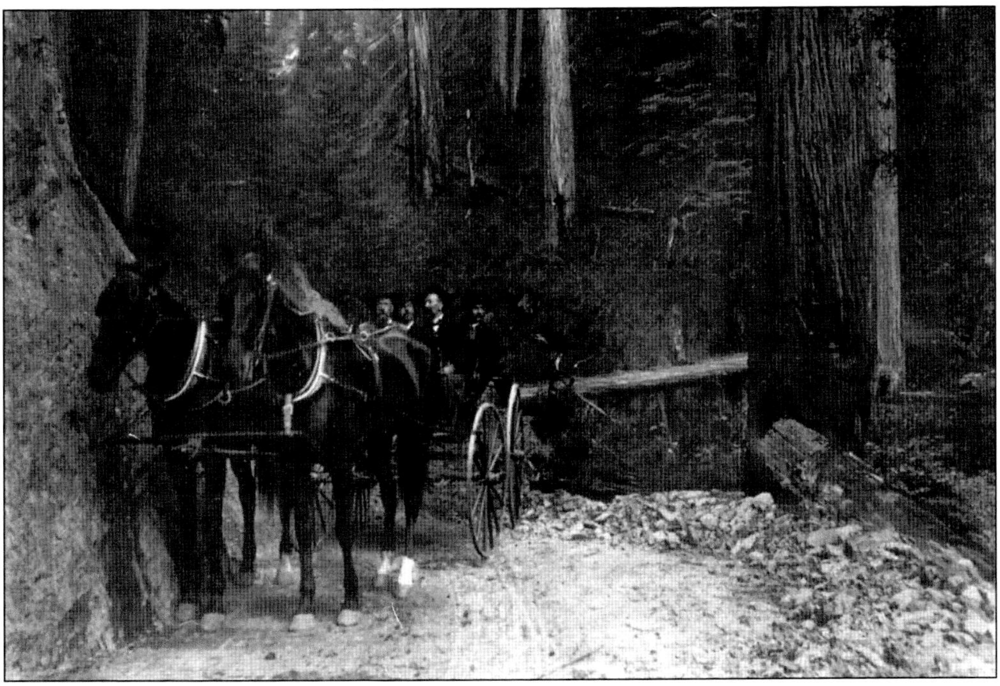

In 1877, the county approved the construction of the Grizzly Bluff and Camp Grant Road to provide more reliable, year-round access to the communities in the southern end of the county. The road was built along the west bank of the river to avoid the need for large bridges or ferries to cross the flood-prone Eel. (Courtesy of the Humboldt State University Library, Humboldt Room, Palmquist Collection.)

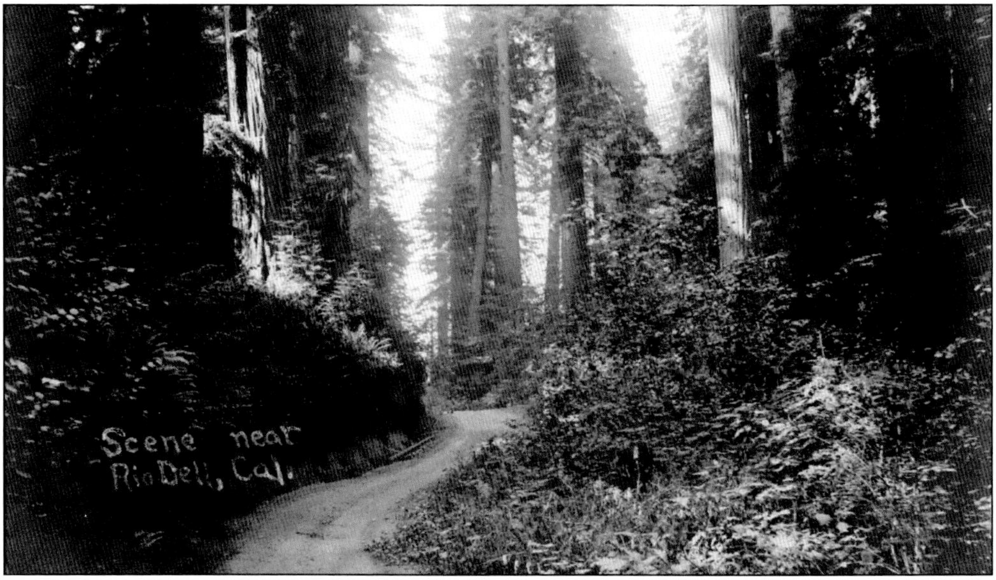

This new wagon trail would come to be known as the West Side Road and ran 28 miles from Grizzly Bluff to Camp Grant, passing through Rio Dell and continuing south on the west bank of the river. By midsummer, the road was seeing frequent use by travelers, and Lorenzo Painter began running a weekly stage to Eureka along the new route. (Courtesy of the Todd-Schuler/Bartleson family.)

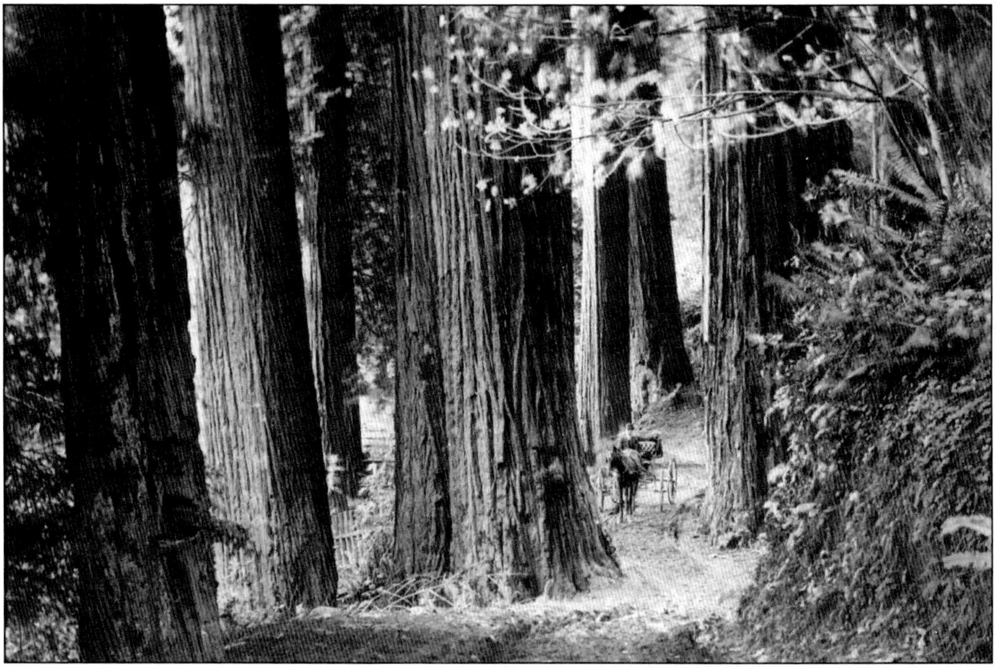

The West Side Road was built along bluffs in several places and was plagued by repeated slides, frequently becoming impassable for wagons. Around the beginning of the 20th century, a massive slide between Rio Dell and Grizzly Bluff at Blue Slide closed this part of the West Side Road to all but horses for the next five decades. (Courtesy of the Humboldt State University Library, Humboldt Room, Neill Collection.)

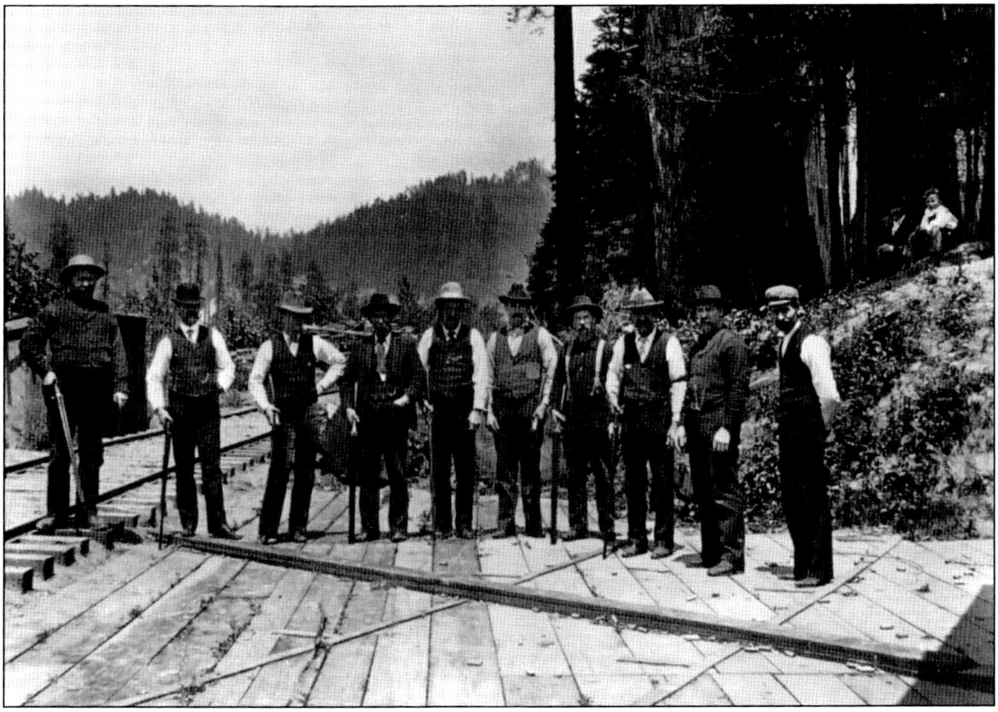

After 1885, timber products and farm goods were increasingly shipped via railroad. In addition to the depot at Scotia, there were railroad stops at Nanning Creek along the Scotia Bluffs and at Robinson across the Eel River north of Rio Dell. Some of Scotia's elite pose here while out hunting next to the tracks in Scotia. (Courtesy of the Fortuna Depot Museum.)

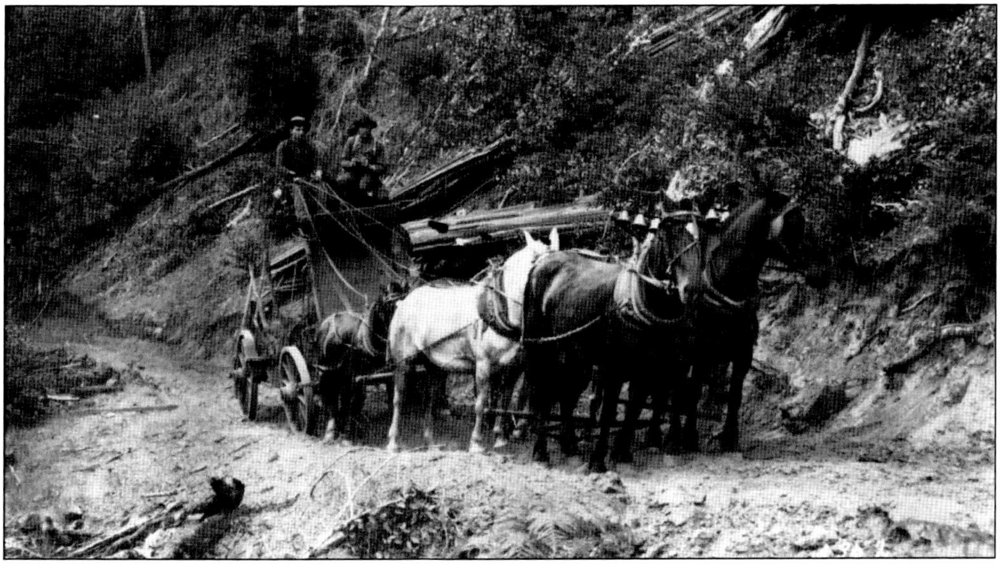

The road south of Scotia remained in use, however, providing a vital link to the rest of the county for wagons, horses, and eventually automobiles. The wet climate, frequent use, logging, and railroad building combined with frequent slides to make this stretch of the road one of the worst in the county. (Courtesy of the Humboldt State University Library, Humboldt Room, Swanlund-Baker Collection.)

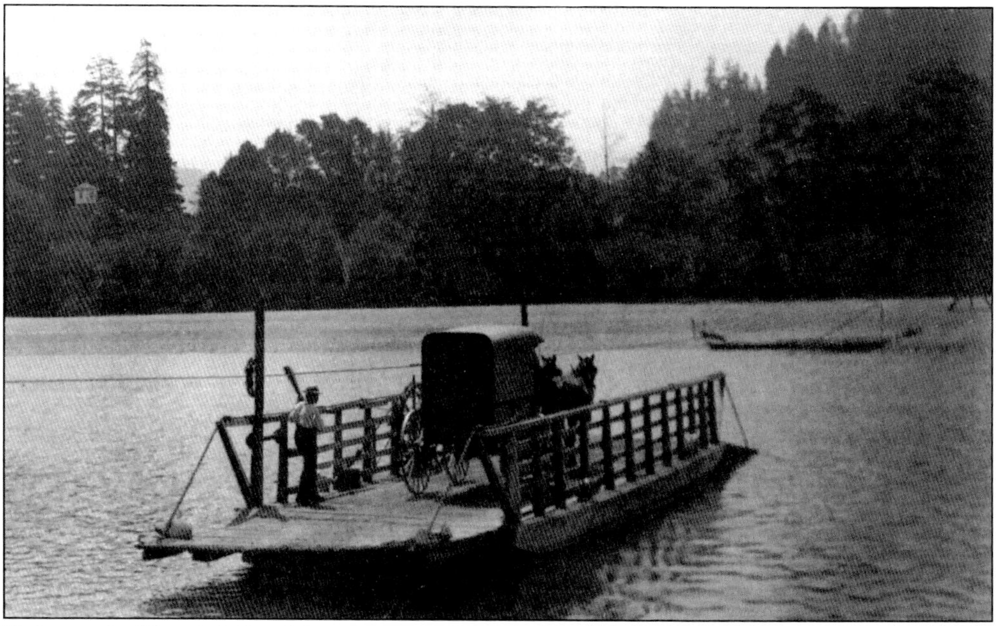

Slides on the West Side Road forced area residents to resume making river crossings when traveling north. Sometime in the 1890s, Bill Robinson's ferry service was established, making it possible to cross from Rio Dell to McDiarmid's Prairie year-round. Bill Robinson operated the ferry and owned a farm across the river from Rio Dell. After the railroad came into the area, the small community that sprang up near the ferry, called Robinson, was the site of a railroad stop where Rio Dell residents could catch the train. Robinson's ferry, later operated by Charlie May, served until the building of the Robinson Ferry Bridge sometime around 1912. (Above, courtesy of the Humboldt State University Library, Humboldt Room, Swanlund-Baker Collection; below, courtesy of the Humboldt County Historical Society.)

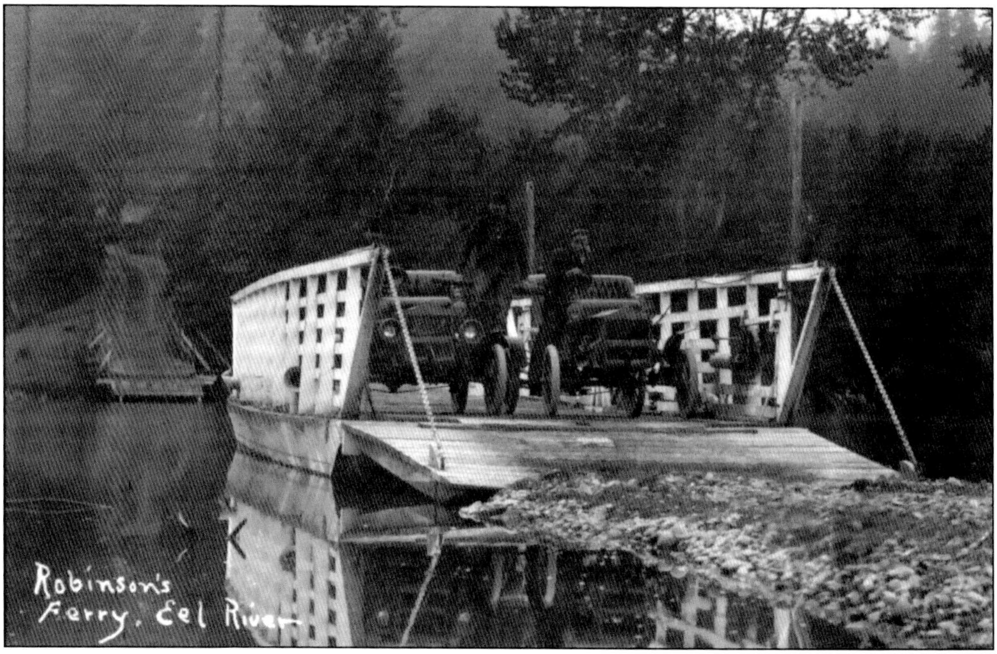

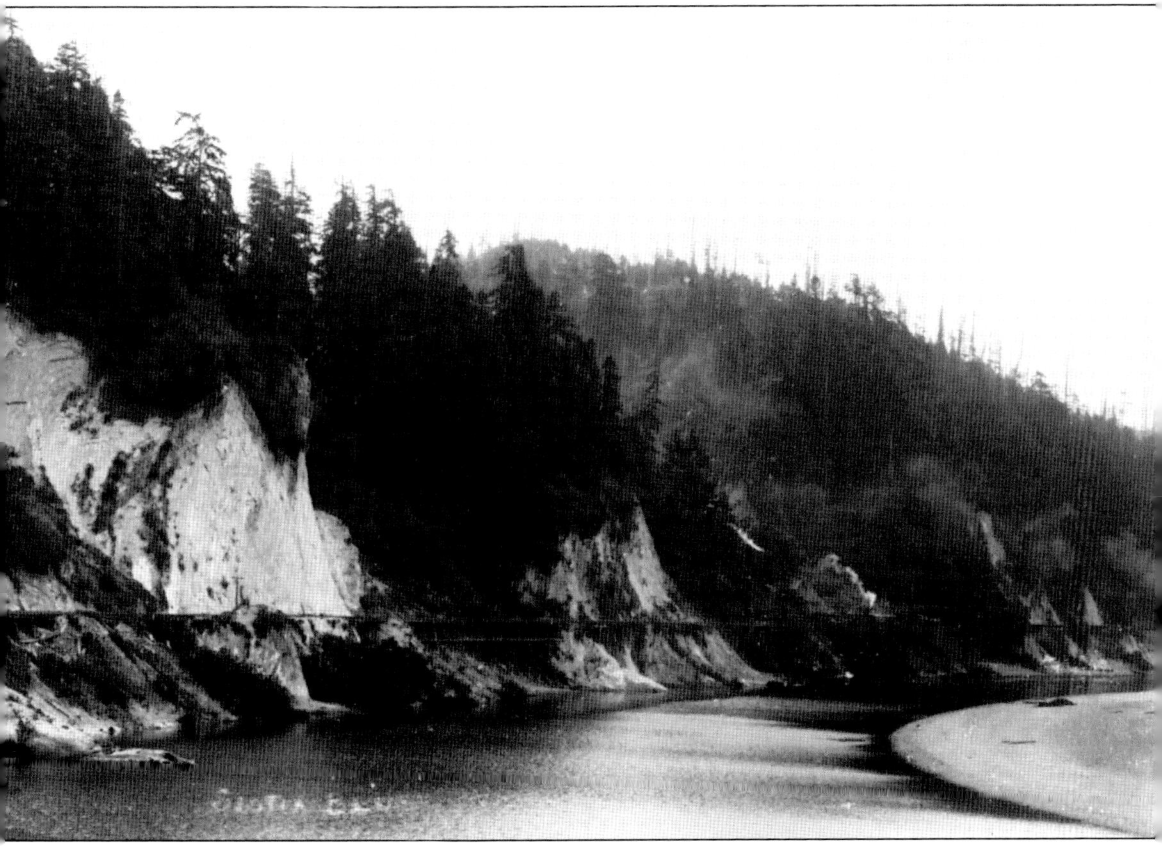

In 1885, the Pacific Lumber Company completed its railroad line from Alton to its new mill site south of Rio Dell. Lorenzo Painter was approached in the early 1880s by the Pacific Lumber Company seeking to purchase a site in Eagle Prairie for its mill, but Painter's price was considered too high, and the company instead purchased land across the Eel River south of Rio Dell from Henry Niebur in a place called Forestville. According to some sources, Painter was again approached by Pacific Lumber when the company sought a right-of-way for its rail line across his land. Painter, knowing that his land was the easiest route for a rail line north from Forestville, allegedly asked for a sum that PL management considered outrageous and flatly refused. After estimating the cost of building and maintaining its line along the bluffs, however, PL reconsidered, only to be rebuffed again when Painter doubled his first price. Another story maintains that all Painter asked for was a railroad station in Rio Dell. (Courtesy of the Humboldt State University Library, Humboldt Room, Swanlund-Baker Collection.)

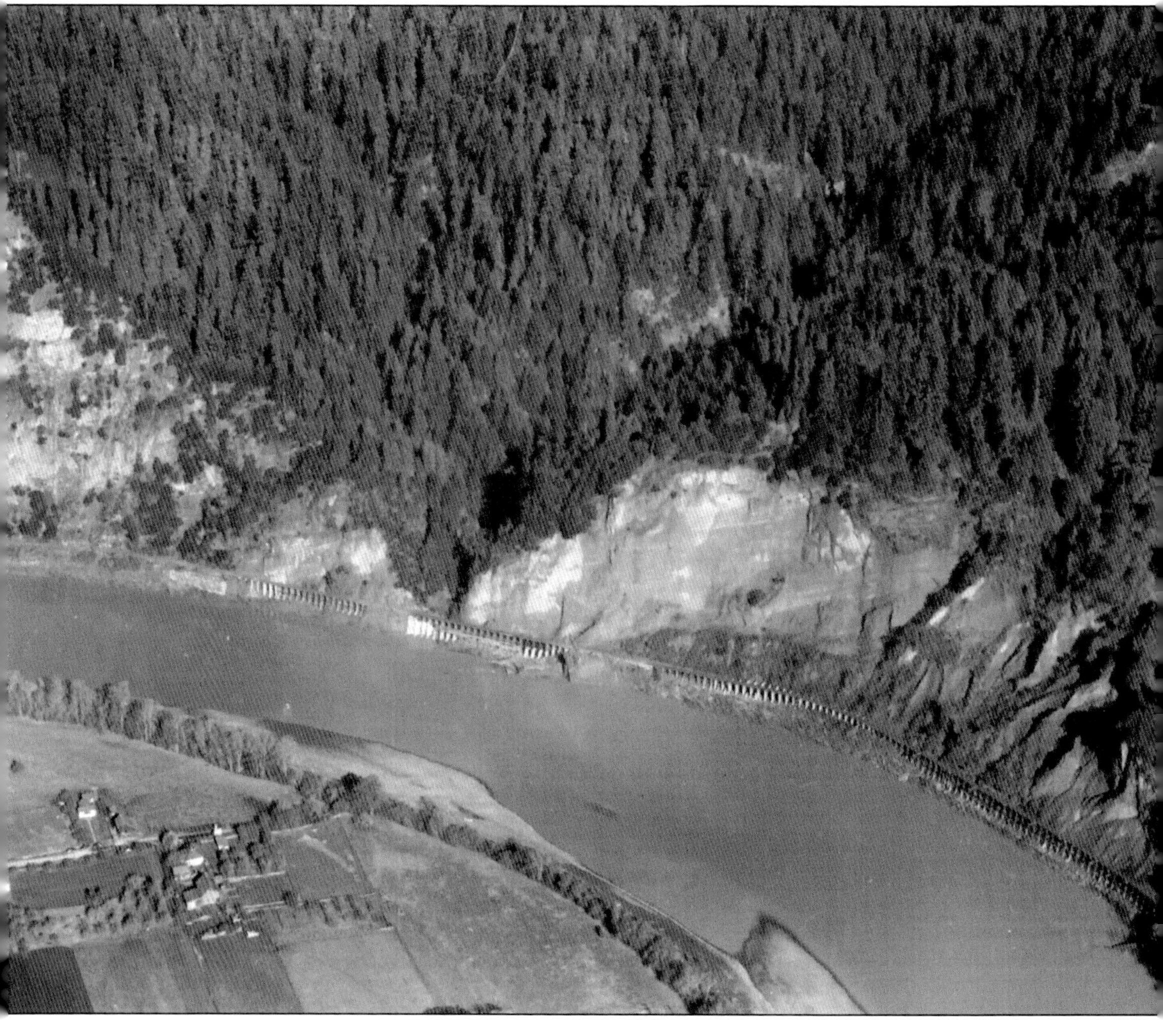

Other sources maintain that Pacific Lumber never intended to build its rail line across Painter's land at all. Two of the company's owners, John Paxton and Allen Curtiss, and the company's first general foreman, George Douglas, were experienced railroad men who would have been well aware of the difficulties they faced. The three had helped to build the Nevada Central Railroad, which extended for 92 miles through rugged and forbidding terrain. They had personally surveyed the timber company's considerable holdings without balking at the prospect of building along what was then known as the Rio Dell Bluffs. However it transpired, Pacific Lumber's railroad bypassed Painter's land, for better or worse, leaving Rio Dell without a railroad depot and PL with one of the most problematic pieces of track ever laid. The company's tracks along the bluffs were plagued by frequent slides and washouts over the next century and required constant and costly upkeep. (Courtesy of the Humboldt County Historical Society.)

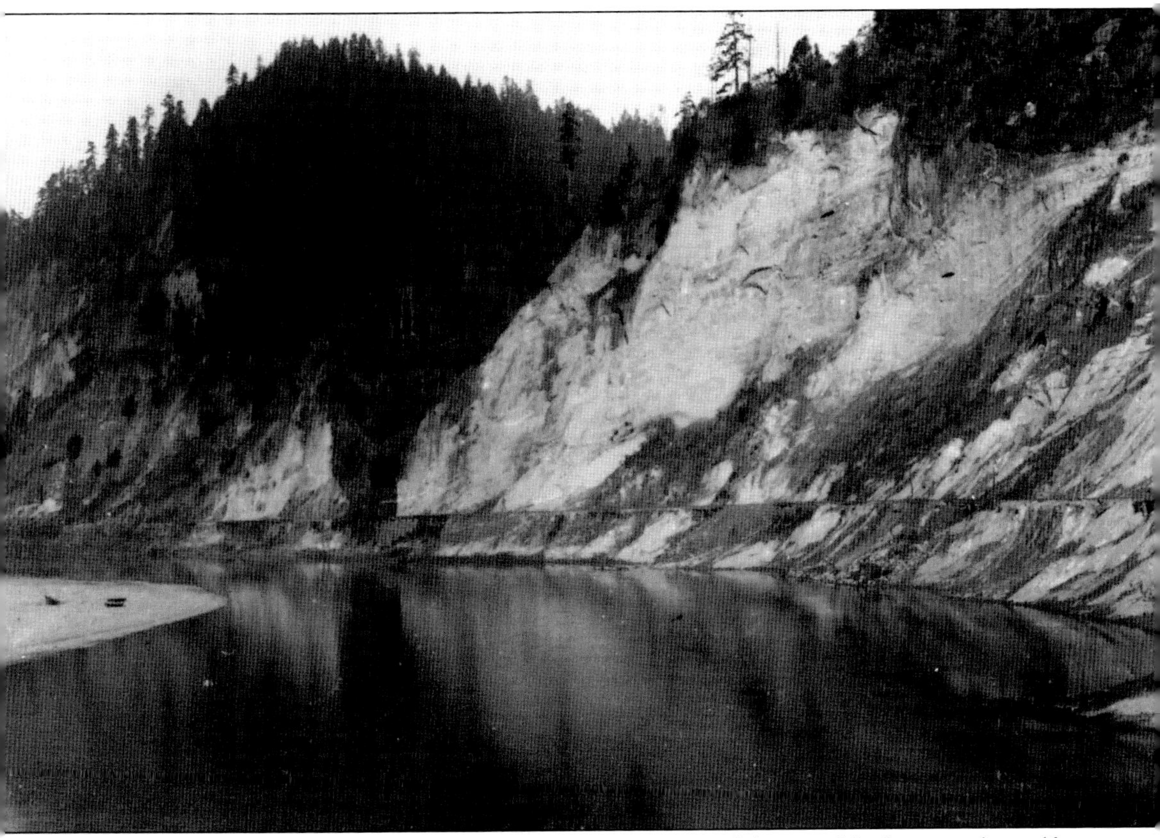

Lorenzo Painter sold off much of his land and, in October 1892, took his own life, drowning himself in the Eel River after suffering from depression over multiple financial losses in the preceding years. A suicide note left by Painter explained that he would rather pass into the "spirit world" than live to see his property taken from him. Painter, who left behind his adult children, widow, and two ex-wives to mourn him, was buried in a small graveyard on his property. His burial site is lost to time, the cross and white picket fence that once surrounded it having long ago burned in a brush fire. Although Rio Dell has no cemetery today, a few families had their own plots in the early years. Most of the area's residents were buried in graveyards in other communities, such as Hydesville, Rohnerville, and Ferndale. (Courtesy of the Humboldt State University Library, Humboldt Room, Swanlund-Baker Collection.)

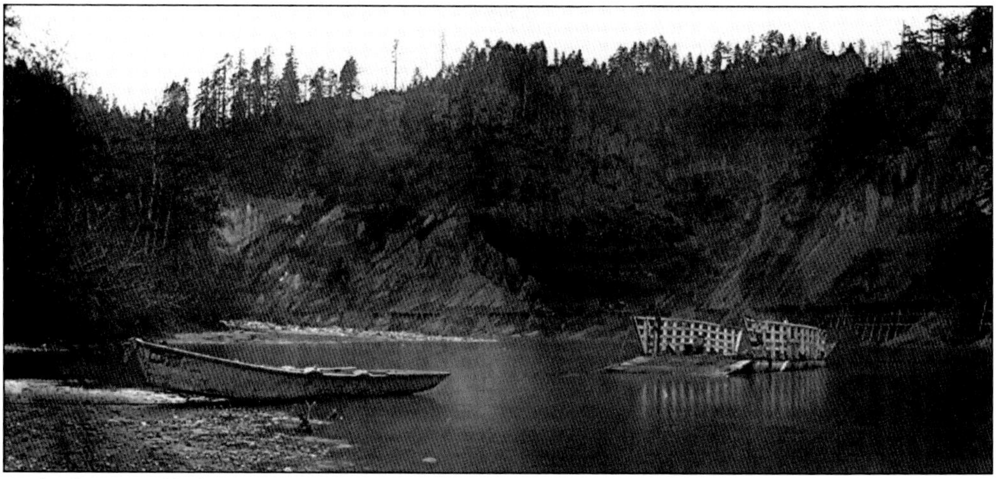

To facilitate traffic between Eagle Prairie and Scotia, a ferry service was established in 1888. Otto Hoffman ran the ferry from 1888 until his death in 1890. Frank Schuler took over the business after he married Hoffman's widow, Anna. Although it changed hands several times, this ferry remained in service until the first bridge was built between the neighboring communities in 1914. (Courtesy of Greg Rumney.)

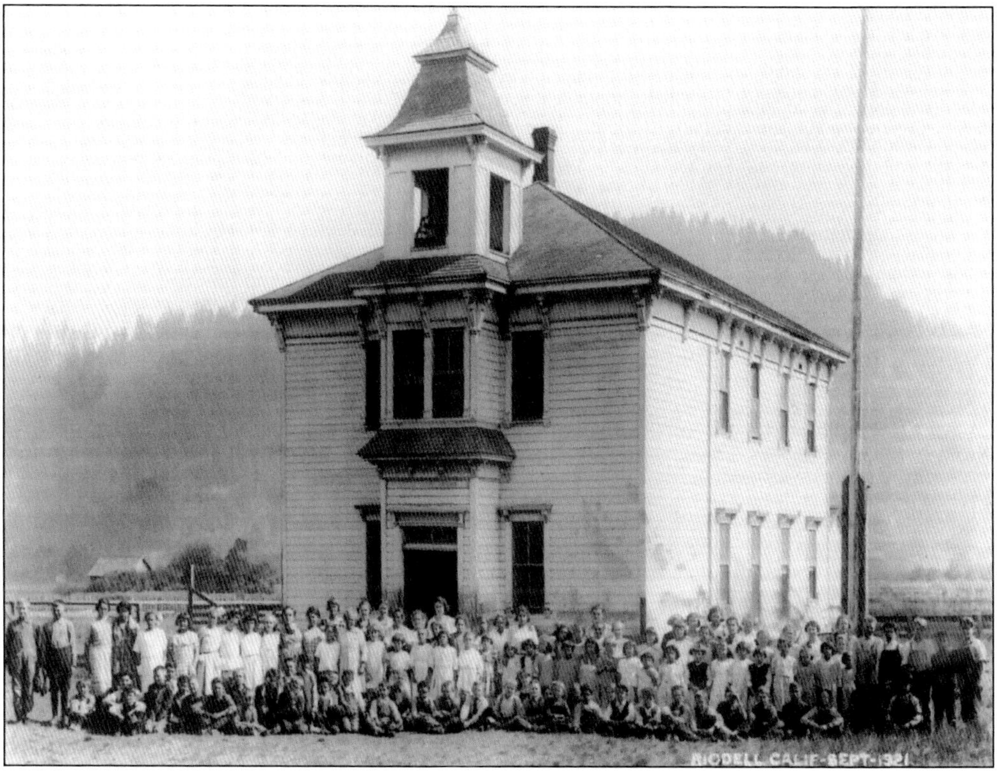

The opening of the Pacific Lumber Company's mill provided jobs for many Rio Dell residents and brought more people into the area. Rio Dell's businesses prospered, providing goods and services for workers and their families. Rio Dell's population slowly grew, and in 1891, property was purchased from Lorenzo Painter for the site of a new, two-story schoolhouse to accommodate all the school-aged children. (Courtesy of the Todd-Schuler/Bartleson family.)

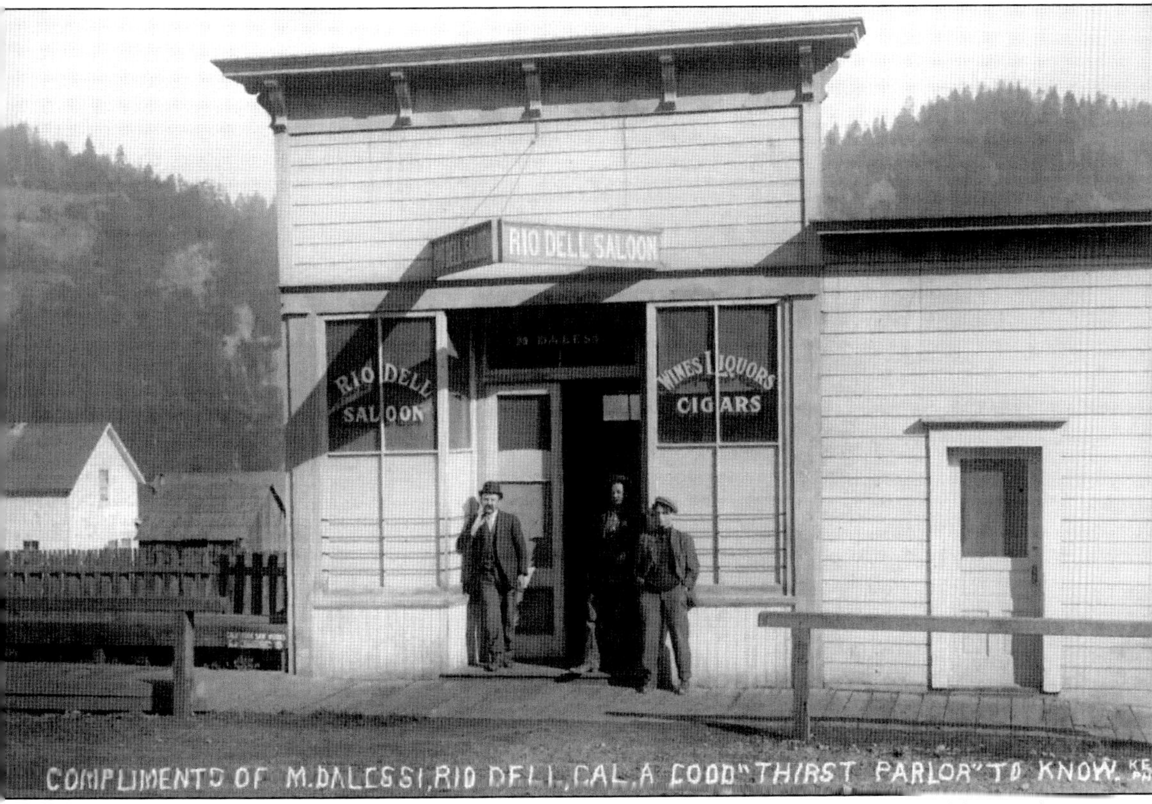

The Pacific Lumber Company employed hundreds of workers and provided for most of the needs of its employees in its town, including room and board. However, many workers looked to Rio Dell for shopping and carousing away from work and out of their bosses' view. Rio Dell's small business district grew to include nearly everything a 19th-century consumer could ask for. What many local loggers and millworkers asked for were saloons, card rooms, and other entertainments. Businessmen in Rio Dell were happy to oblige, and the small town began developing a reputation with loggers and millworkers as a wild place to spend time off. With mill owners, the town became known for the negative effects its rowdy bars and questionable liquor had on their employees. Painter's village hosted several bars, including the Rio Dell Hotel Saloon, operated by barman Thomas Haney, and the Exchange Saloon, operated by the town's barber, B.F. Sears. Rio Dell would be home to many more saloons, bars, speakeasies, and cocktail lounges over the next century. (Courtesy of the Todd-Schuler/Bartleson family.)

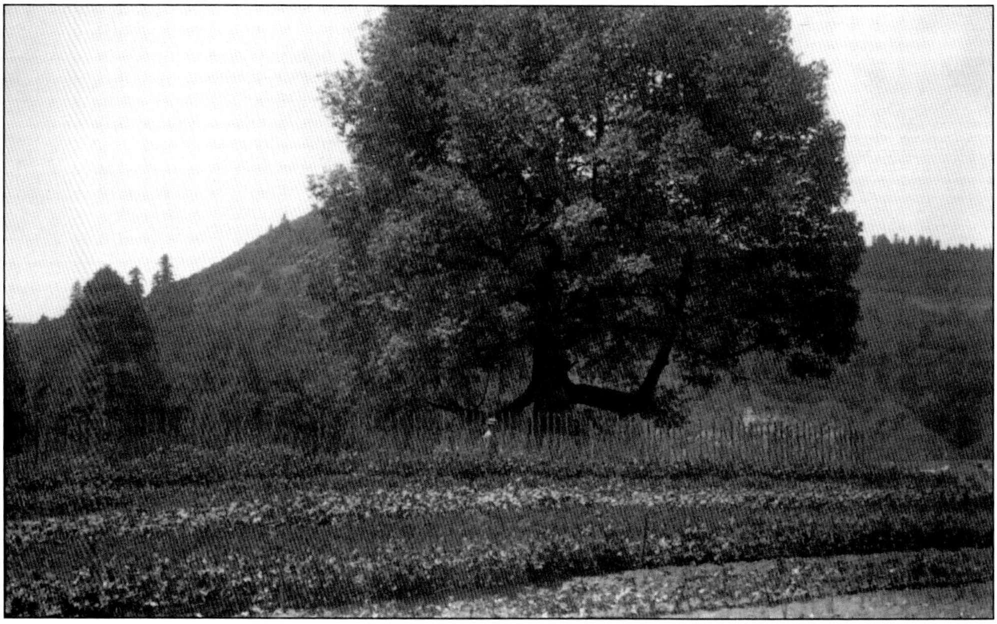

Farming and ranching remained an important way of life for many in the Rio Dell area. Harvests of hay, wheat, potatoes, and apples were bountiful, providing a good living for Rio Dell residents. Farming families were able to provide for many of their own needs and sell their excess crops in markets throughout the county. (Courtesy of the Humboldt State University Library, Humboldt Room, Swanlund-Baker Collection.)

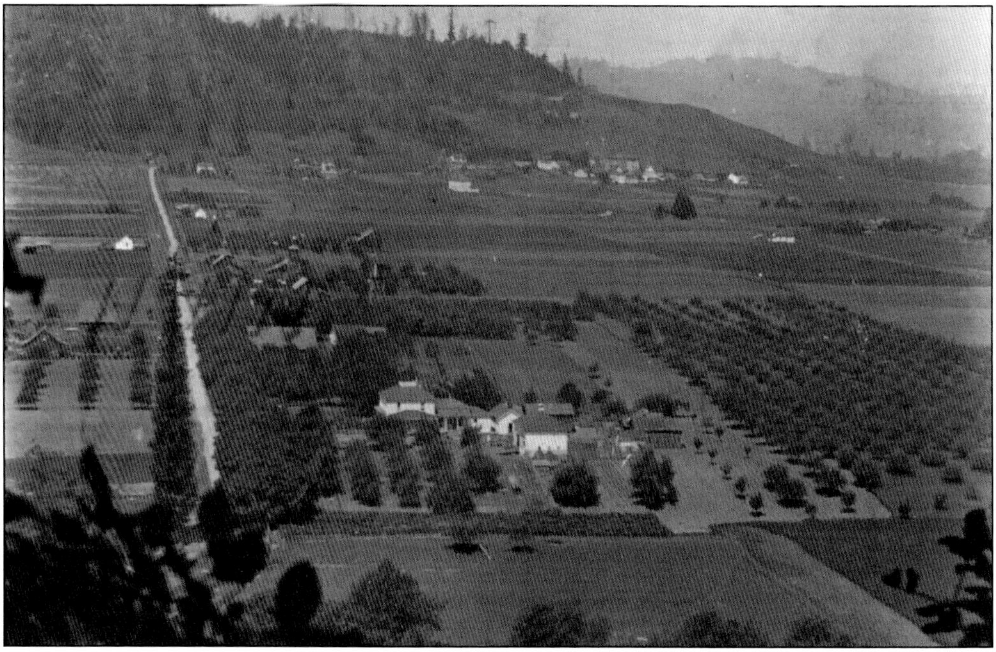

John W. Davis, a longtime resident of Humboldt County, purchased 15 acres on the east side of the prairie from Lorenzo Painter in 1886 and started a farm and an orchard. He married Maude Whitehouse of Rio Dell, and they sold their produce to the Pacific Lumber Company and their apples to Clendenen's Cider Works in Fortuna. (Courtesy of the Todd-Schuler/Bartleson family.)

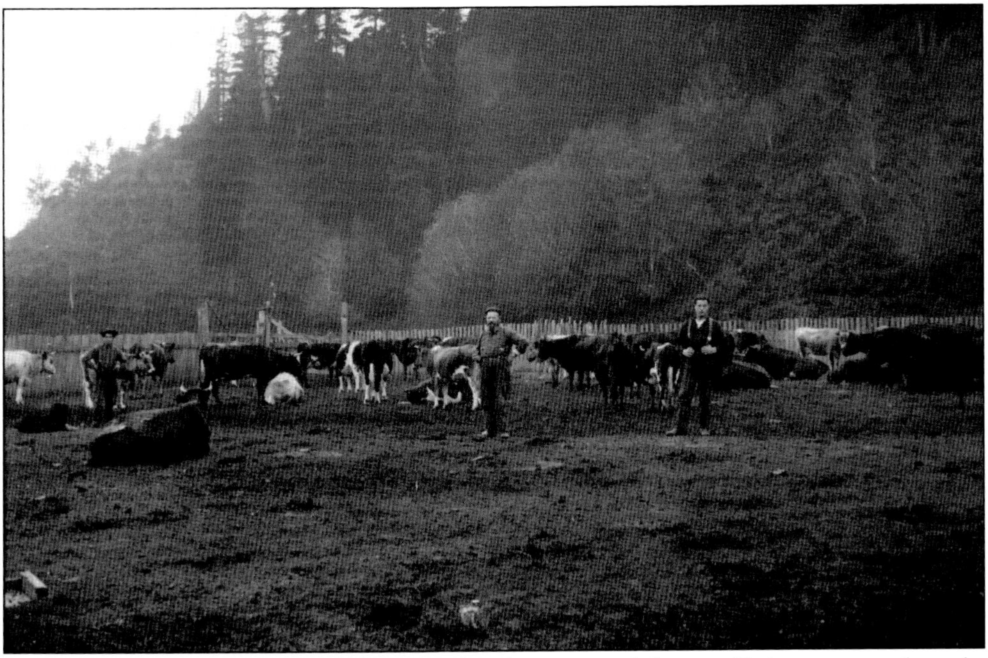

Rio Dell was home to several small dairy ranches during its early history. Dairy cows were brought into the county as early as the 1850s, both to meet the demands of the growing population and to capitalize on the high prices at the goldfields, where butter reportedly sold for $10 a pound. (Courtesy of the Humboldt State University Library, Humboldt Room, Swanlund-Baker Collection.)

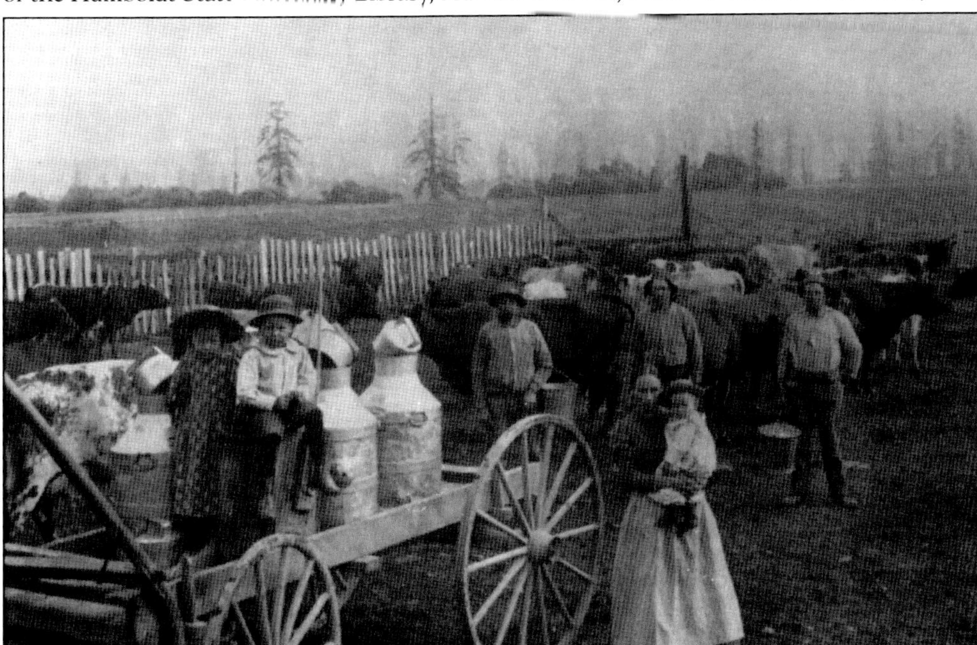

In the 1890s, milk from Eagle Prairie farms would be taken to a creamery across the Eel River to the north in McDiarmid Prairie. This prairie is known today as Metropolitan after the lumber company that once operated there. (Courtesy of the Humboldt State University Library, Humboldt Room, Palmquist Collection.)

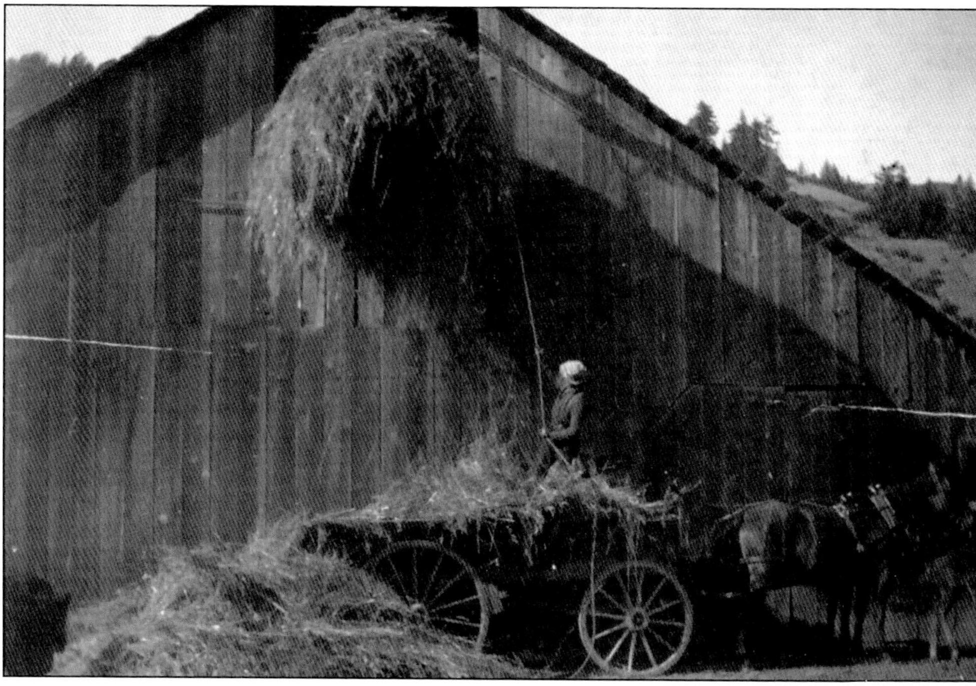

Cutting and storing hay was one of many big jobs that needed to be done each summer and one that required many hands. Hay was cut using sickles and scythes before the development of mechanical reapers in the 1860s. The hay then had to be transported to a barn to be stored out of the weather. (Courtesy of the Humboldt State University Library, Humboldt Room, Palmquist Collection.)

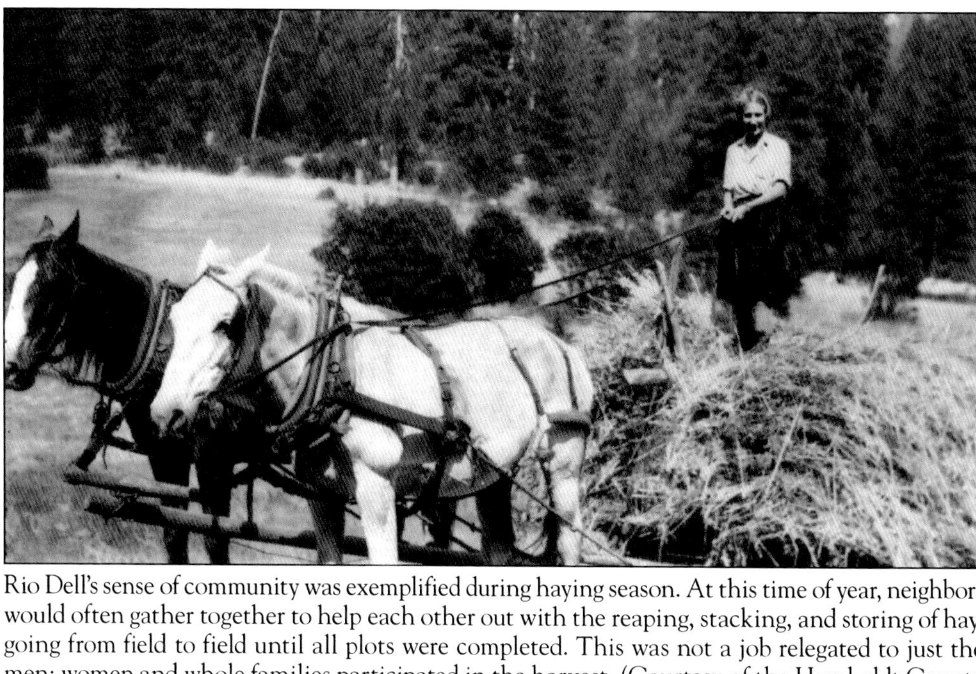

Rio Dell's sense of community was exemplified during haying season. At this time of year, neighbors would often gather together to help each other out with the reaping, stacking, and storing of hay, going from field to field until all plots were completed. This was not a job relegated to just the men; women and whole families participated in the harvest. (Courtesy of the Humboldt County Historical Society.)

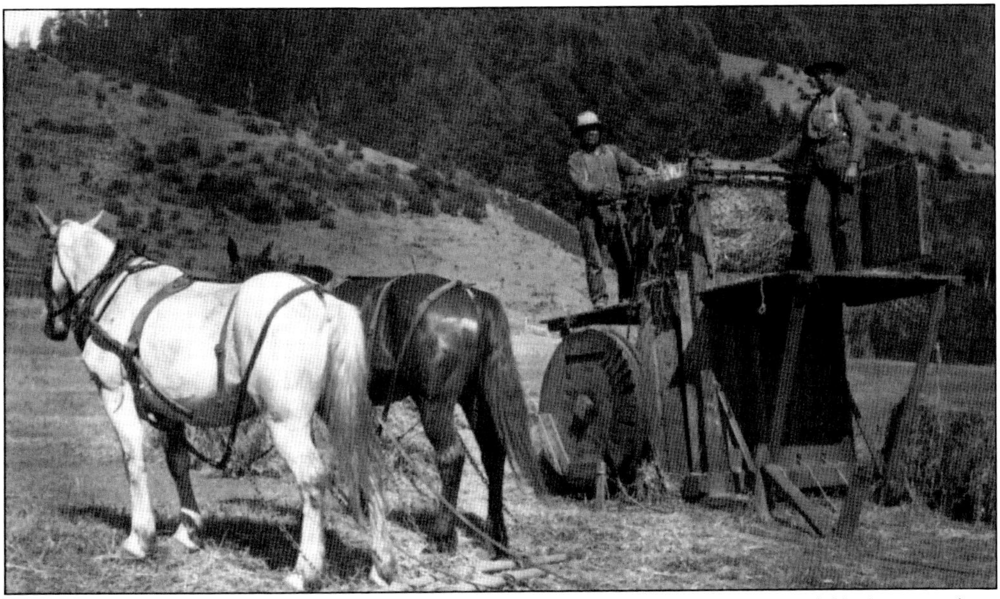

Portable man- or horse-powered balers were invented in 1863. A good crew could bale more than 70 bales a day, allowing for more efficient handling and storing of their hay. Baling machinery was often used by hay dealers, who would buy hay from area farmers, then bale it before taking it to market. (Courtesy of the Humboldt State University Library, Humboldt Room, Swanlund-Baker Collection.)

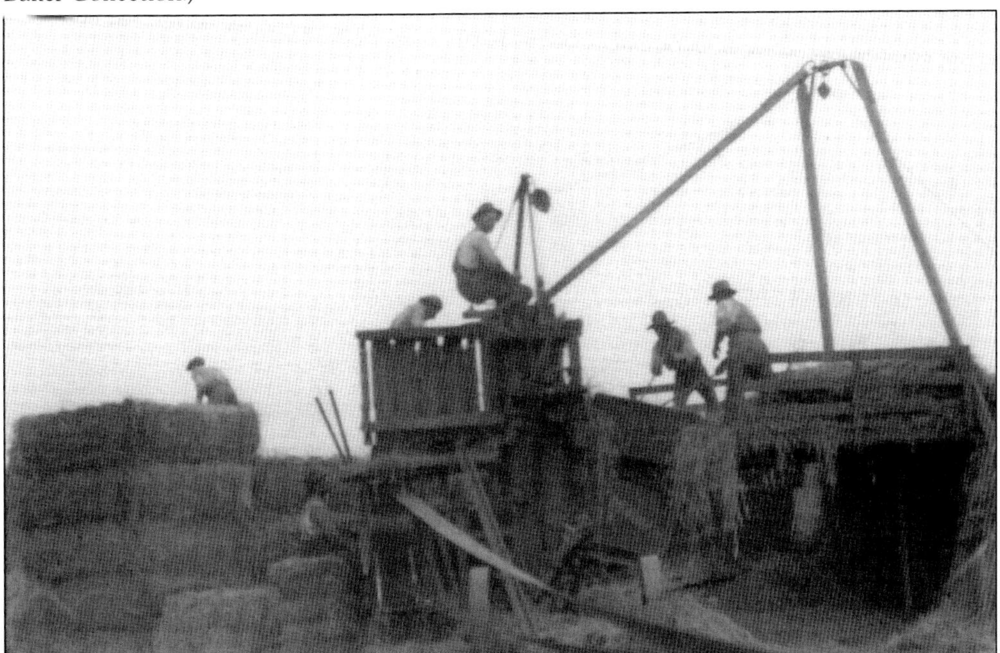

The introduction of steam-powered, belt-driven balers made the job even easier and more efficient and left farmers more time to attend to other work. These machines used long leather drive belts to transfer power from a portable steam engine. Some of these steam-driven machines continued to be used into the 1940s. (Courtesy of the Fortuna Depot Museum.)

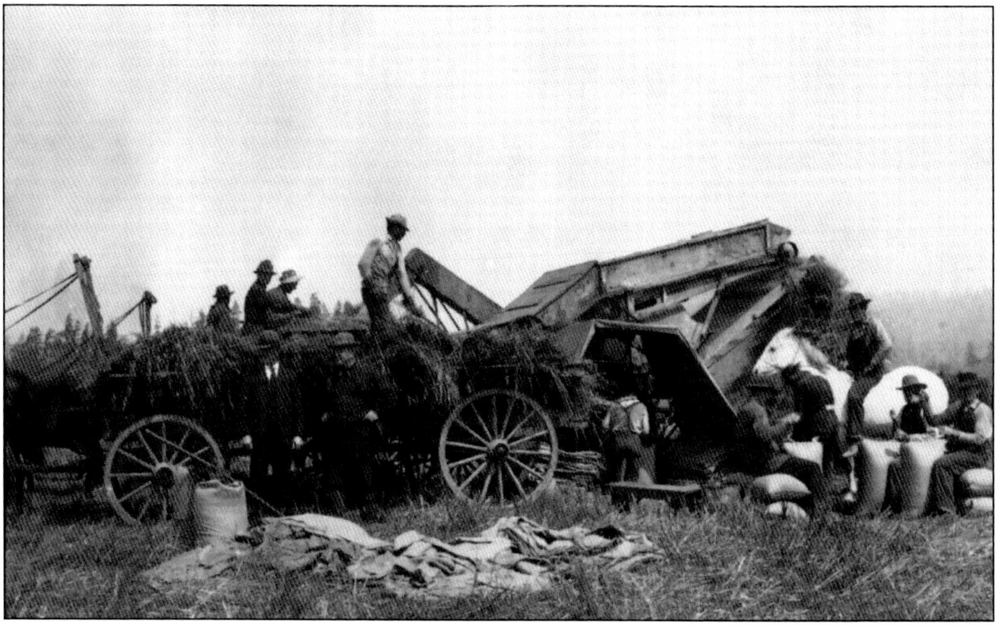

Steam-powered threshing machines were another welcome addition to area farming, allowing for faster harvest times and larger grain yields. Threshers replaced slower methods of removing the stalks and husks from grain and saved farmers time and wages in getting their crops to market. (Courtesy of the Humboldt State University Library, Humboldt Room, Swanlund-Baker Collection.)

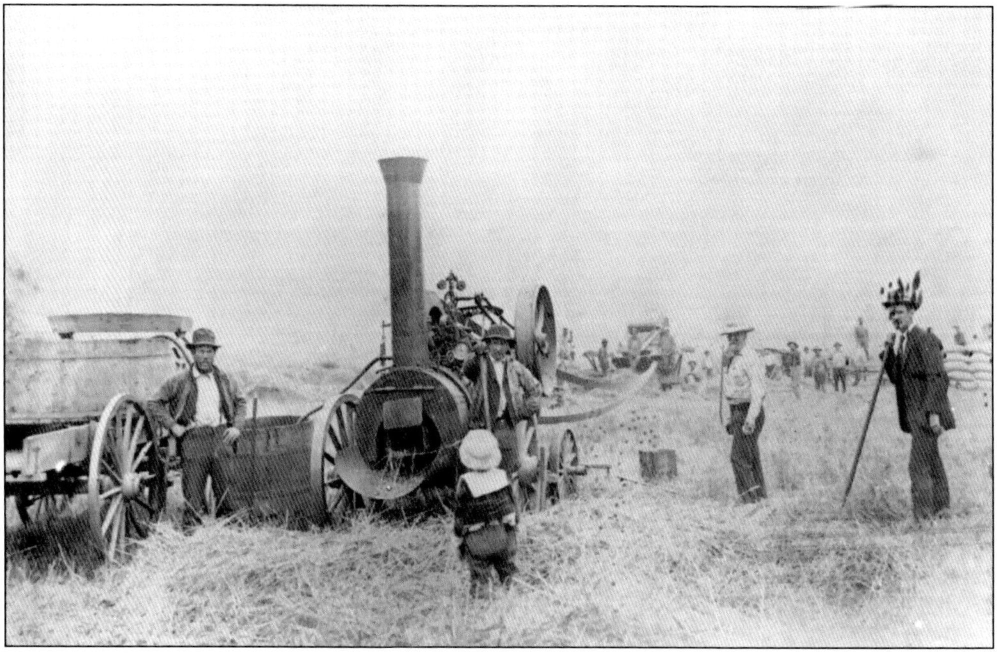

Expensive farming equipment was often beyond the reach of Rio Dell's small-scale farmers. Sometimes, machinery was purchased jointly by multiple families who would share the equipment and help each other with the harvest. Scotia historian Fred Elliot identified this equipment as belonging to Charles Stone, who owned a ranch across the Eel River to the north of Eagle Prairie. (Courtesy of the Fortuna Depot Museum.)

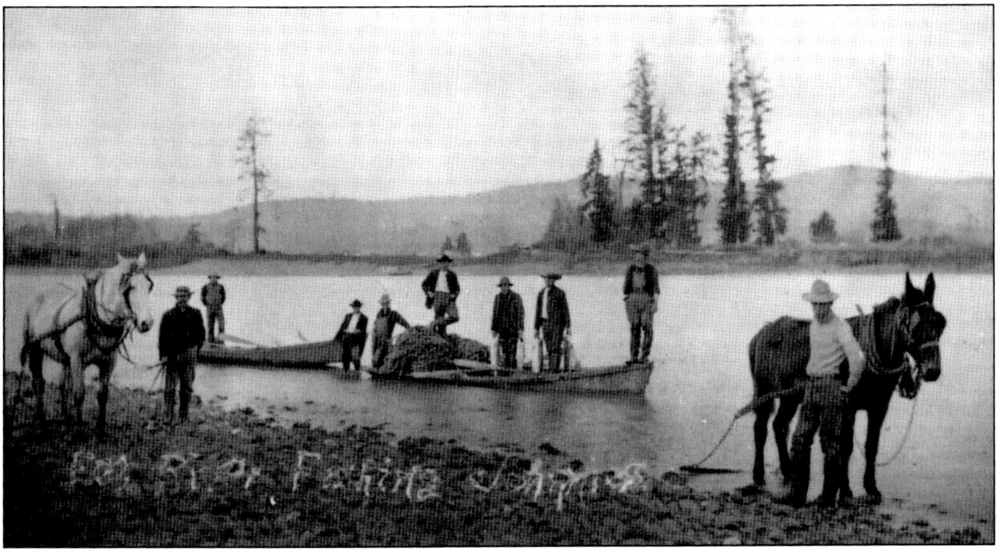

Salmon, steelhead, and trout were abundant in the Eel River, providing a favorite pastime and source of food for many, as well as a source of income for some. In the early 1900s, residents began to fish salmon commercially in the Eel River as far up as Rio Dell. Using horses to pull in their nets, these men hauled in heavy loads of the valuable fish, one group netting seven tons in 1909. The fish were taken north by wagon to canneries that had been established along the Eel River at Fortuna, Port Kenyon, and Loleta. Humboldt Bay and Eel River salmon was considered a superior product and was shipped to markets throughout the Pacific Basin and New York. (Both, courtesy of the Humboldt State University Library, Humboldt Room, Palmquist Collection.)

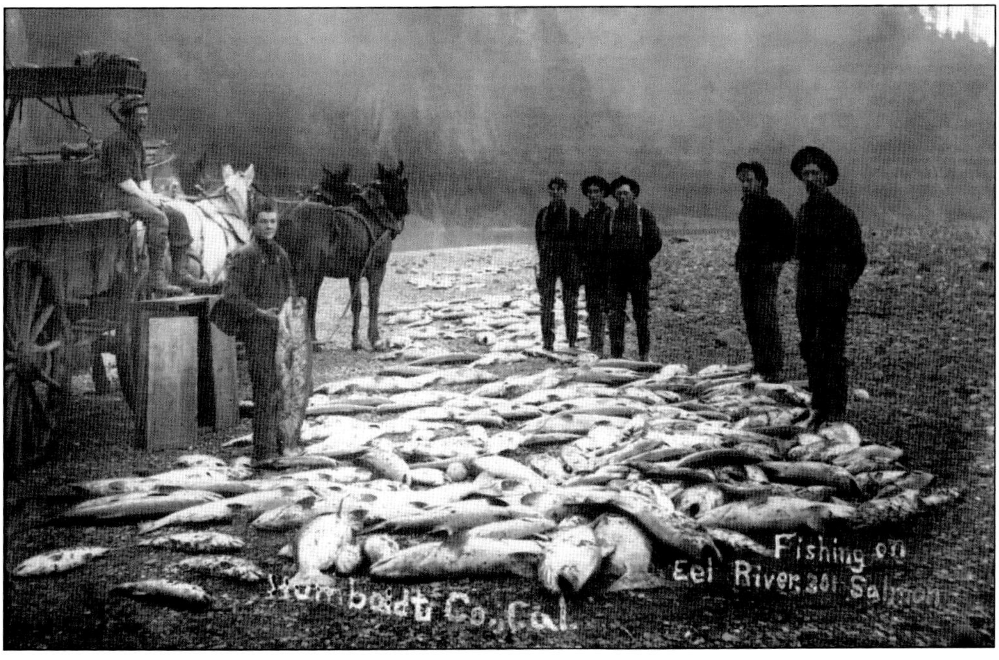

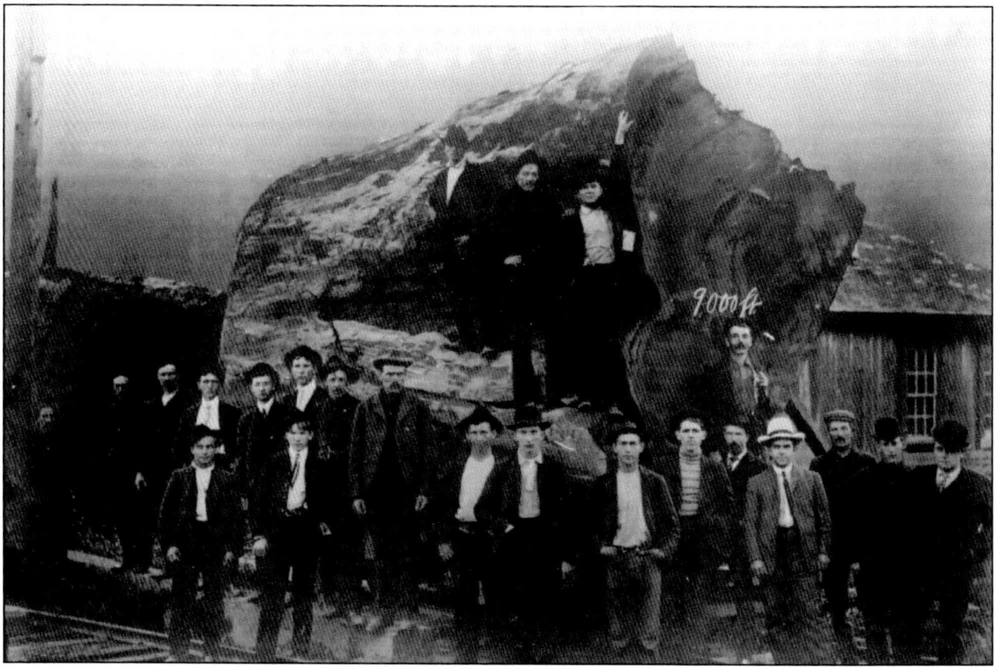

Logging began in earnest in the area after the completion of Pacific Lumber's railroad and mill. The railroad allowed for the easier transport of timber to the mills and a connection to the shipping ports in Humboldt Bay. This allowed PL to operate its business but also provided opportunities for local workers and landowners to profit from the sudden demand for their labor and timber. (Courtesy of the Fortuna Depot Museum.)

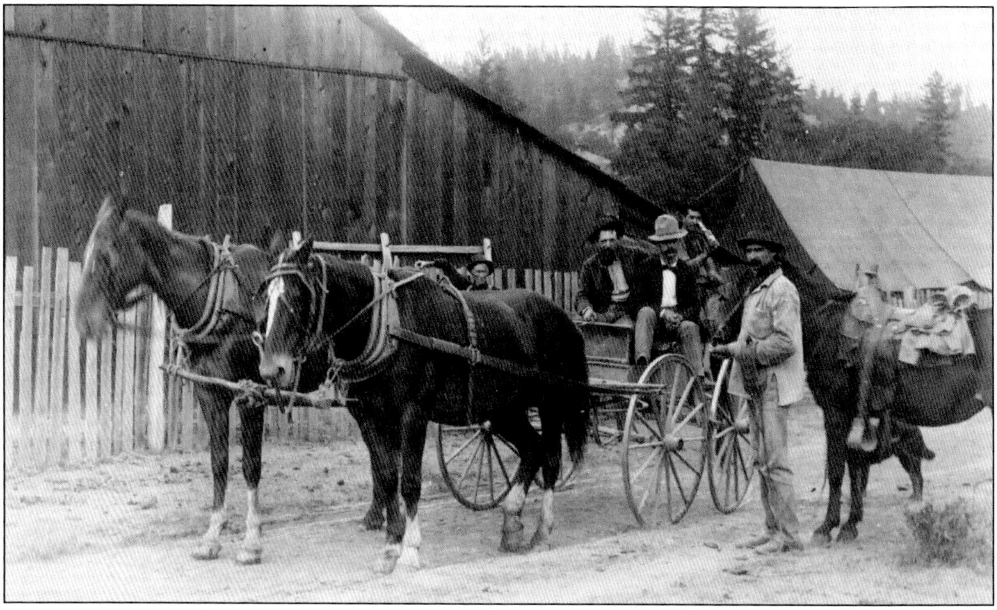

In 1898, Monroe Whetstone, with help from the Pacific Lumber Company, opened a shingle mill near Mill Creek at the north end of Eagle Prairie. He was supplied with wood primarily from the property of Natale Sacchi on the hills west of Rio Dell. (Courtesy of the Humboldt State University Library, Humboldt Room, Palmquist Collection.)

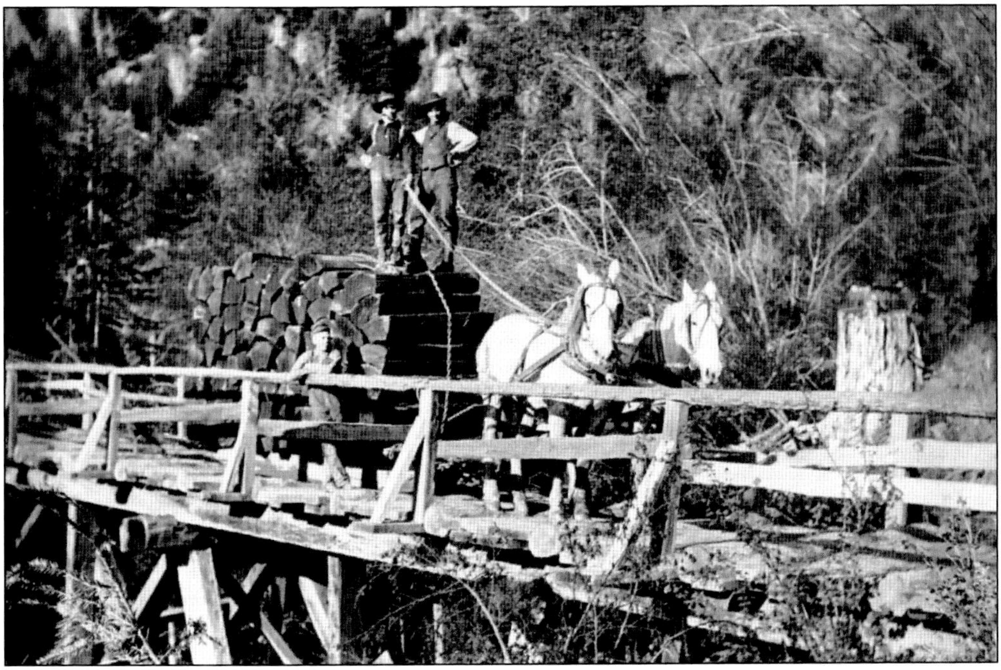

Edwin Ogle was an insurance agent and business owner in Rio Dell. Arriving in town in 1903, Ogle bought the town's waterworks, the grocery store, and the Whetstone mill. He set to work logging the rest of the redwoods on the Sacchi ranch. Ogle contracted to supply shingle bolts to PL, which hauled them to Scotia from Robinson. (Courtesy of the Humboldt State University Library, Humboldt Room, Palmquist Collection.)

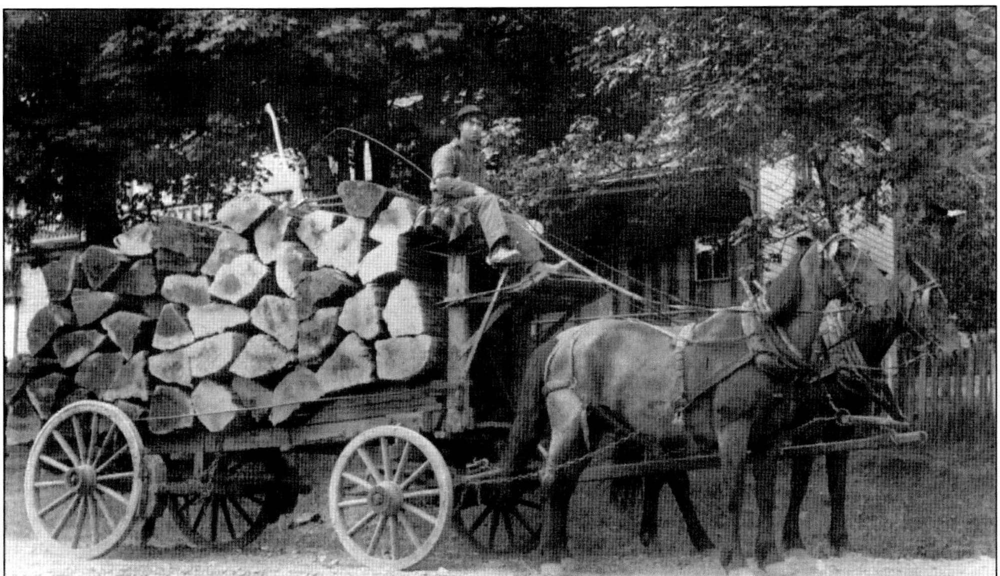

Ogle logged Belleview and Riverside, and on the hillside above the south end of town. He built another mill in the Dean Creek area in Rio Dell, and later another in Holmes Flat. As he expanded his operations, he became one of Rio Dell's biggest employers, keeping a crew of 20 to 50 men busy in the woods and at the mills. (Courtesy of the Humboldt County Historical Society.)

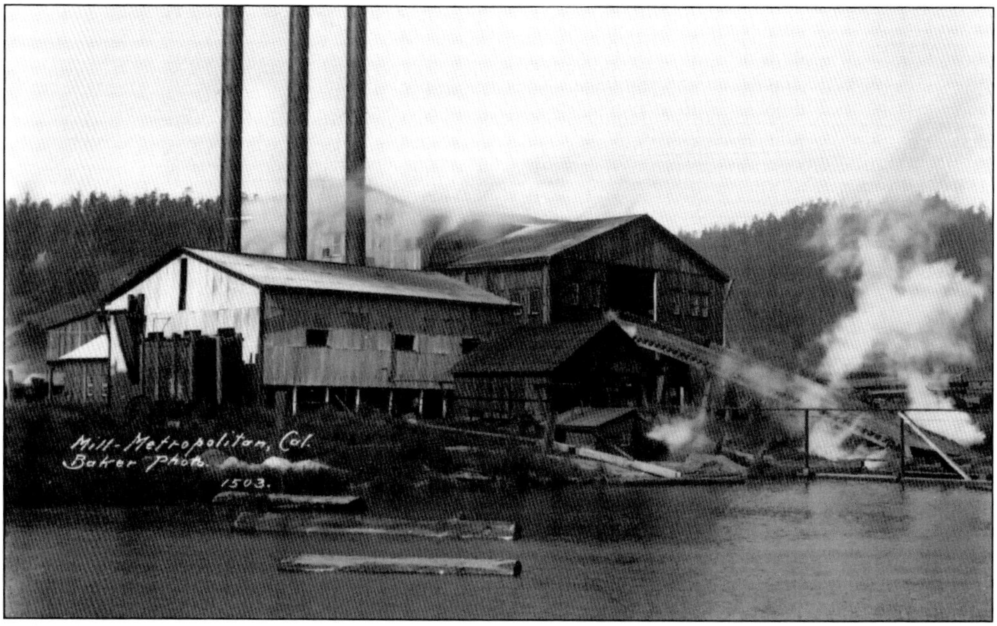

Other logging operations in the area included the Metropolitan Redwood Lumber Company (MRLC), which logged the hillside above Rio Dell and at Slater Creek near Blue Slide beginning in 1904, and the Bayside Lumber Company, which began cutting timber along Nanning Creek on the Scotia Bluffs by 1909. (Courtesy of the Humboldt State University Library, Humboldt Room, Swanlund-Baker Collection.)

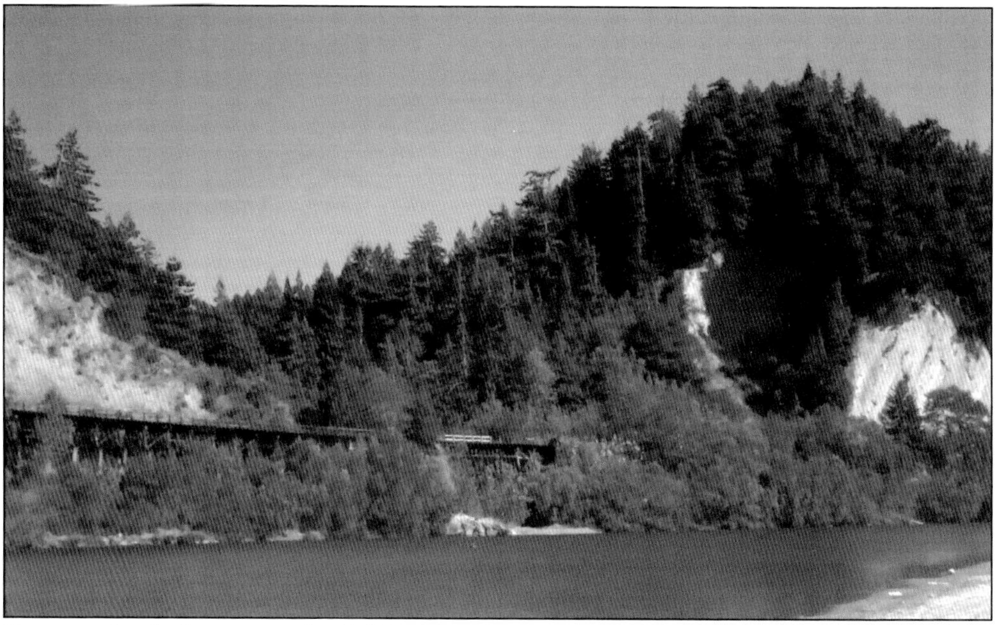

Nanning Creek drains into the Eel River at the Scotia Bluffs, across from the eastern end of Eagle Prairie. The Bayside Lumber Company built a spur line into the steep, narrow canyon and started a logging camp. Bayside logged Nanning Creek during the summer, but workers had to find other places to live and work during the winter, when the creek flooded. (Courtesy of the Garrison Collection.)

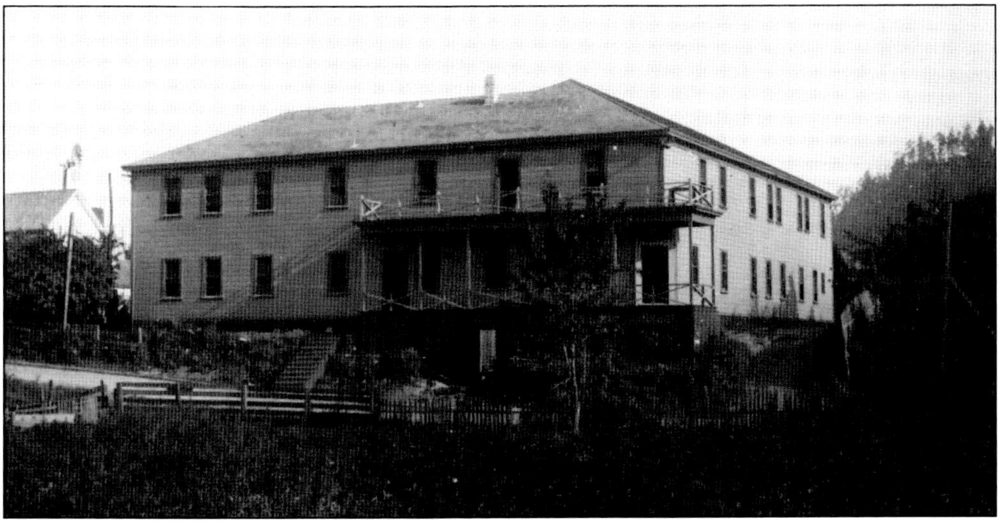

Most of Metropolitan Lumber's workers lived in company housing, including in the Metropolitan Motel, and Bayside's woods crews lived in their camp up Nanning Creek. However, many of these workers spent their time off, and their wages, in Rio Dell. Surrounded by paternalistic company towns, Rio Dell's businesses flourished, particularly those that offered services not found across the river. (Courtesy of the Humboldt State University Library, Humboldt Room, Swanlund-Baker Collection.)

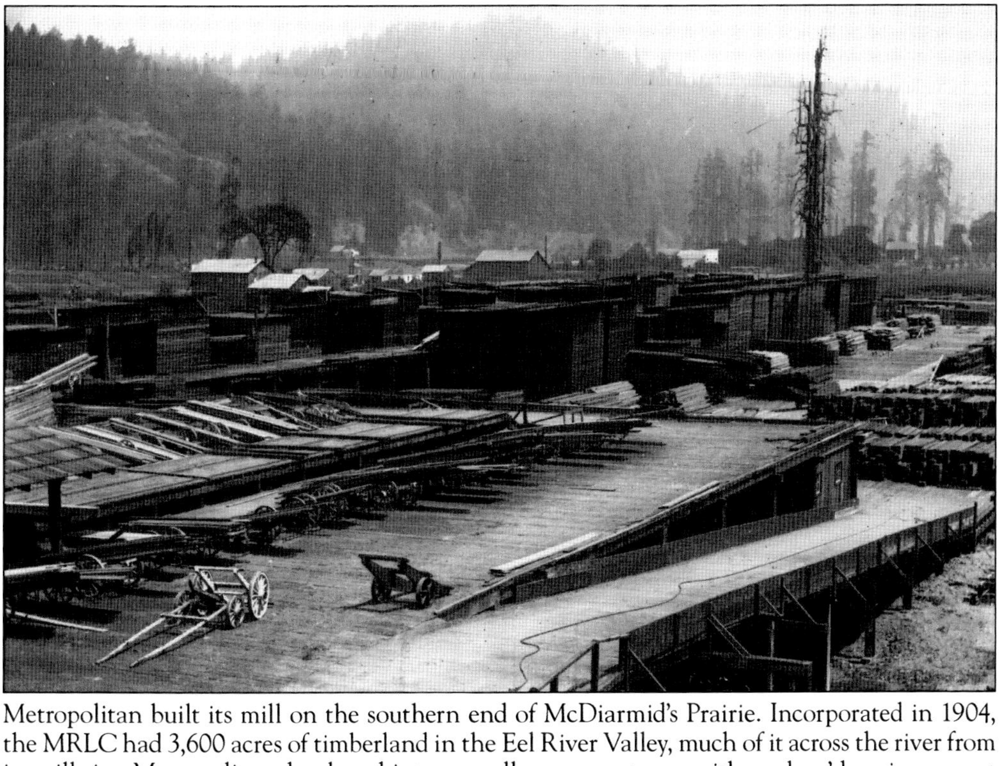

Metropolitan built its mill on the southern end of McDiarmid's Prairie. Incorporated in 1904, the MRLC had 3,600 acres of timberland in the Eel River Valley, much of it across the river from its mill site. Metropolitan developed into a small company town, with workers' housing, a post office, a general store, a hotel, and a saloon. (Courtesy of the Humboldt State University Library, Humboldt Room, Swanlund-Baker Collection.)

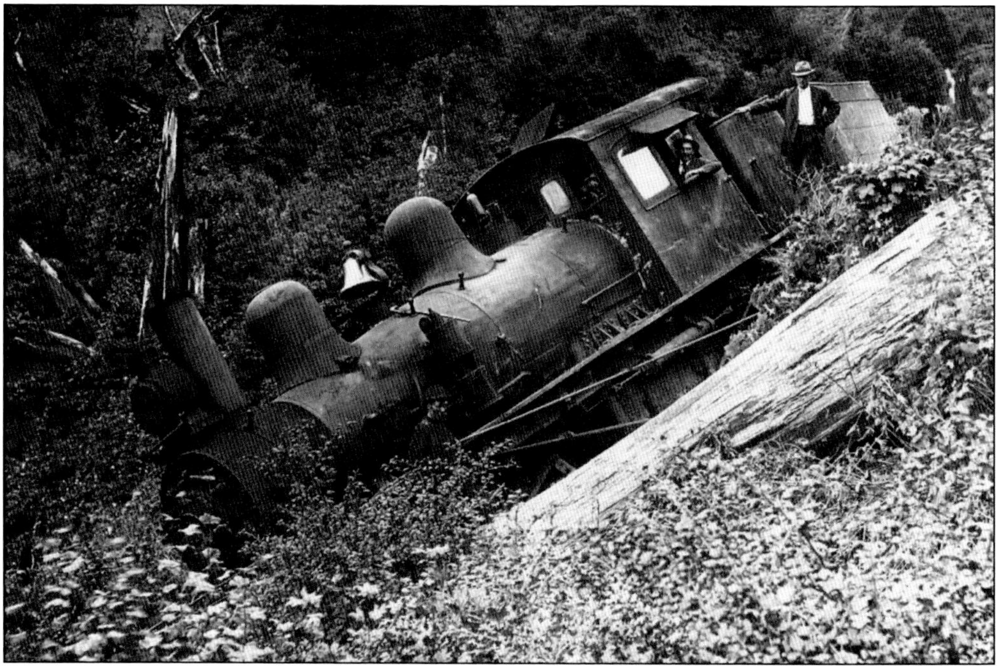

To facilitate its logging operations, Metropolitan constructed a railroad trestle over the Eel River at Slater Creek and had tracks connecting the mill to the main rail line to Humboldt Bay. Slater Creek was a treacherous stretch of tracks and was the site of multiple train wrecks, one costing the lives of four trainmen. (Courtesy of the Humboldt State University Library, Humboldt Room, Palmquist Collection.)

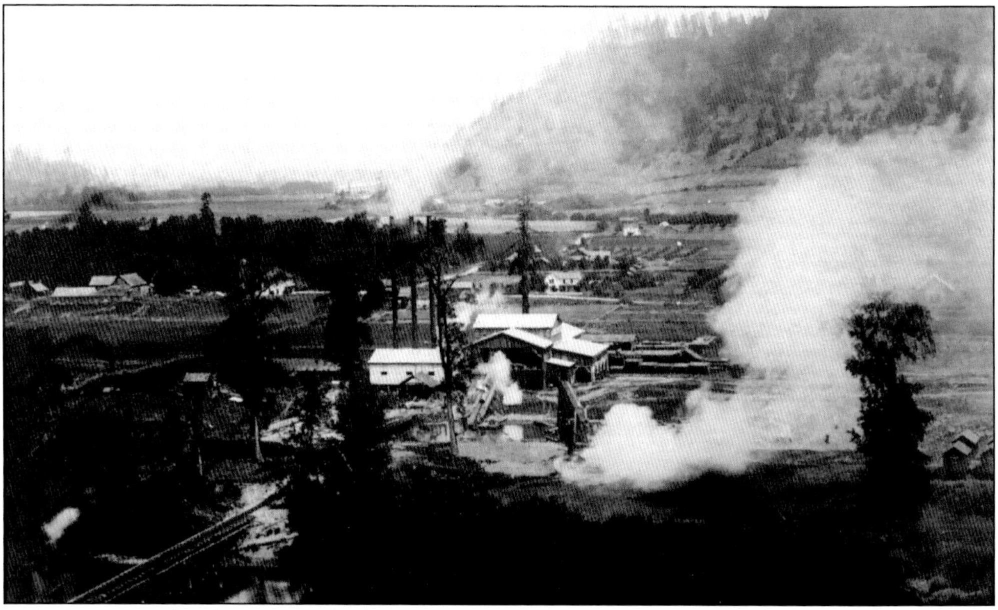

MRLC remained in business only as long as its accessible timber held out, and the mill closed in 1925. After the mill's closure, the machinery and equipment was sold, as were the houses. All that remains of Metropolitan are a few houses surrounded by what has become pastureland. (Courtesy of the Humboldt State University Library, Humboldt Room, Palmquist Collection.)

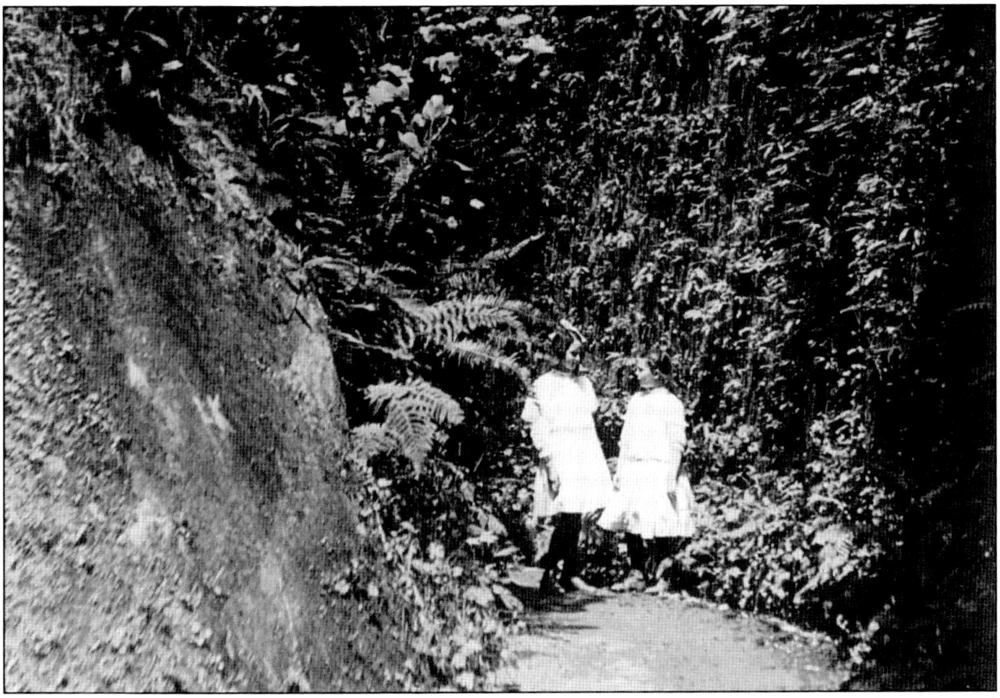

Although people in the area were focused primarily on the timber industry, Rio Dell continued to be a popular vacation spot. In the 1890s, Jacob T. Jacobson established Canyon Park near Rio Dell. Located on McDiarmid's Prairie, the park was named for its narrow canyon entrance. (Courtesy of the Humboldt County Historical Society.)

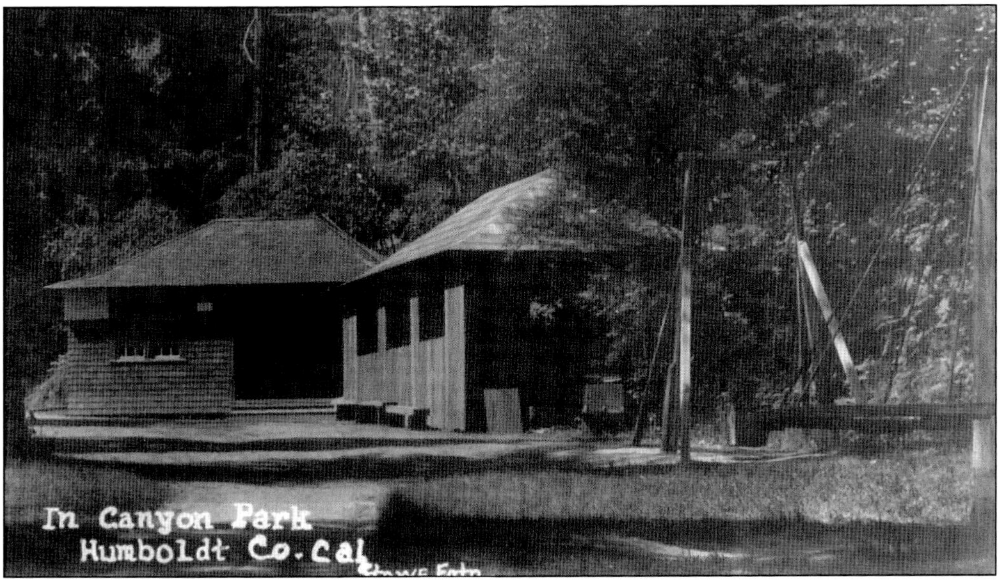

Jacobson transformed his 40 acres of old-growth property into a recreational area, complete with a pavilion, bandstand, concessions, and a four-person swing ride, in addition to many well-groomed paths. Known for its abundant ferns and mosses that created a sylvan setting, the park was a popular spot for hiking and picnics and hosted many gatherings. (Courtesy of the Humboldt County Historical Society.)

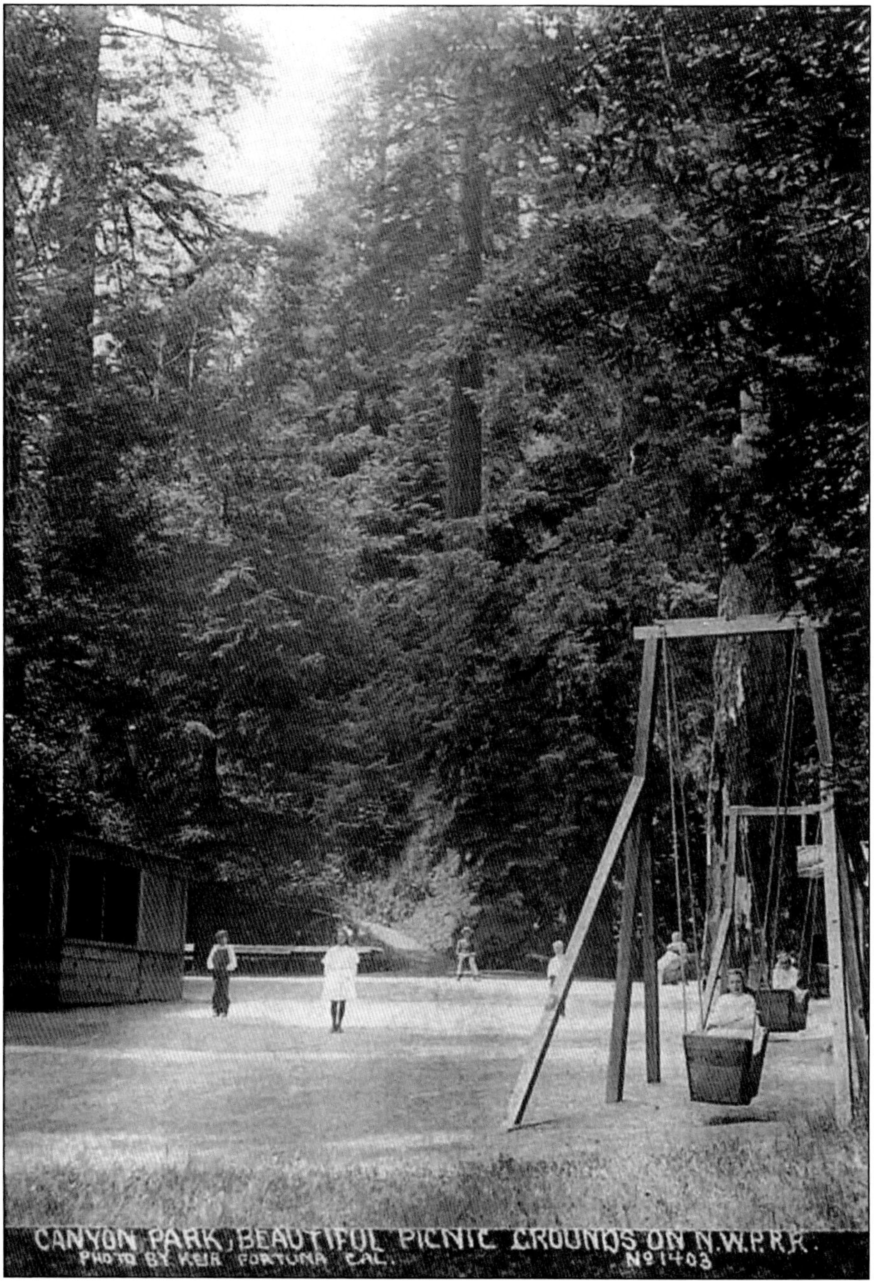

Canyon Park was the site of many Swedish and Danish picnics before lodges were built in the area by these groups. The railroad ran weekend excursion trains to Canyon Park, just a two-hour ride from Arcata, and more people were able to travel into the area for outdoor fun and relaxation. The Jacobsons sold ice cream and pastries and charged 25¢ for admission. The park was meticulously maintained and remained a county favorite for years. Jacobson continued to operate his park until the 1920s. After his death in 1930, the family sold the property. Despite some interest in reviving the park in the 1960s, it remained closed, and Canyon Park's stand of old-growth redwoods was logged for the first time in 1992. The park now lies choked with brush and all but forgotten by the communities it once meant so much to. (Courtesy of the Todd-Schuler/Bartleson family.)

Two

FROM FORESTVILLE TO SCOTIA

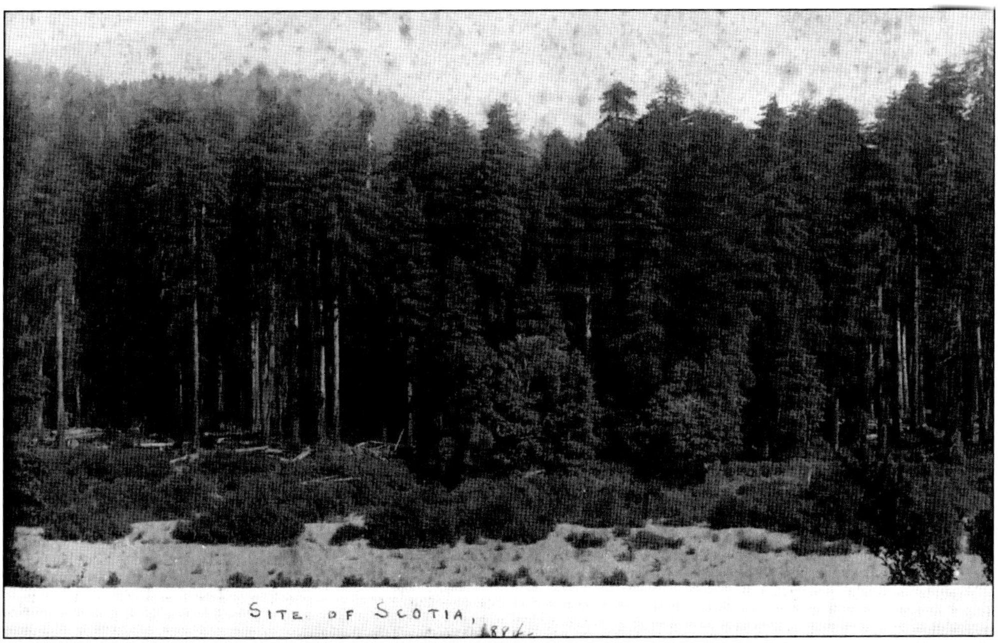

In 1883, the Pacific Lumber Company purchased land from Henry Niebur for its new mill south of Rio Dell. Known at the time as Forestville, the site would soon become the town of Scotia and the home of the Pacific Lumber Company and its workers. (Courtesy of the Humboldt State University Library, Humboldt Room, Palmquist Collection.)

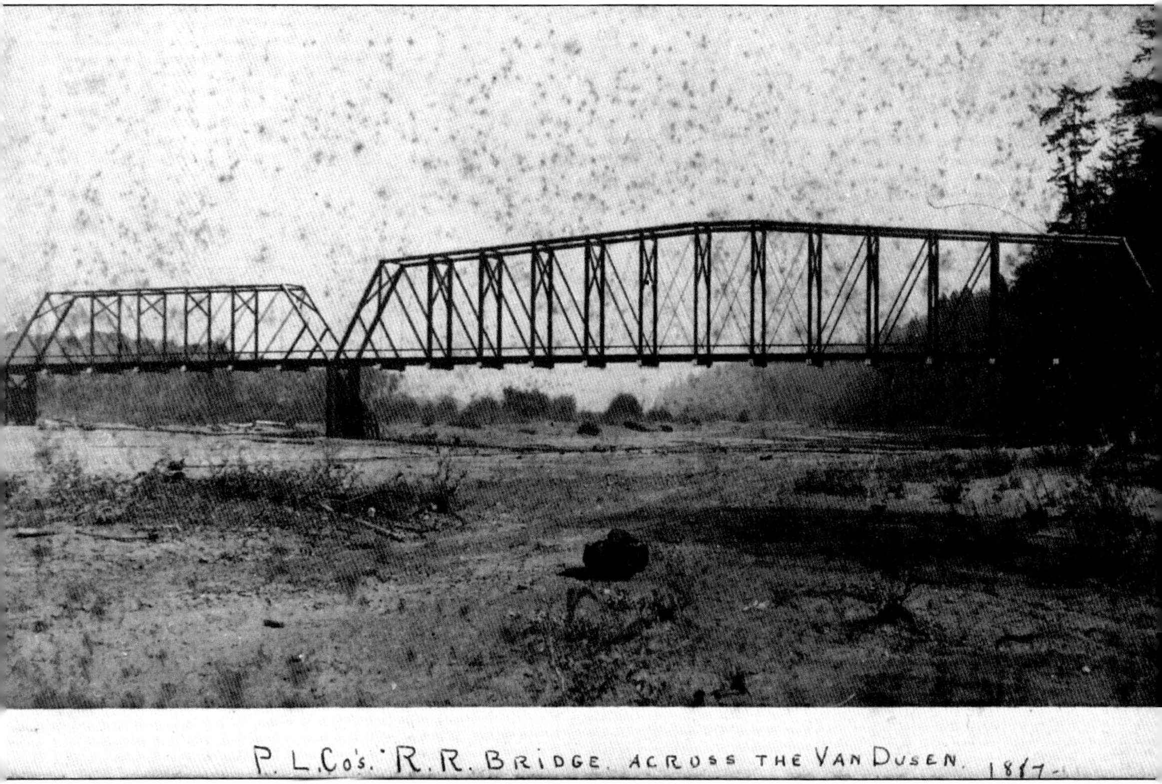

The first order of business for the Pacific Lumber Company was the construction of a railroad line, an essential part of its redwood logging operations. Railroads were used to get logs to the mills, crews to the woods, and finished lumber to the company's docks for shipping. George Douglas, a railroad engineer who had worked on the Nevada-Central Railroad, was hired as PL's general foreman in 1885. Arriving in Humboldt County in June of that year, Douglas brought with him a crew of experienced Chinese railroad workers. While 100 men labored to build a railroad bridge across the Van Duzen River, another 150 men worked at completing the line along the Scotia Bluffs to Forestville. A tent city was erected south of Alton, and bunkhouses were built to house the workers at the planned mill site. Cookhouses were maintained at both ends of the line to feed the hungry workers. (Courtesy of the Humboldt State University Library, Humboldt Room, Palmquist Collection.)

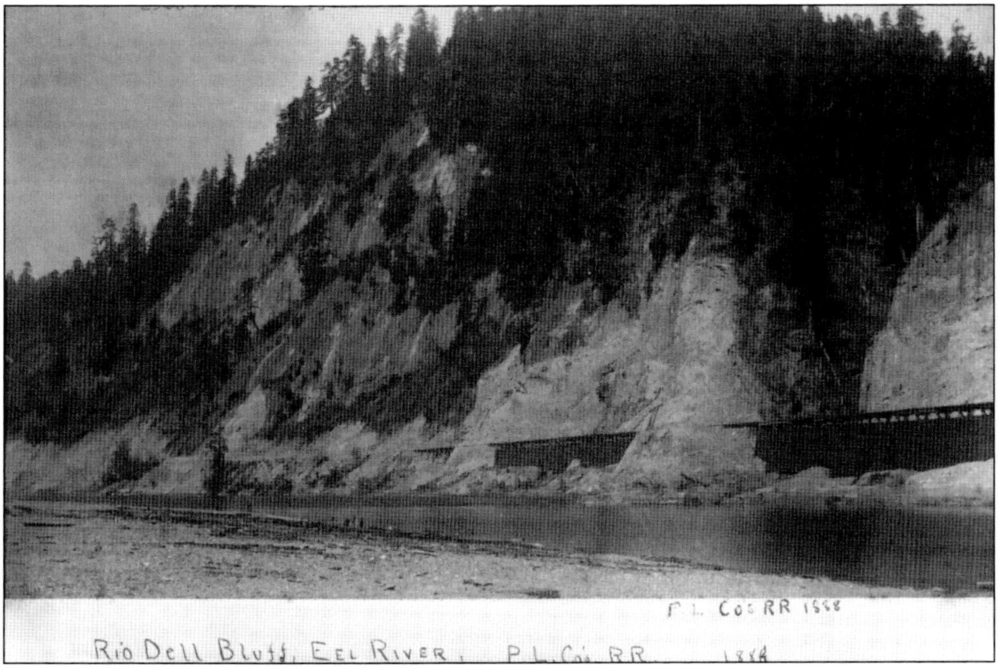

The construction of the rail line around the Scotia Bluffs was no easy task. Composed of marine sandstone and mudstone, the fossil-rich bluffs are plagued by frequent slides in the flood-prone Eel River Valley. The rail line entailed an elaborate series of retaining walls, benches, and trestles approximately 50 feet above the river during summer. (Courtesy of the Humboldt State University Library, Humboldt Room, Palmquist Collection.)

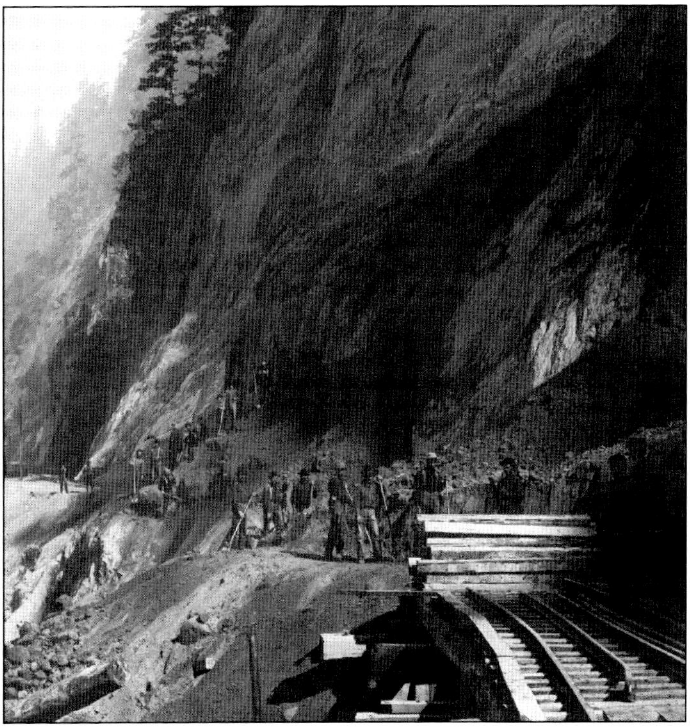

Although this stretch of railroad was completed in August 1885, work on this section of tracks never really ended, as they were almost constantly under repair. Because rail service was frequently interrupted by slides or flooding, a railroad bridge crew was assigned to work exclusively on the Scotia Bluff trestles from 1916 through 1959. (Courtesy of the Humboldt State University Library, Humboldt Room, Humboldt County Collection.)

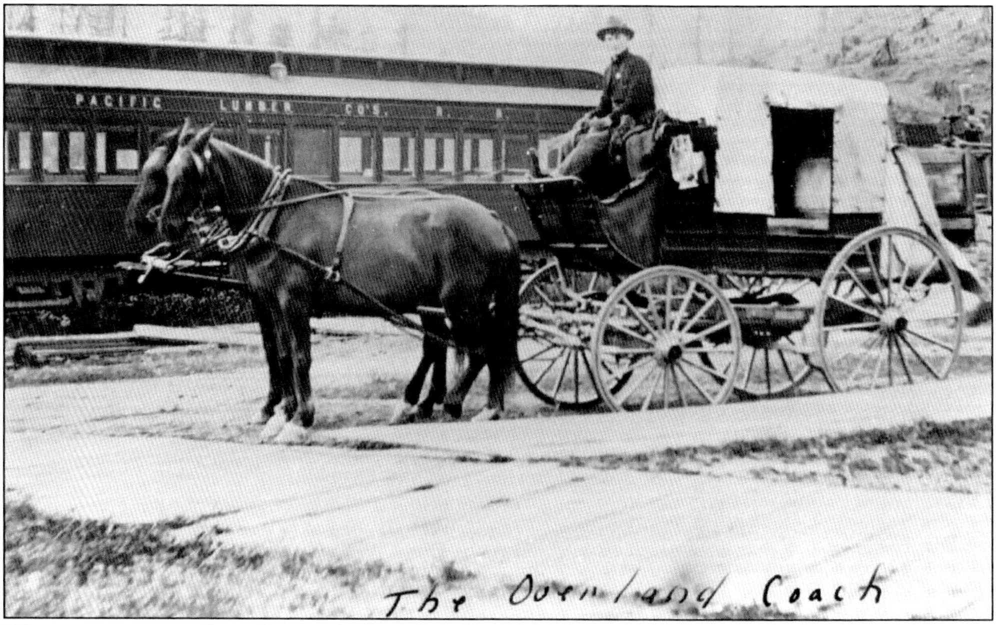

The construction of Pacific Lumber's railroad was essential to its logging operations but was also a highly anticipated boon to people living in the secluded, and undeveloped, southern end of the county. The rail line made it far quicker and easier for residents of these remote communities to get to Eureka and also encouraged people living in town to visit some of the county's more out-of-the-way places. In addition to providing passenger, freight, and mail services to these isolated areas, the railroad also ran excursion trains to Scotia, offering Eureka residents an opportunity for sight-seeing and picnicking. Horseback riding, picnicking, and hiking were popular activities in Scotia's scenic backcountry. (Both, courtesy of the Fortuna Depot Museum.)

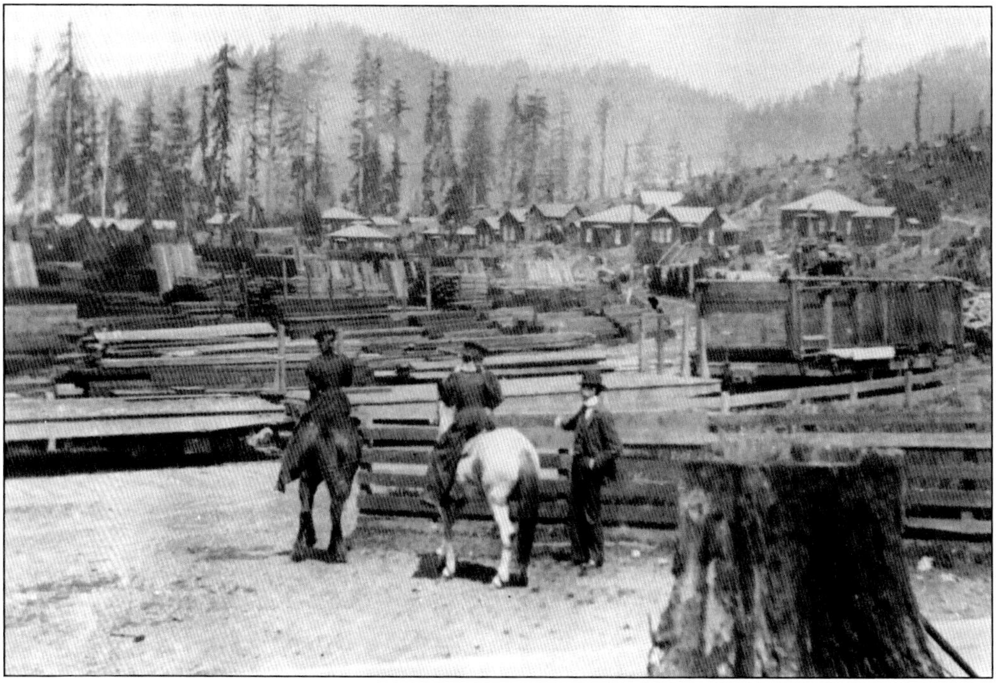

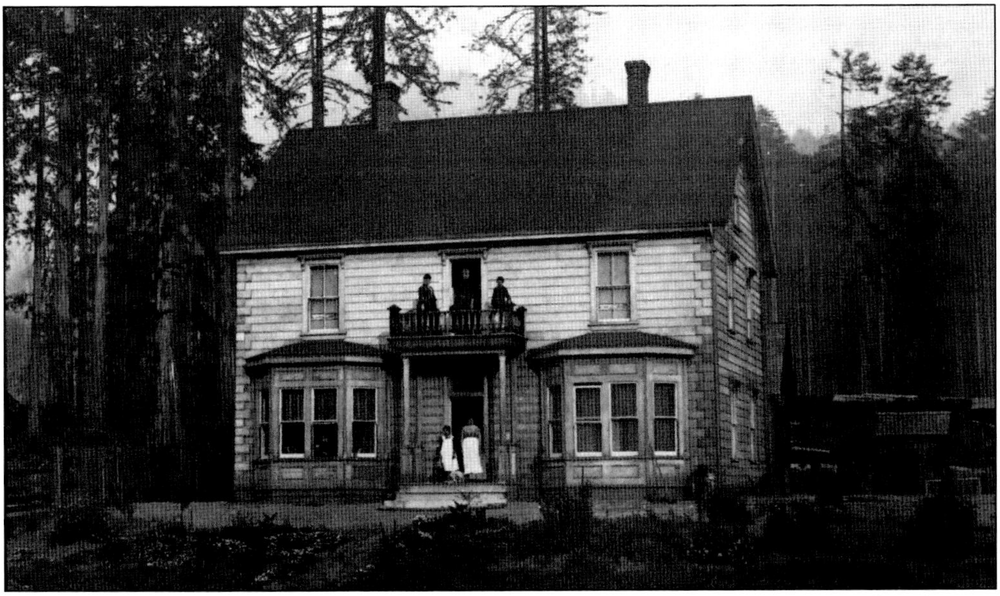

On completion of its rail line to Alton, PL laid off all but a few workers in the winter of 1885–1886. Those who remained were put to work building the home of company superintendent James A. Rigby, shown here. This was one of the first buildings constructed in Forestville by the Pacific Lumber Company. (Courtesy of the Humboldt State University Library, Humboldt Room, Palmquist Collection.)

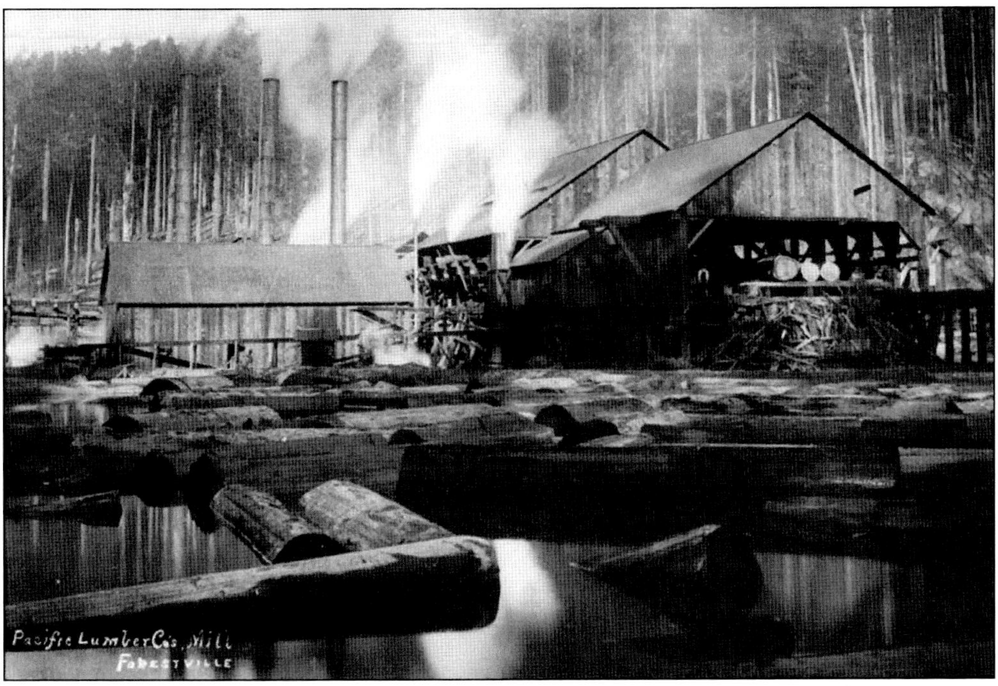

In April 1886, the company put on 150 men and began operations, starting with construction of its first sawmill using timber that was cut in Bluff Prairie and floated downriver to Forestville by William Shively. When the mill was completed, it was equipped with two circular saws, two edgers, hand trimmers, and three or four old-style planers. (Courtesy of Eldon Whitehead.)

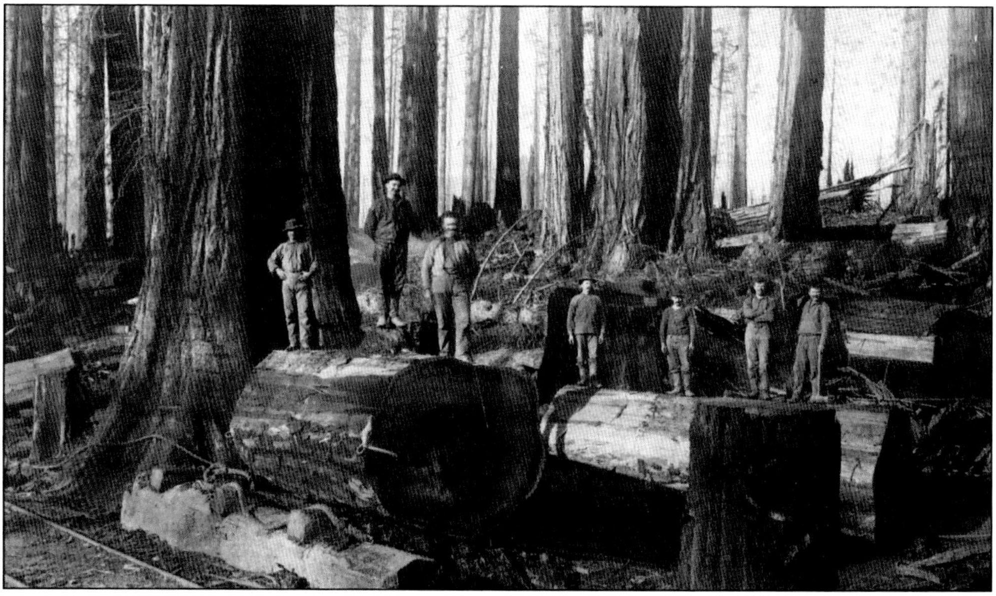

The following winter, timber fellers worked at clearing the area around the mill. Fellers went out in pairs, and each pair could usually take down one or two of the giant trees each day using axes, wedges, and saws. Much of what was cut that first year was used in the building of the company's facilities. (Courtesy of the Humboldt State University Library, Humboldt Room, Palmquist Collection.)

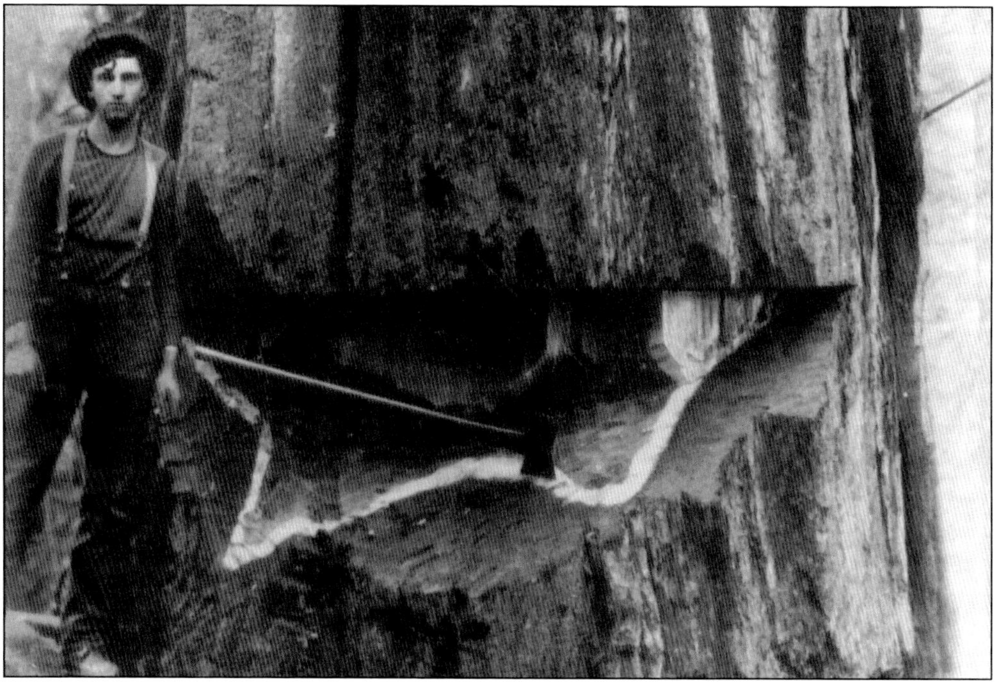

Before the introduction of industrial technologies, the work of cutting, hauling, and processing timber was performed by men and draft animals. Logging the redwoods was no easy task; felling and transporting a single tree could take up to a week to accomplish and required the efforts of a crew of men and animals. (Courtesy of the Fortuna Depot Museum.)

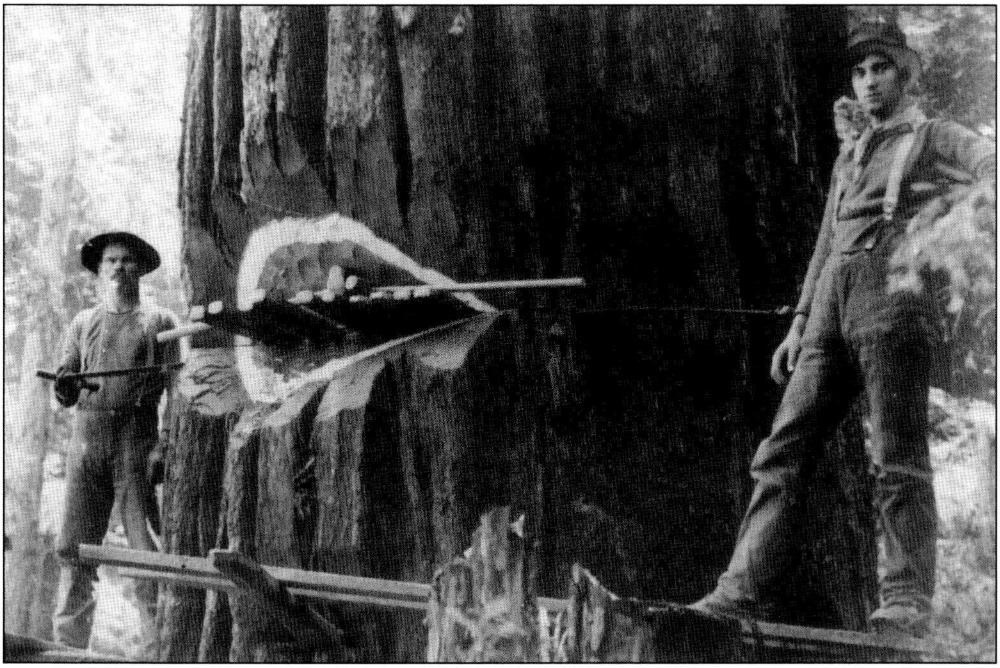

Using only hand tools, loggers in Scotia cut many acres of timber each season. A pair of veteran fellers could take down a tree like this in only a day. The first cut was made on the side of the tree facing the direction the loggers wanted the tree to fall, usually the uphill side. After cutting a notch, called an undercut, the choppers made the back cut from the opposite side. Axes were all that was used in the early days before the introduction of crosscut saws large enough to cut through the redwoods' massive trunks. (Above, courtesy of the Fortuna Depot Museum; below, courtesy of the Humboldt State University Library, Humboldt Room, Swanlund-Baker Collection.)

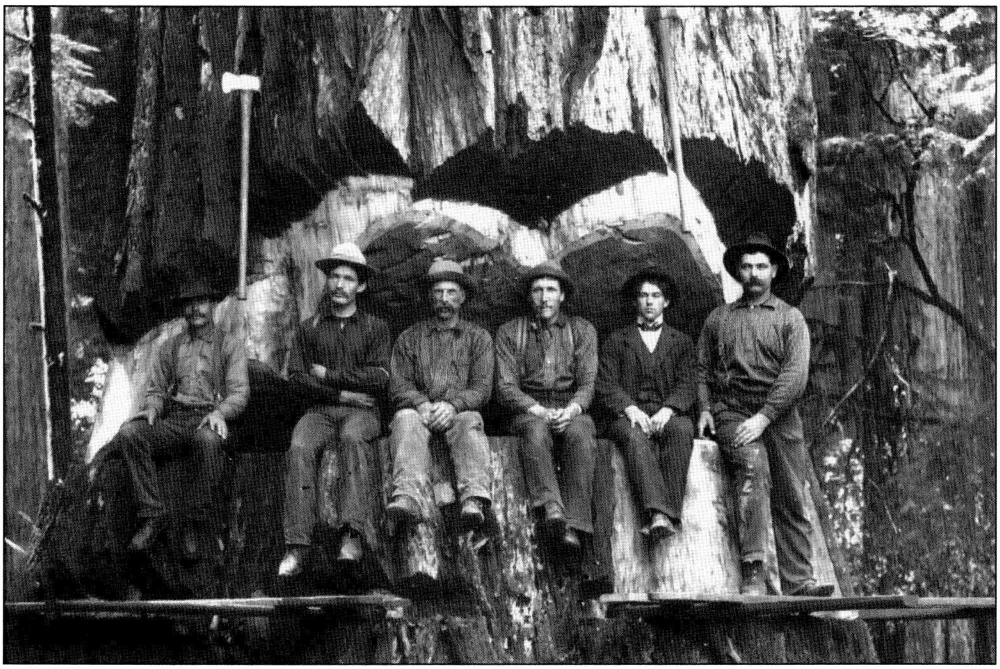

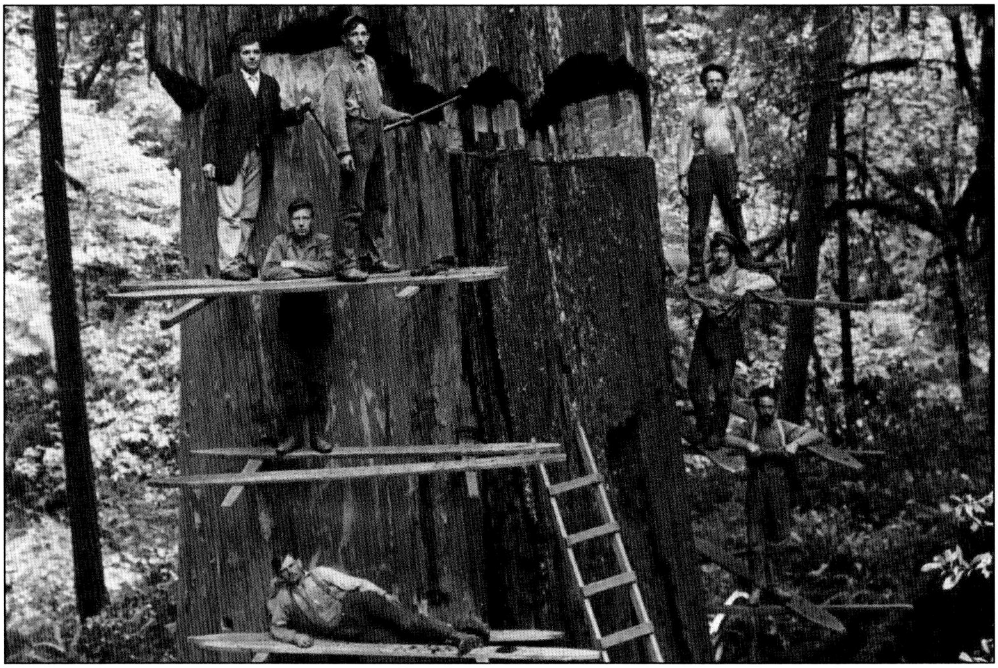

Early loggers usually built staging to stand on while they worked at felling the oversized redwoods. Working from these platforms, fellers began their cut above the often considerably larger and irregularly shaped bases of the trees. The base was often not as straight-grained as the rest of the tree and was harder to cut. (Courtesy of the Humboldt State University Library, Humboldt Room, Palmquist Collection.)

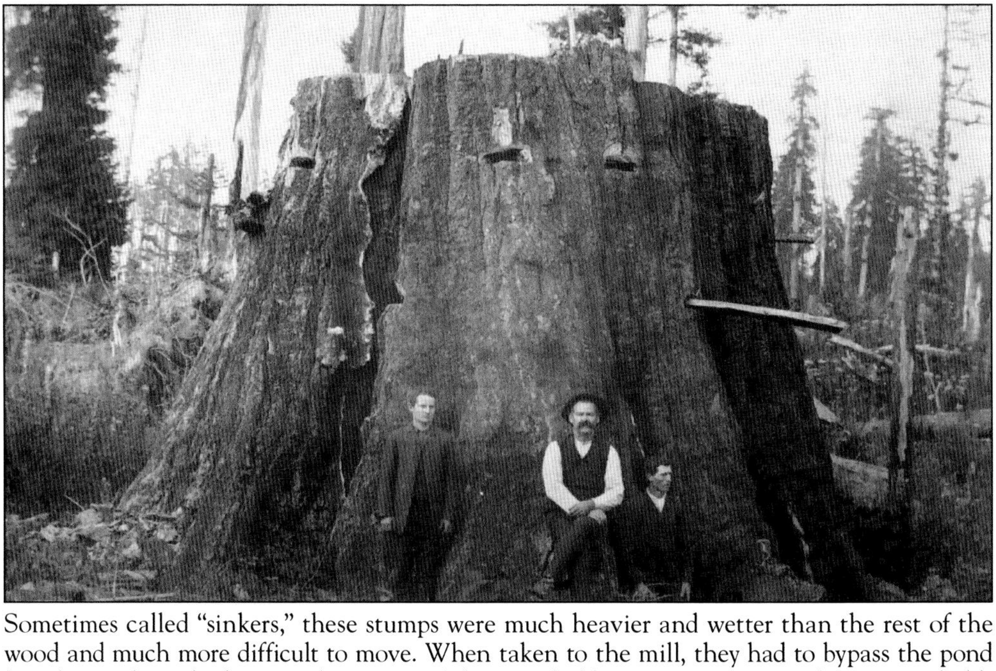

Sometimes called "sinkers," these stumps were much heavier and wetter than the rest of the wood and much more difficult to move. When taken to the mill, they had to bypass the pond lest they sink to the bottom. (Courtesy of the Humboldt State University Library, Humboldt Room, Palmquist Collection.)

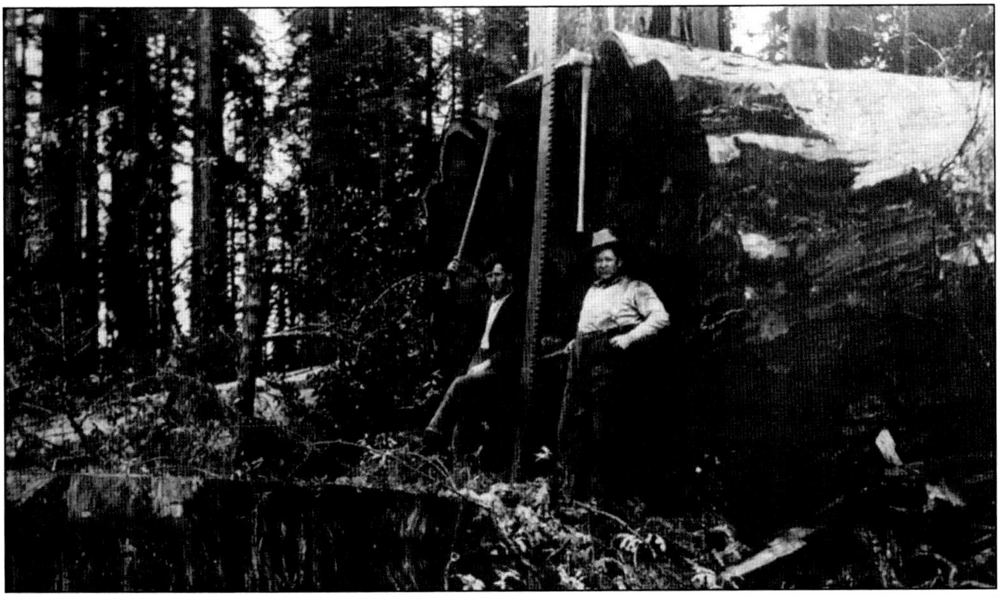

Felling the immense old-growth redwoods not only demanded a sharp axe and saw, it also required preparation and planning. Loggers would fell smaller trees across an area, creating a "bed" for the huge trees to fall into. Without this preparation, the colossal trees posed a serious risk to life and limb but could also be crushed by their own weight, splintering the wood and making it unusable as lumber. (Courtesy of the Humboldt State University Library, Humboldt Room, Boyle Collection.)

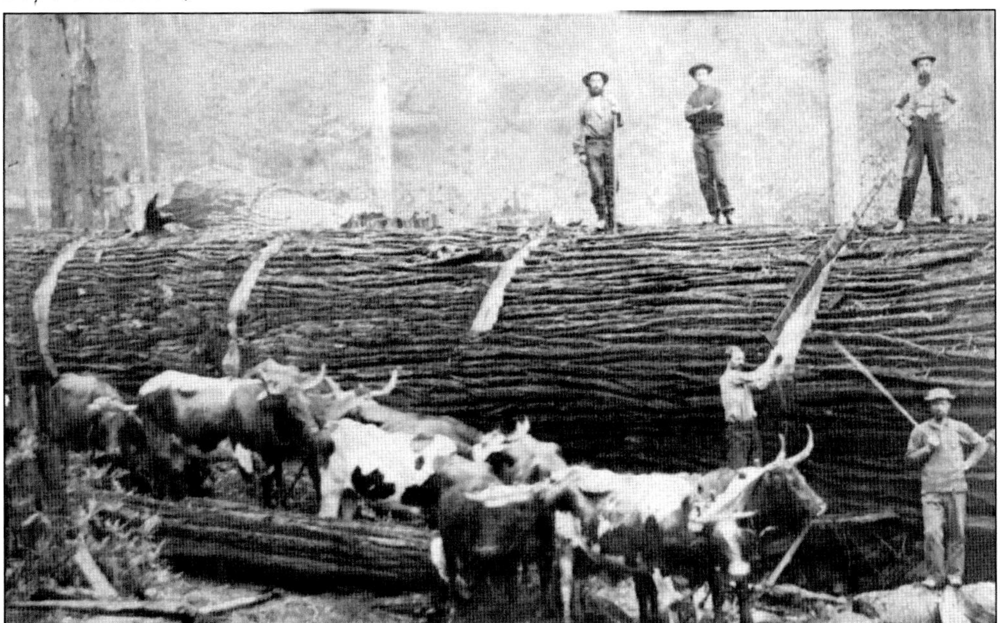

The massive trees had to be cut into lengths small enough to be dragged out of the woods. For many years, the job of felling and "bucking" these monsters down to size was accomplished using long, hand-drawn saws. These saws were known by those who used them as "misery-whips." (Courtesy of the Humboldt State University Library, Humboldt Room, Palmquist Collection.)

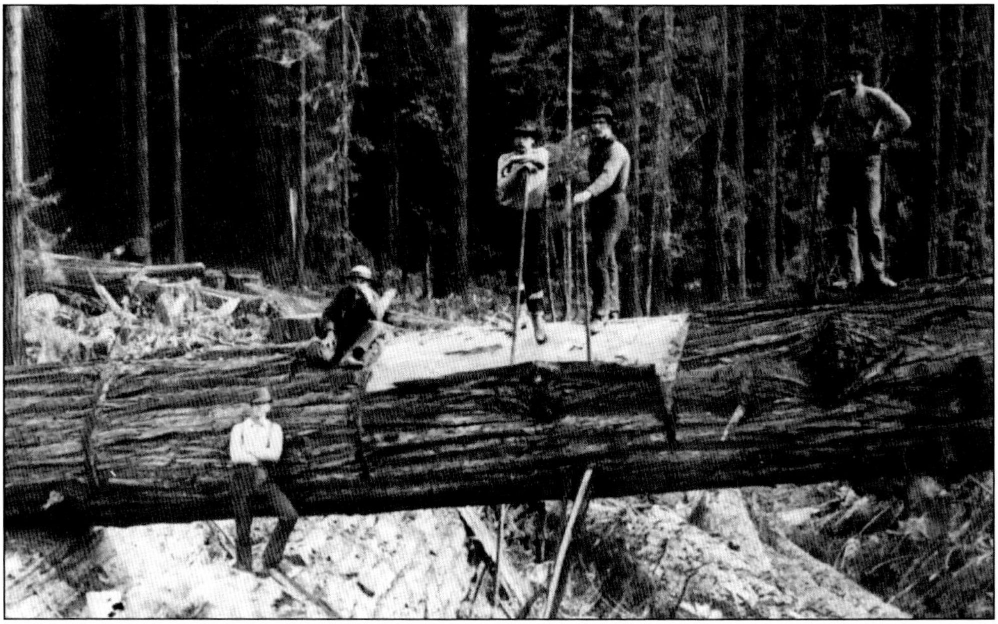

Once the work of felling the tree was completed, and before it could be hauled away by a team of draft animals, the strenuous task of removing the branches and bark began. In the early years, the bark was stripped in the woods, allowing the logs to slide more easily while being dragged out. Before the invention of heavy machinery to accomplish this, the work of peeling these fallen titans fell to men with axes and pry bars. In later years, the bark would often be left on the tree until it got to the mill. (Both, courtesy of the Humboldt State University Library, Humboldt Room. Above, Palmquist Collection; below, Swanlund-Baker Collection.)

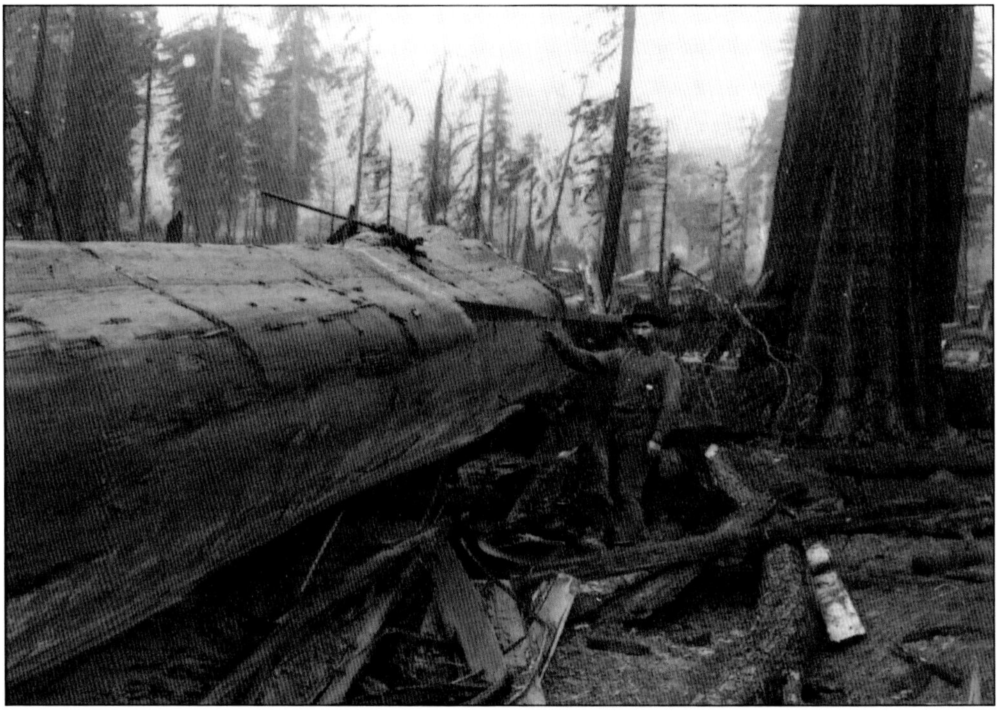

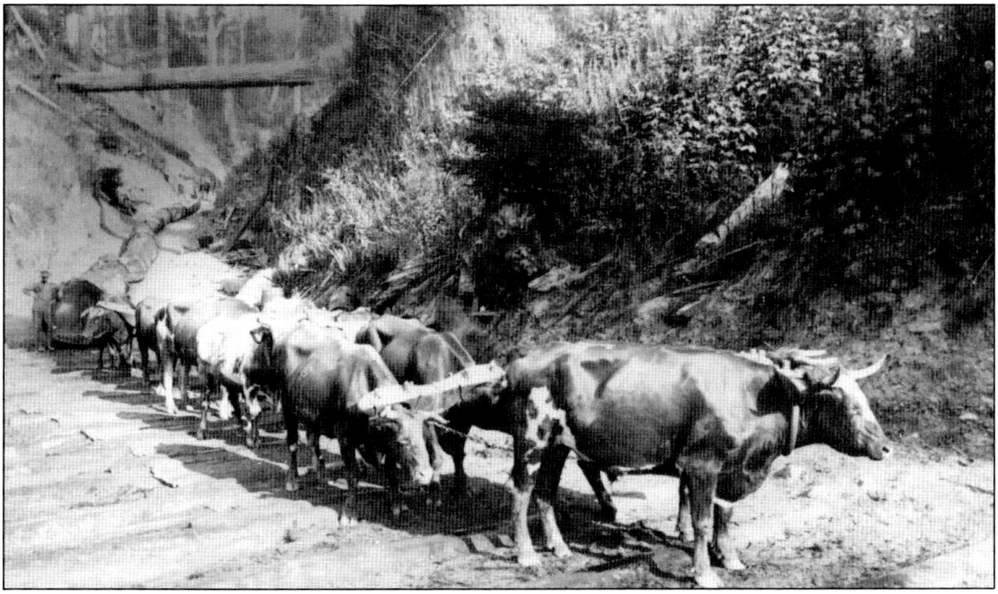

Beasts of burden were the heavy equipment of their day, and clever drivers were able to use them to lighten the workload for the human crew. For the first four to five years of operation, Pacific Lumber used teams of horses or oxen to haul the cut logs out of the woods. This job was made easier by the construction of skid roads. Sometimes called "corduroy roads," they were built by laying logs down side-by-side and filling in the gaps with dirt. These bumpy roads provided purchase for the draft animals to drag their burdens over the smooth, slick surface of the exposed logs. These logs would sometimes be wetted or greased to facilitate the movement of heavier burdens. Logs were dragged on the skid road to where they could be loaded onto one of PL's rail cars bound for the mill pond. (Both, courtesy of the Town of Scotia Company.)

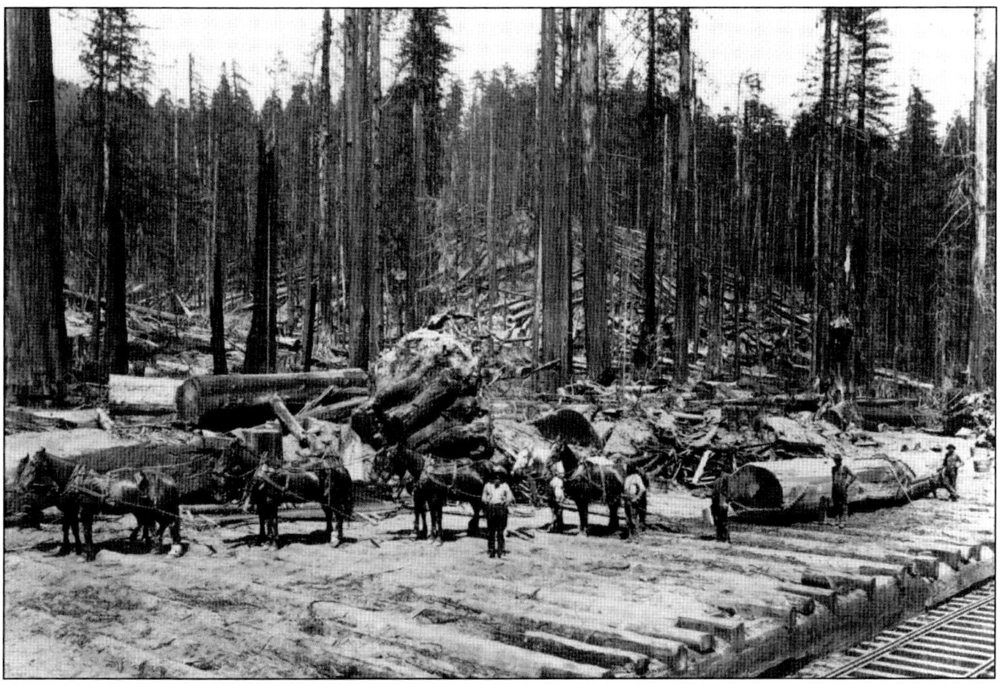

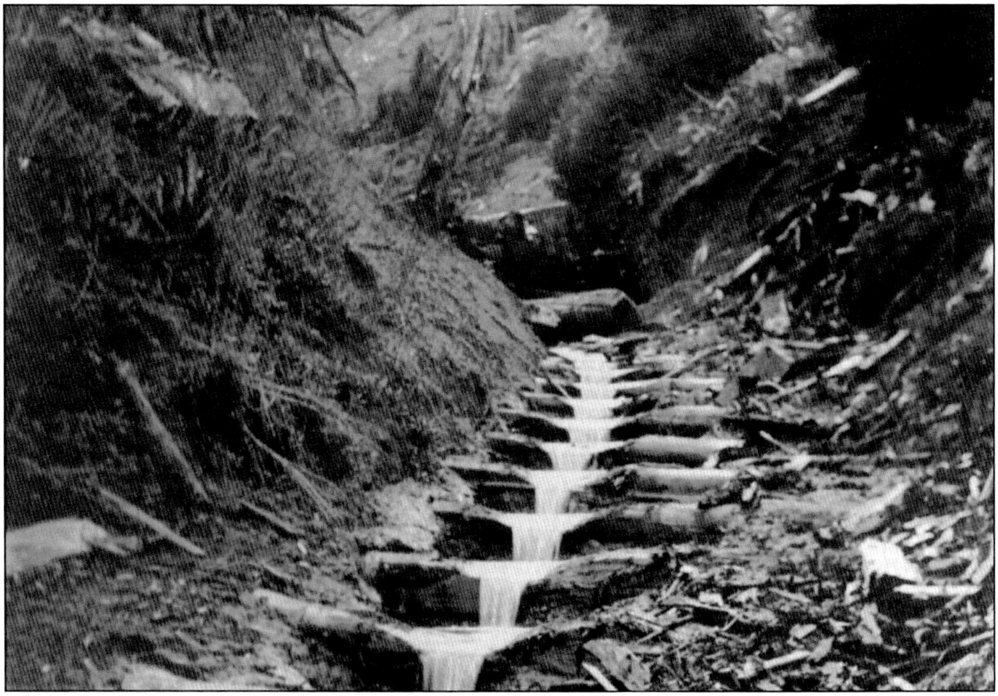

Logging companies built skid roads up nearly every creek-bed in the county. Most of these were left to be reclaimed by nature after logging had ceased. Redwood is a sturdy material, however, and a determined hiker can still find evidence of these corduroy roads in the backwoods of the county. (Courtesy of the Humboldt State University Library, Humboldt Room, Neill Collection.)

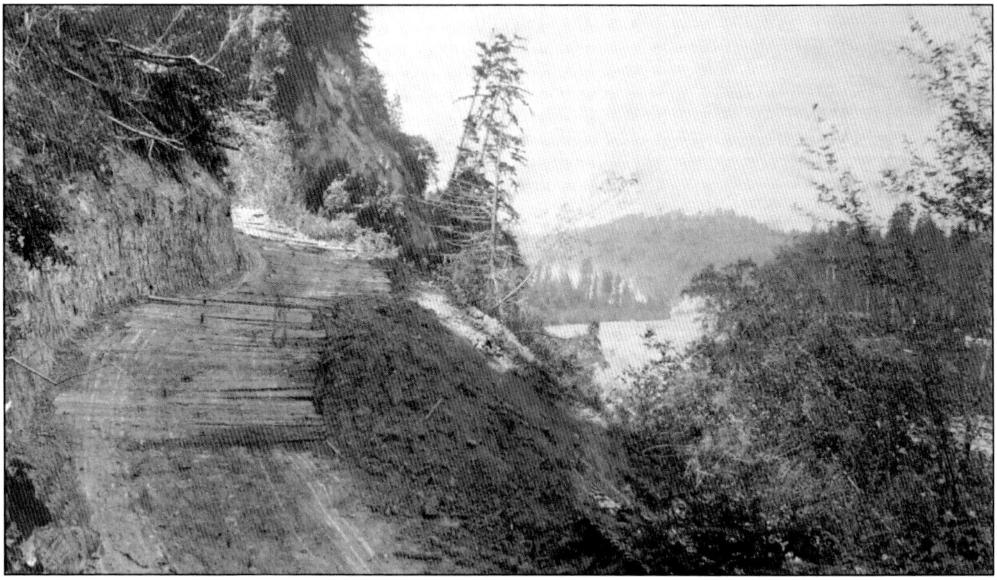

Loggers were not the only ones to make corduroy roads. Logs and planks of wood were often laid in roadbeds to prevent wagons from becoming stuck in the mud. This was a risk at any time of year in the damp Humboldt climate, and these log- and plank-studded roads made travel easier in the days before blacktop. (Courtesy of the Humboldt State University Library, Humboldt Room, HCC collection.)

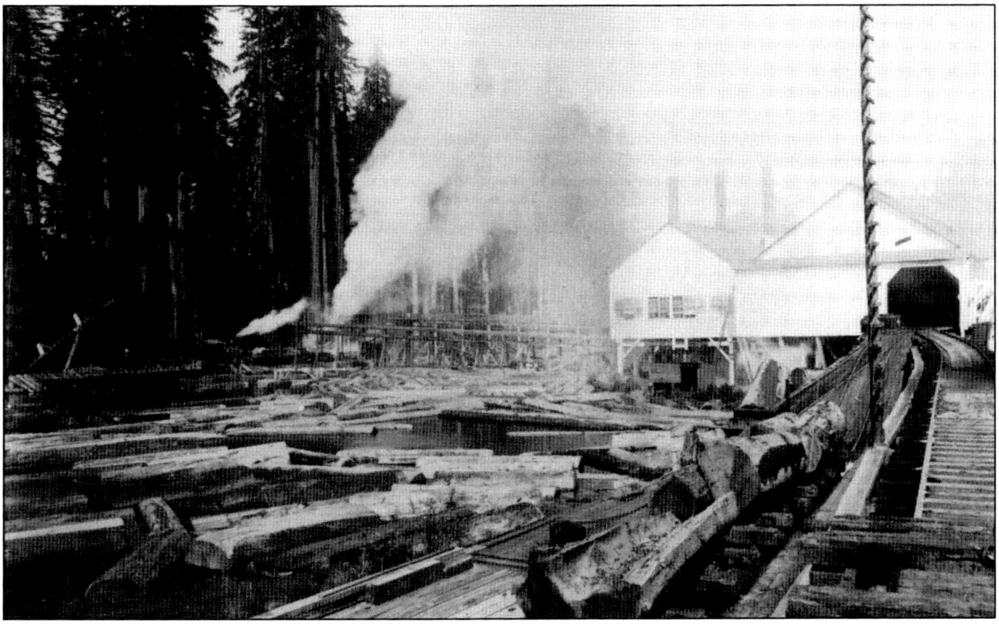

The sawmill was fired up for small-scale production in March 1887, and Pacific Lumber made its first shipment of lumber in June. It also constructed a shingle mill that year that was soon producing 200,000 shingles each day. This mill processed shingle bolts supplied by local contractors, who salvaged much of the waste wood left behind after logging operations. (Courtesy of the Humboldt State University Library, Humboldt Room, Palmquist Collection.)

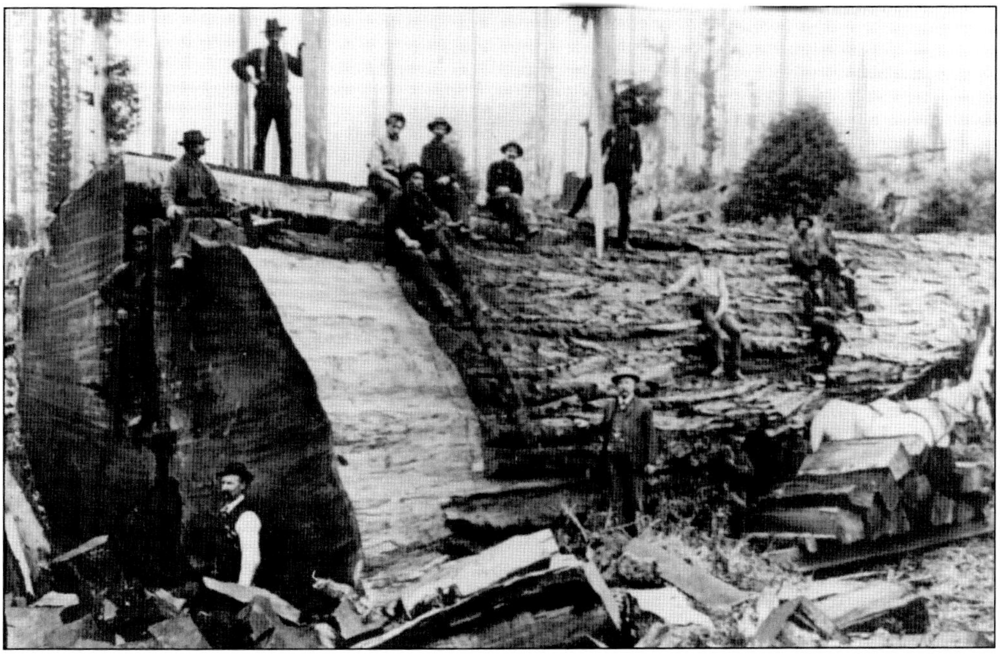

Within a year, Pacific Lumber was one of the country's biggest producers of shingles. The production of split redwood products—shake and shingle bolts, rail ties, fence posts, and grape stakes—continued to be an important source of income for many area families for generations. (Courtesy of the Humboldt State University Library, Humboldt Room, Palmquist Collection.)

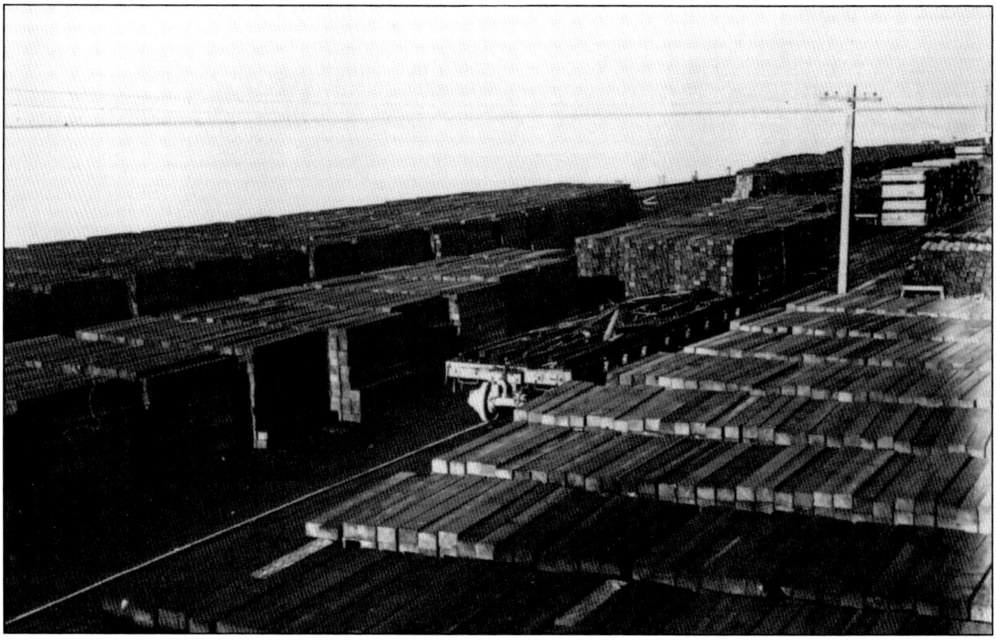

A wharf was built in Fields Landing using pilings and lumber cut in Scotia, the first wood to be shipped out on the company's railroad. The Pacific Lumber Company's dock was 200 by 800 feet and had several turntables for turning railcars. The wharf is shown here heavily laden with thousands of railroad ties awaiting shipment. (Courtesy of the Humboldt State University Library, Humboldt Room, Swanlund-Baker Collection.)

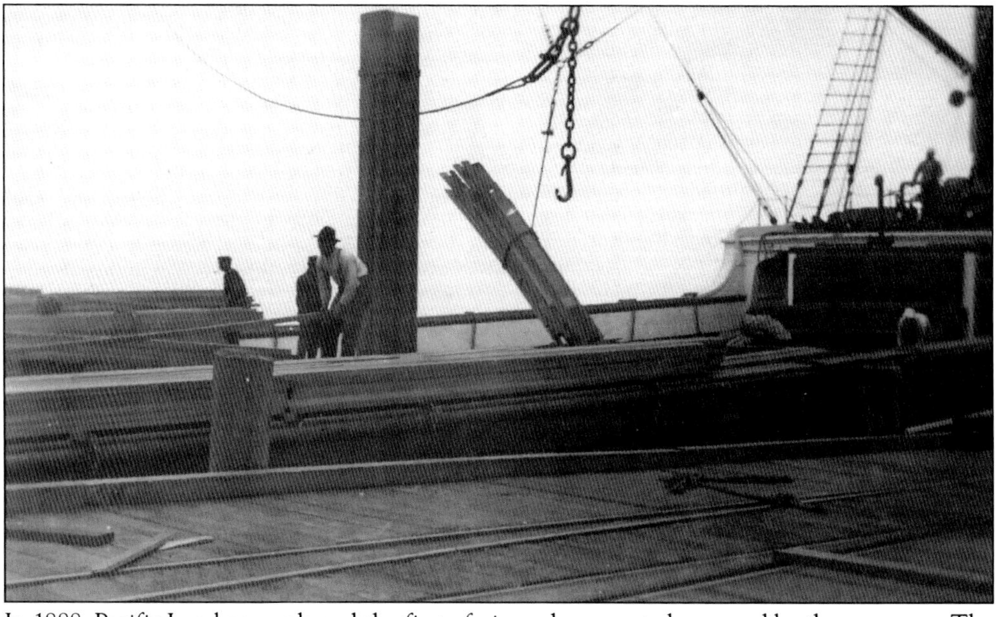

In 1888, Pacific Lumber purchased the first of nine schooners to be owned by the company. The ship was named the *Allen A.*, in honor of company president Allen A. Curtis. The company later added the ships *Hellen N. Kimball, National City, John A., Aberdeen, Despatch, Prentiss, Temple E. Dorr*, and the *William H. Murphy* to its fleet. (Courtesy of the Humboldt State University Library, Humboldt Room, Neill Collection.)

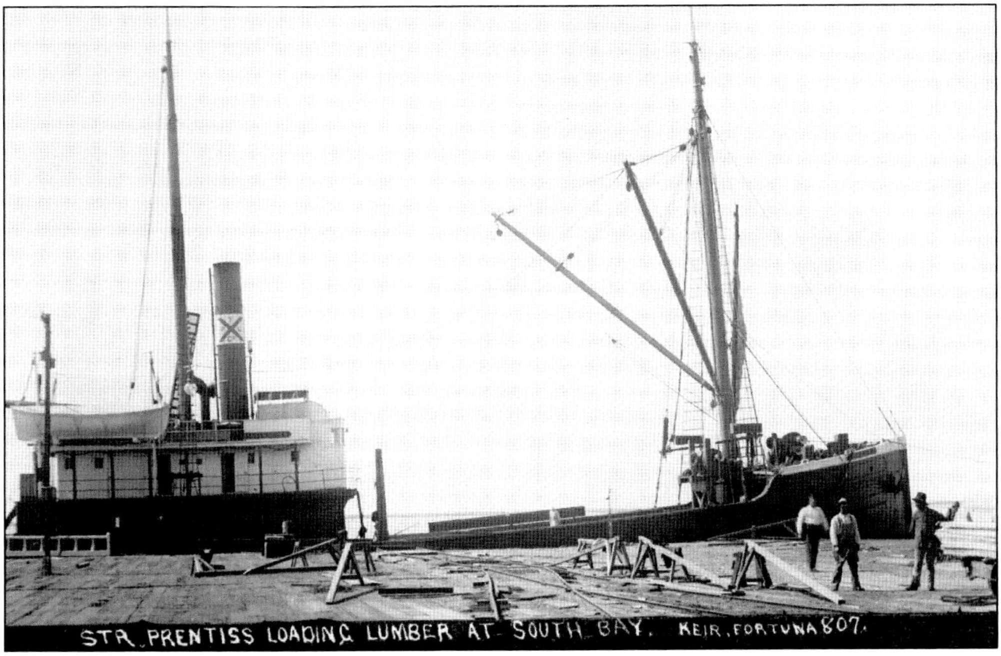

Bearing the distinctive "TPLCo" trademark on its smokestack, the *Prentiss* is shown being loaded at the company dock in Fields Landing. Lumber schooners, first sail-powered and later steam-driven, were the only means of transporting lumber out of the area before 1914. (Courtesy of the Humboldt State University Library, Humboldt Room, Palmquist Collection.)

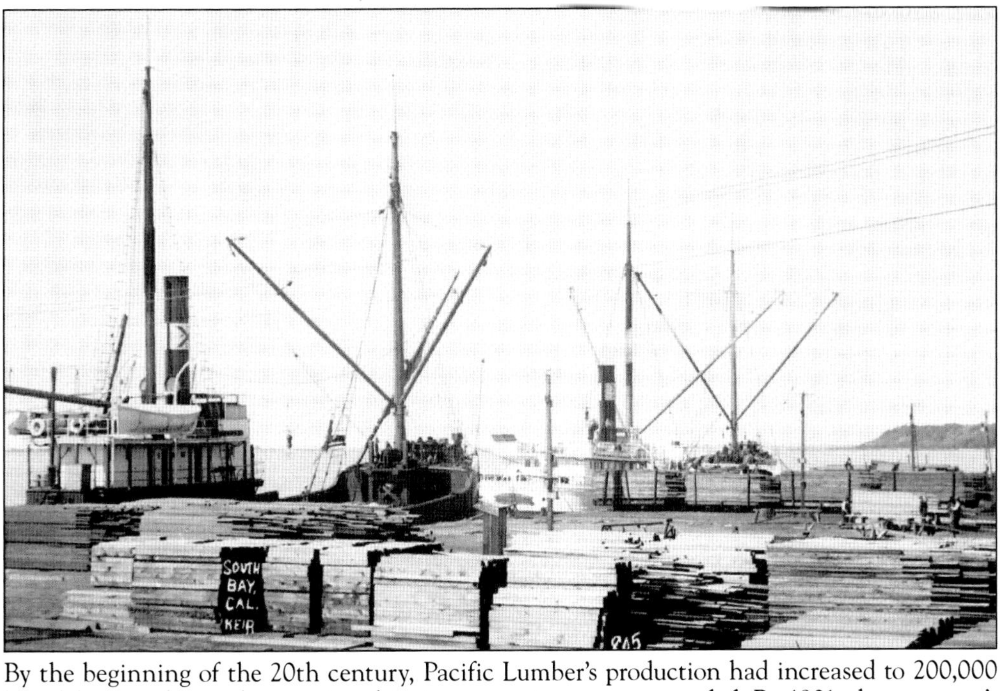

By the beginning of the 20th century, Pacific Lumber's production had increased to 200,000 board feet per day, and its marine shipping operations were expanded. By 1901, the company's fleet of schooners began exporting lumber to Hawaii and Japan. (Courtesy of the Humboldt State University Library, Humboldt Room, Palmquist Collection.)

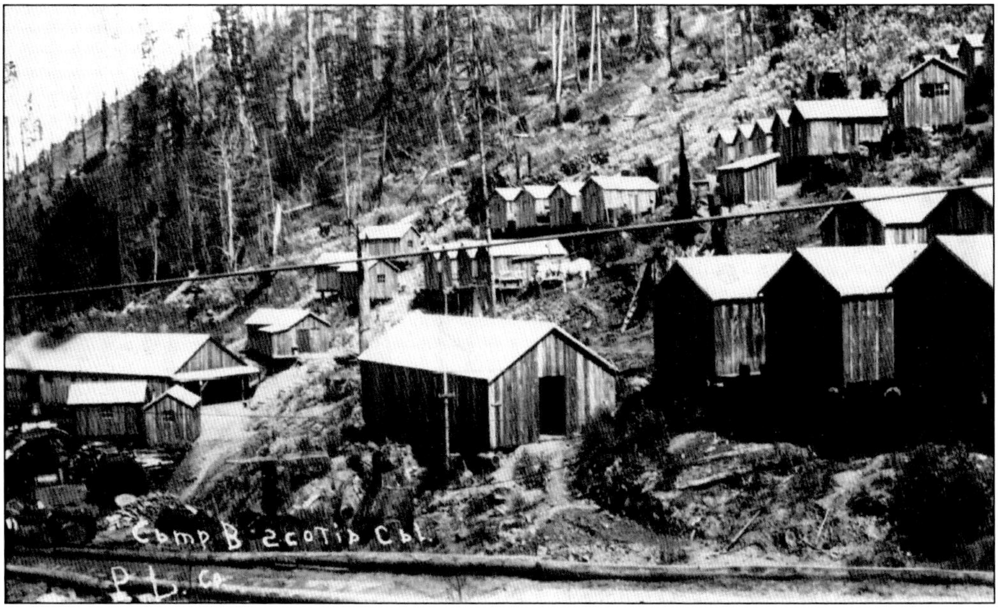

Many of Pacific Lumber Company's workers lived in camps like those shown here. These camps consisted of little more than bunkhouses and a cookhouse. Early PL bunkhouses were simple one-room shacks with bunks for six to eight men. PL built logging camps in many places to serve the needs of its timber operations. (Courtesy of the Humboldt State University Library, Humboldt Room, Palmquist Collection.)

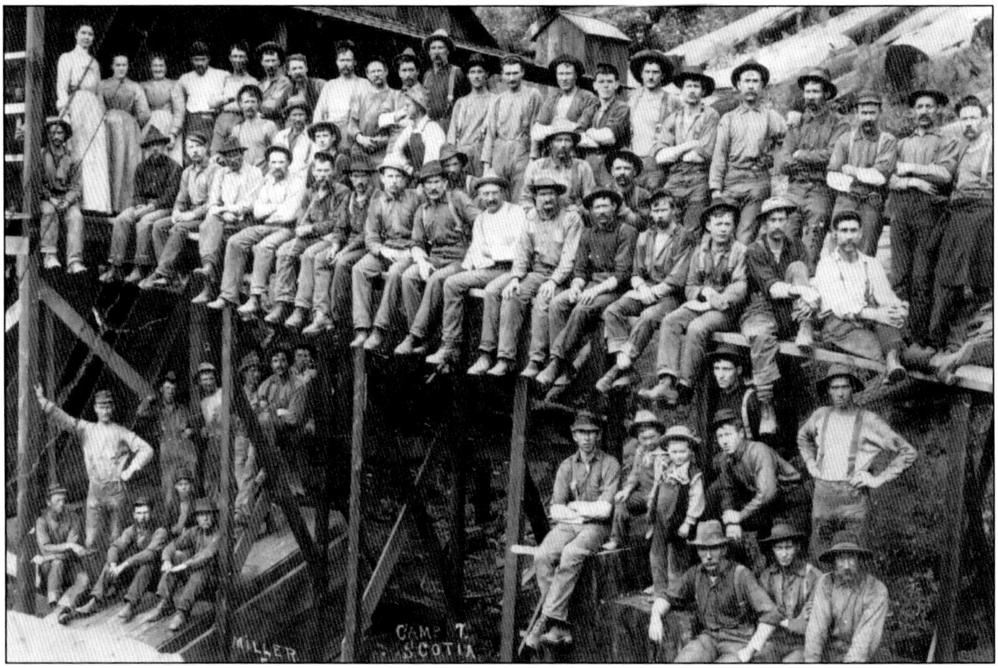

People living in these logging camps worked long hours, and this was particularly true for the camp cooks. Some of the few female employees working for the company, these women were reported to work from well before sun up until long into the evening preparing hearty meals for large crews of hungry men. (Courtesy of the Town of Scotia Company.)

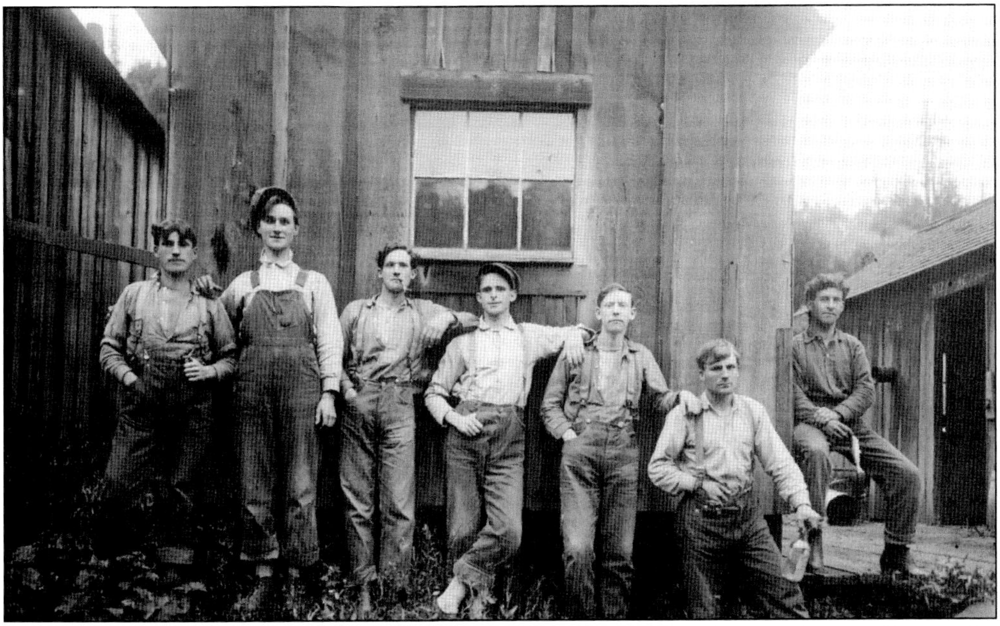

Much like their logging camp counterparts, many of Pacific Lumber's workers in Forestville slept in bunkhouses. These were a no-frills affair in the 1880s and 1890s, and tired lumbermen could expect a dry bunk and a wood stove for heat, but not much else. They could also expect to share their quarters with a half-dozen or more of their fellow laborers. (Courtesy of the Town of Scotia Company.)

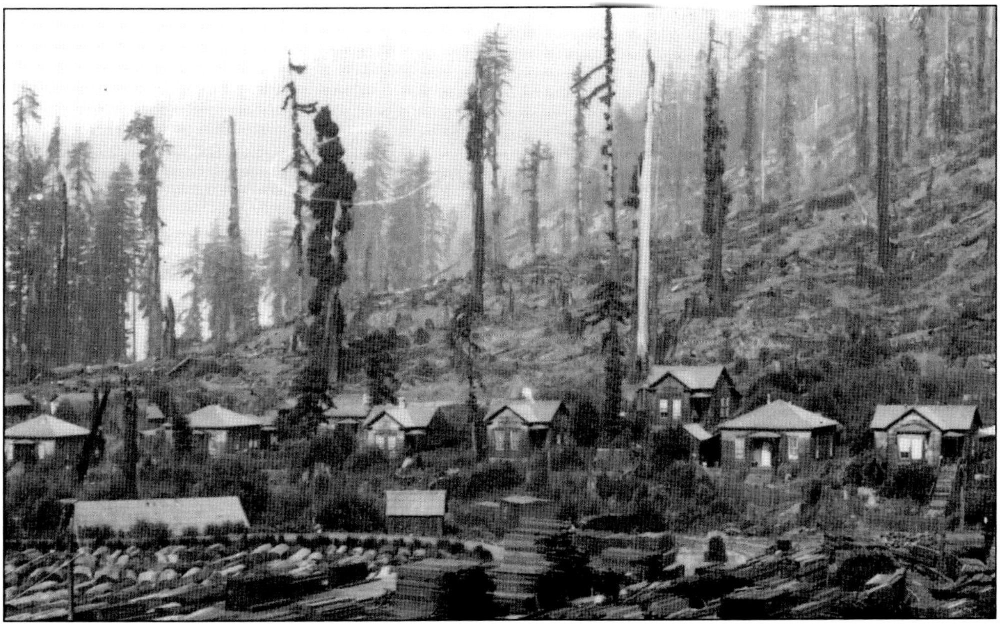

In addition to the bunkhouses, Pacific Lumber also began building houses for married men and their families. The first family homes in the company's town were for the company managers, but by the 1890s, as married men came to be seen as more reliable and less likely to fall to drink or walk off of the job, more family housing was built. (Courtesy of the Humboldt State University Library Humboldt Room, Palmquist Collection.)

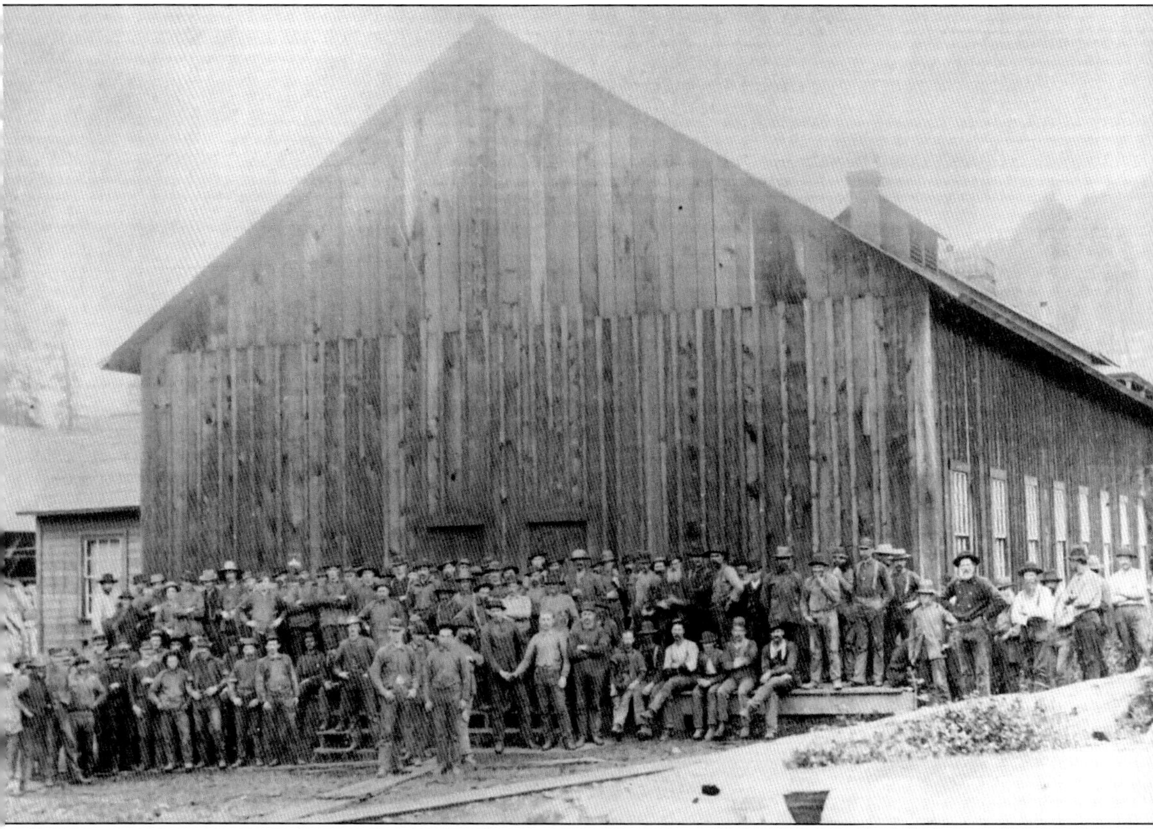

Cookhouses were erected in Forestville and at the company's logging camps. The Pacific Lumber Company's cooks and cookhouses were seen as a vital part of maintaining a productive workforce. These cookhouses served the workers three meals a day, and some employed over a dozen people to provide the hard-working men with hearty meals. Good food and lots of it was an important part of retaining good workers, and timber companies competed with each other to have the best cooks. PL provided its cooks with beef from the company's herd and produce and dairy products from its own gardens and from other local producers. Dinner in the cookhouse was often the only thing a tired, single worker had to look forward to after a long shift, and the company tried to keep quality as high as possible. (Courtesy of the Fortuna Depot Museum.)

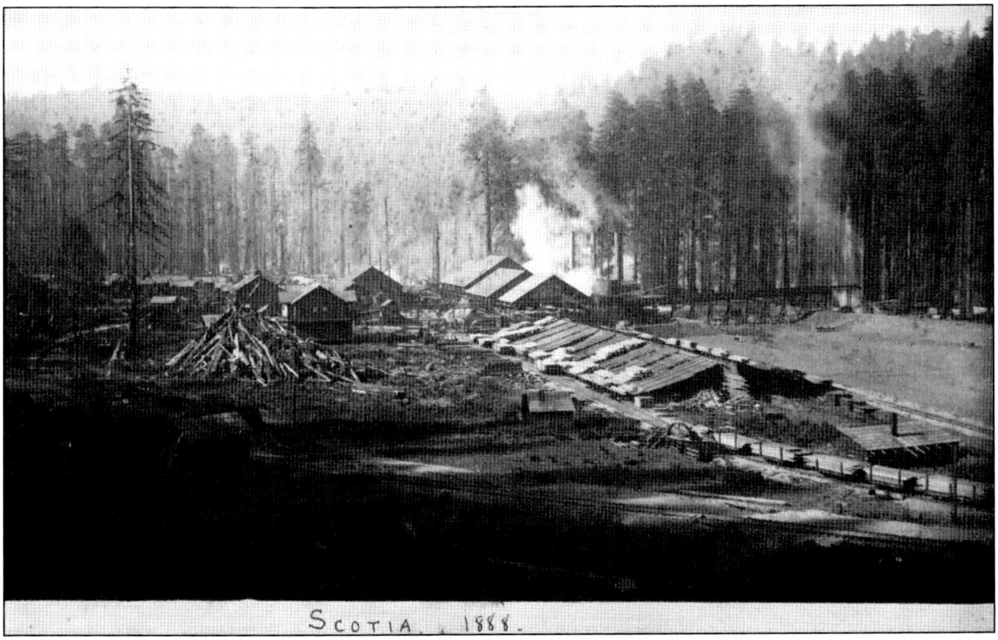

The Pacific Lumber Company's operations slowly turned Forestville into a company town. One hundred houses were built and a boardinghouse constructed that would soon be expanded to become the first Scotia Hotel. When a post office was established in 1888, the town's name was officially changed to Scotia, as there was already a town named Forestville in Sonoma County. The name Scotia is said to have been chosen by coin toss, the other possibility being Brunswick. Both names were evidently chosen for the Canadian loggers who made up a large percentage of the early workforce at Pacific Lumber. (Both, courtesy of the Humboldt State University Library, Humboldt Room, Palmquist Collection.)

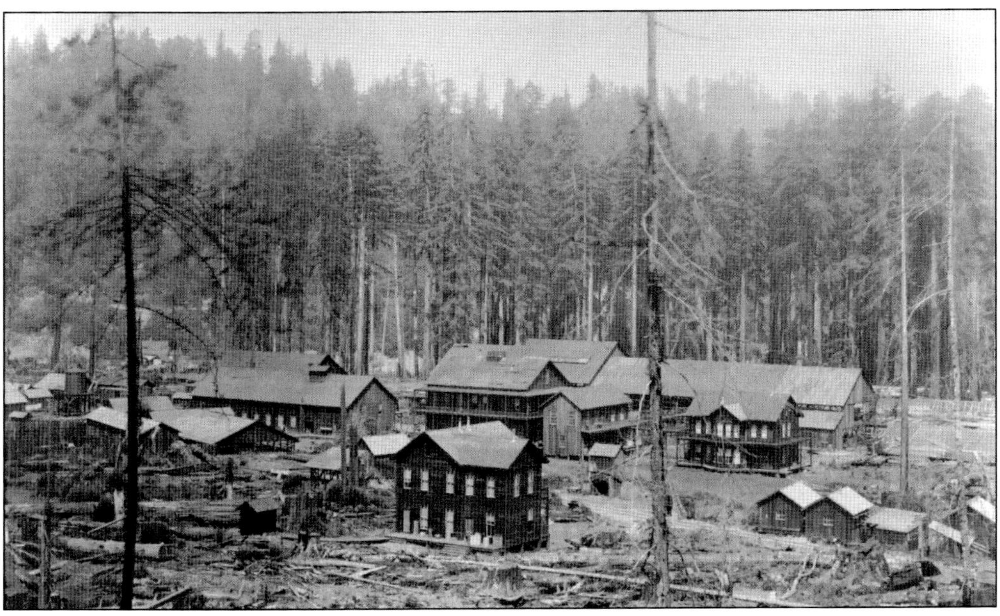

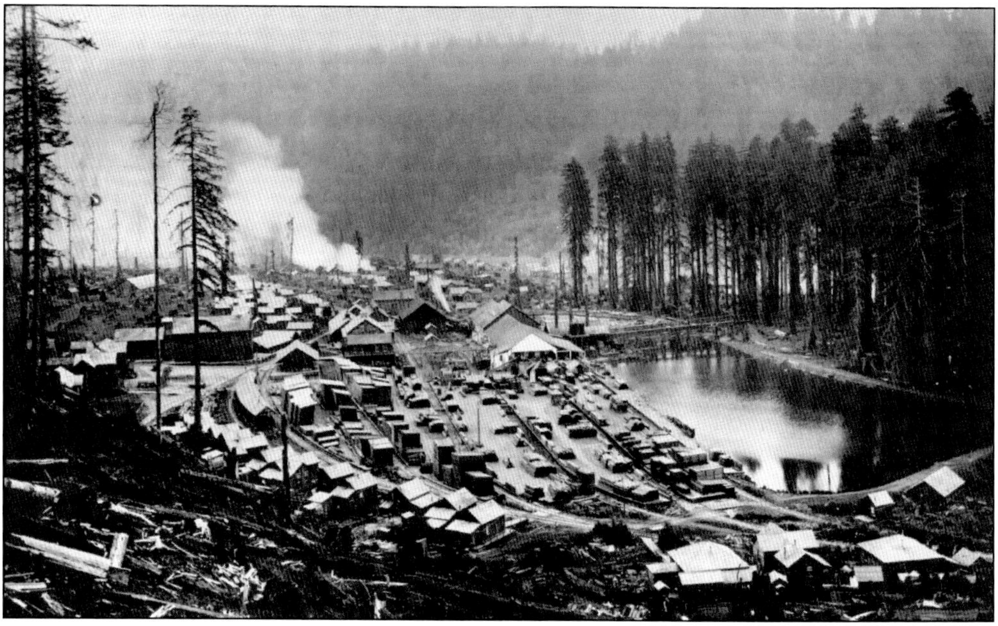

A Southern California housing boom in the late 1880s created an increased demand for redwood timber products, and Pacific Lumber stepped up production. The town grew, and by 1890, included a hotel, a telegraph office, a mercantile, a drugstore, a liquor store, and a schoolhouse, which also served as a church on Sundays and was at first served by a circuit-riding pastor. (Courtesy of the Town of Scotia Company.)

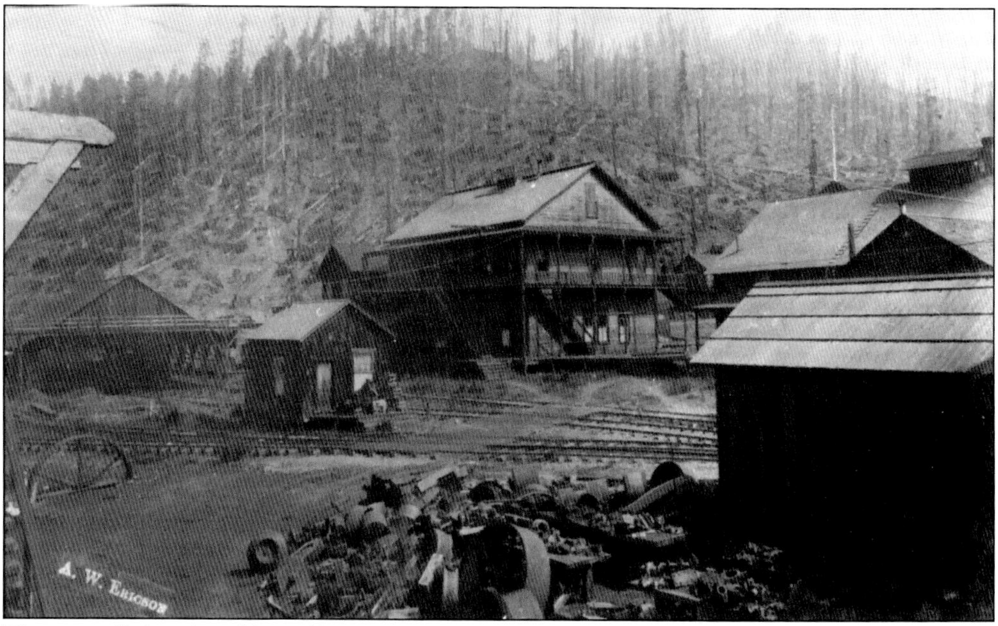

The sawmill, hotel, stables, offices, and company store were all supplied with electric lights by 1890, powered by PL's first power plant. The company store was located in the first floor of the building shown here, with Pacific Lumber's offices located above. The store carried a wide variety of goods, from boots and rain gear to toiletries and postcards. (Courtesy of the Humboldt County Historical Society.)

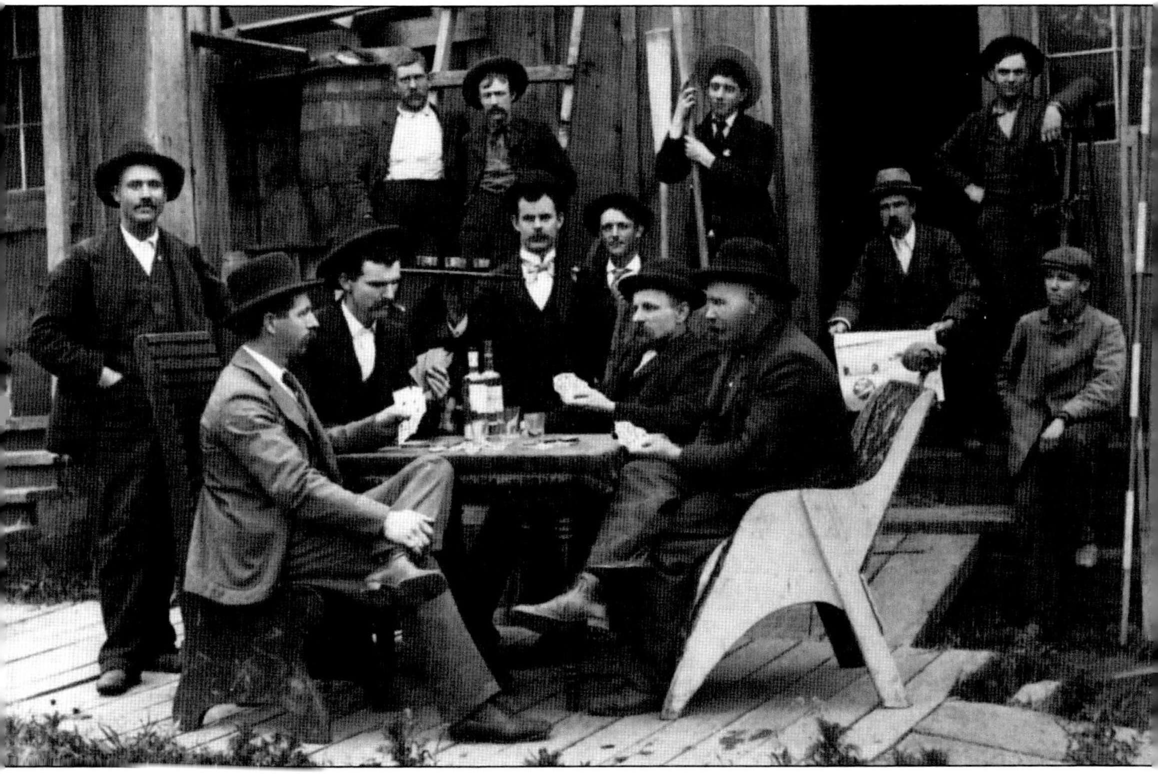

Workers in need of goods or services not offered in Scotia, or who just wanted to drink and carouse out of sight of the boss, would often cross the river to Rio Dell. A night of such festivities in Rio Dell sometimes left Pacific Lumber workers too sick to function, a problem the company blamed on bad, "rot-gut" whiskey. When asked by company president Allen Curtis how they should combat the problem, superintendent George Douglas replied, "build a saloon in Scotia and stock it with the best liquor we can buy." The company took this advice, building the company's saloon in 1888; it stayed open in Scotia until after the turn of the century. Scotia's other drinking establishment was the Green Goose, a gambling den and drinking parlor run by Gene Emerson and his wife. It was located near the picnic grounds until PL management encouraged the Emersons to move farther upriver. (Courtesy of the Humboldt State University Library, Humboldt Room, Palmquist Collection.)

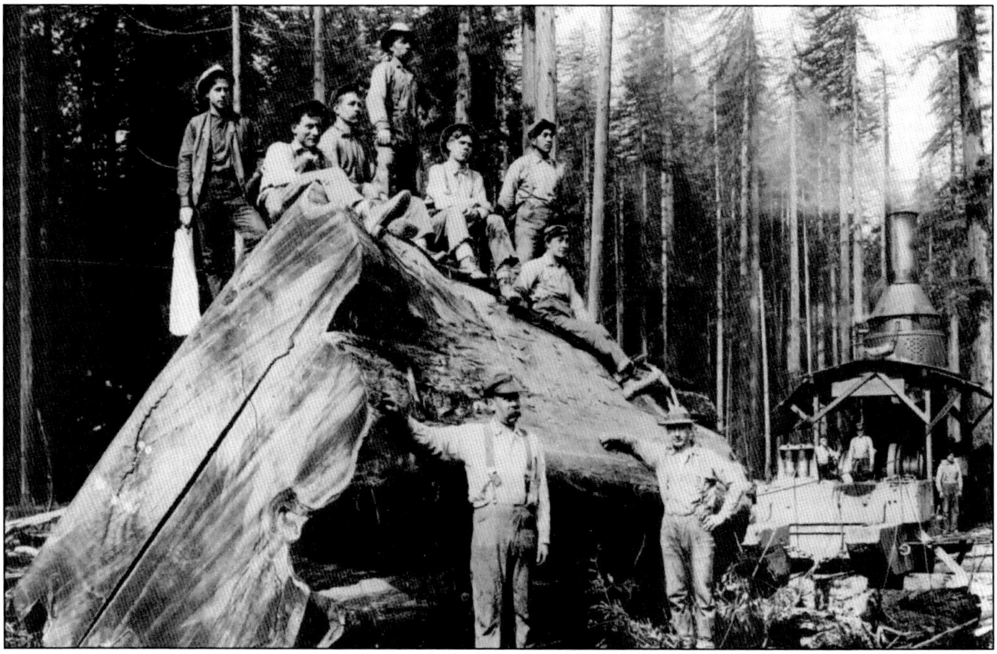

John Dolbeer's logging engine, invented in Humboldt County and patented in 1881, revolutionized the timber industry. Dolbeer's engine, commonly known as the steam donkey or donkey engine, was a steam-powered winch that gradually replaced horses and oxen as the primary means of moving the huge logs out of the woods. (Courtesy of the Town of Scotia Company.)

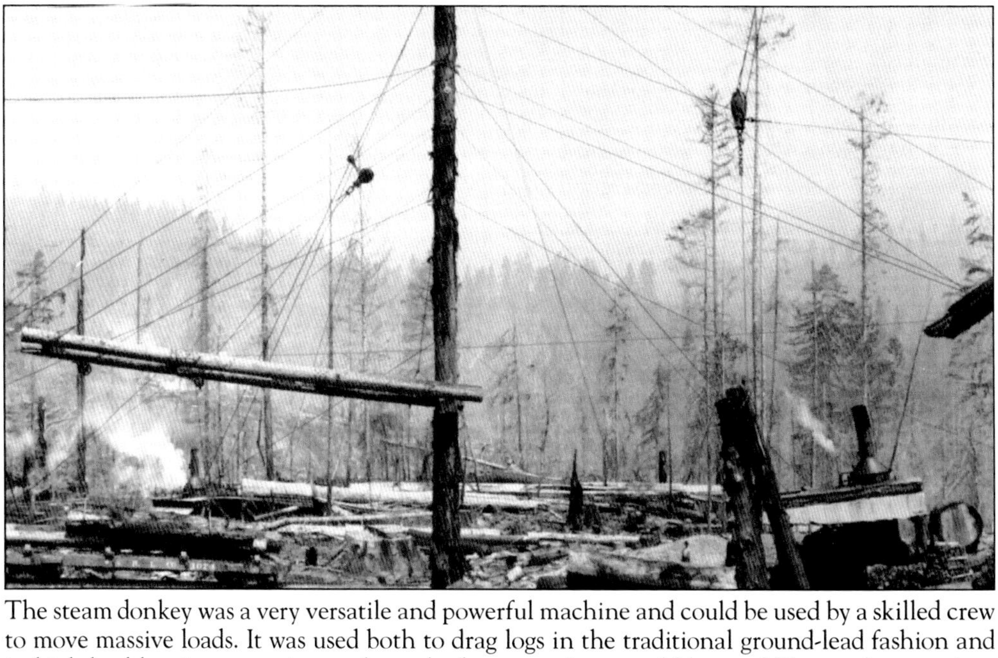

The steam donkey was a very versatile and powerful machine and could be used by a skilled crew to move massive loads. It was used both to drag logs in the traditional ground-lead fashion and in high-lead logging operations, where the larger engines would be used like modern yarders, attaching the logs to a mainline and pulling them on this line to a landing from which they could be transported to the mill. (Courtesy of the Humboldt State University Library, Humboldt Room, Palmquist Collection.)

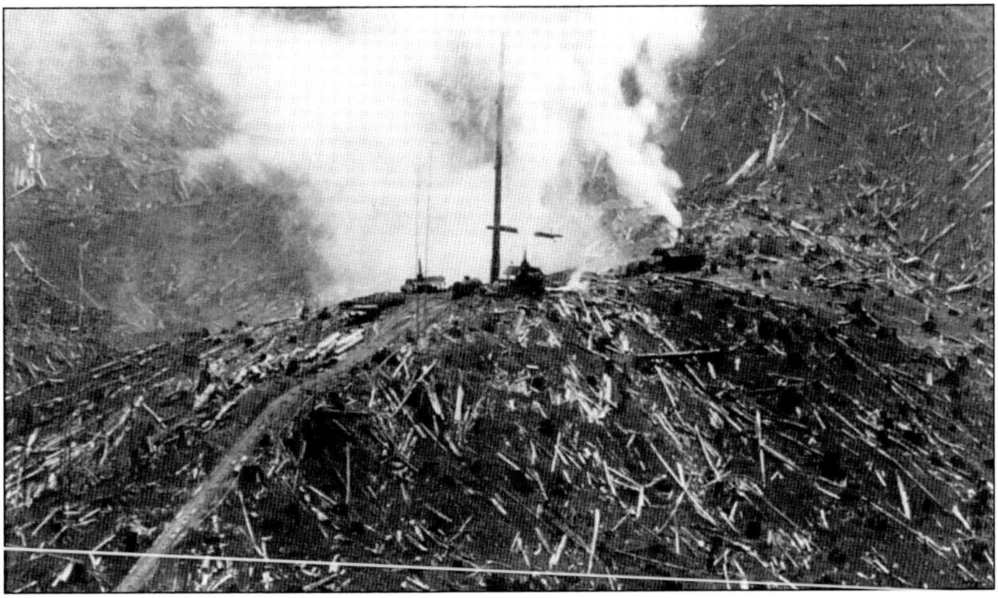

The introduction of high-lead logging using Dolbeer's engines made clear-cutting the most expedient means of harvesting the redwoods. Selective cutting of mature trees, as was done in the days of horse and oxen, was abandoned in favor of methods that would clear the worksite of obstacles. Selective harvest in the redwoods would not be considered practical again until the introduction of the gas-powered tractor. (Courtesy of the Humboldt State University Library, Humboldt Room, Boyle Collection.)

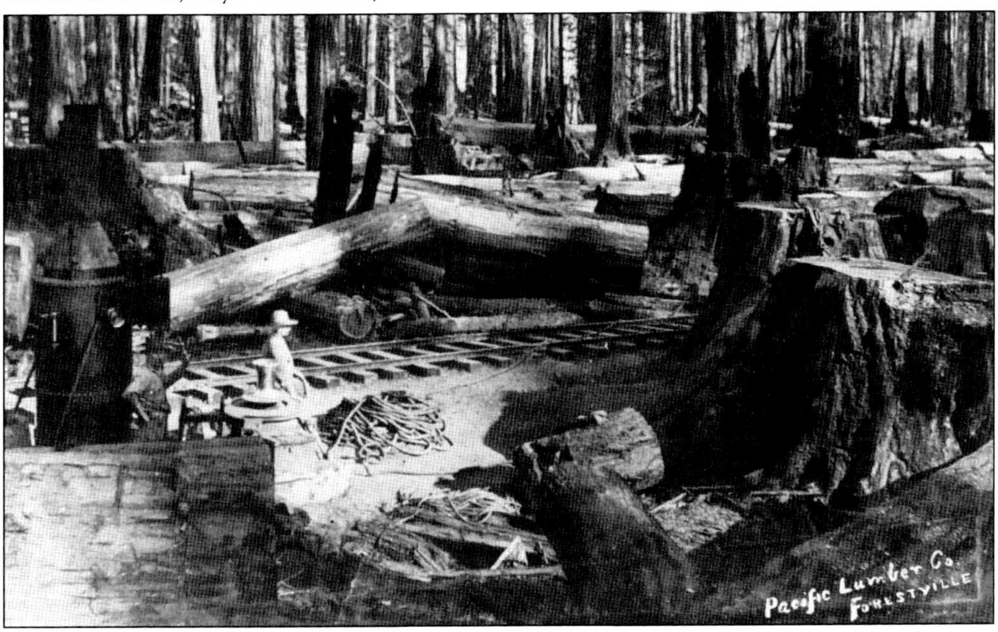

For decades, steam provided the power needed to sustain the county's timber industry both in the woods and at the mills. Also powered by steam was the company's fleet of locomotives, the steam-driven technology that allowed Pacific Lumber, known to many local railroad enthusiasts as TPL, to become one of the most successful operations on the Pacific Coast. (Courtesy of the Town of Scotia Company.)

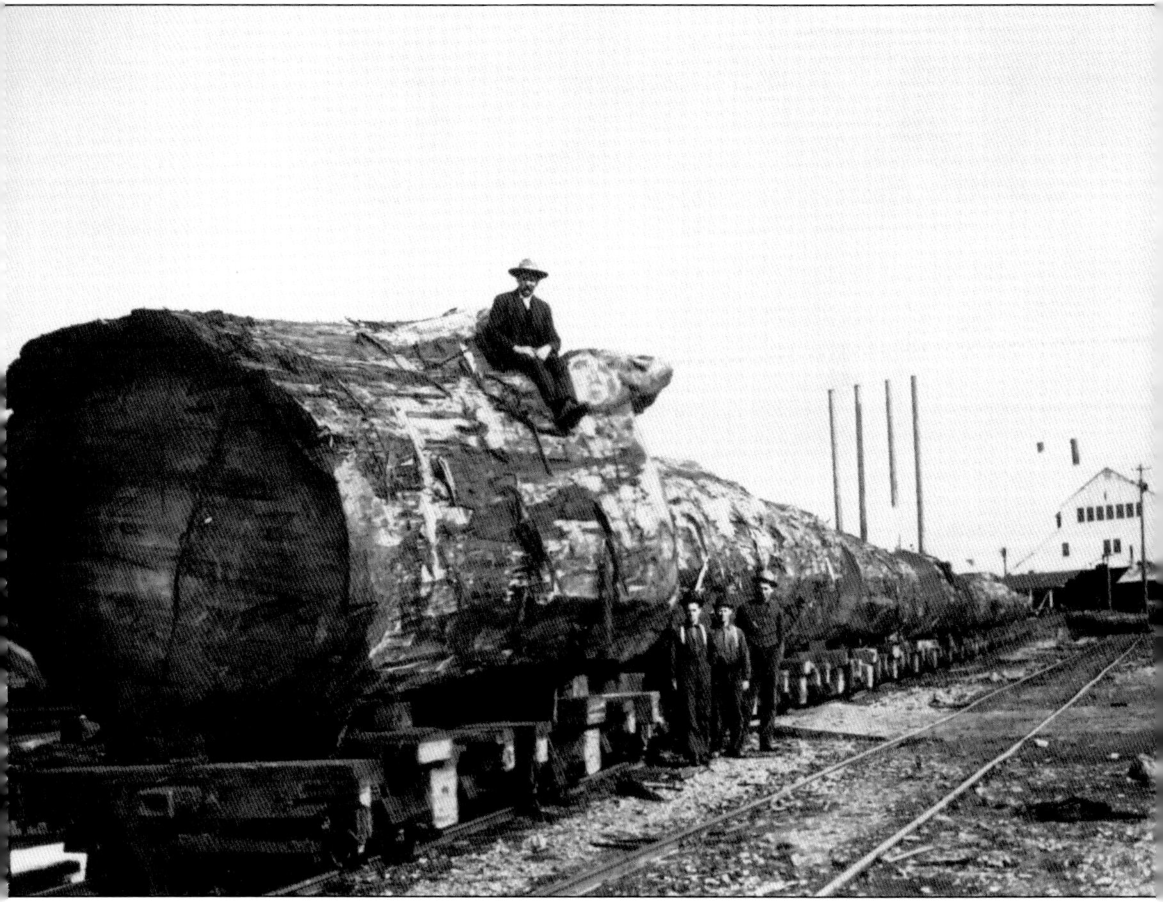

The sheer size of the redwoods in Humboldt County presented a unique problem; despite the ability to cut the trees and fell them without major damage, the behemoths were often deep in the forest and far from the mill. Transportation would prove to be one of the most vital aspects of the timber industry, and the railroad would allow for repetitive, efficient movement of this product. Shown here destined for the mill, likely at the turn of the 20th century, a single tree fills a log train. These short, wooden railcars are known as disconnect trucks. Different from a rigid flatcar, a pair of trucks would hold one log, and they could be placed at the end of logs of any length. These steel rails would become the first redwood highway. (Courtesy of the Humboldt State University Library, Humboldt Room, Palmquist Collection.)

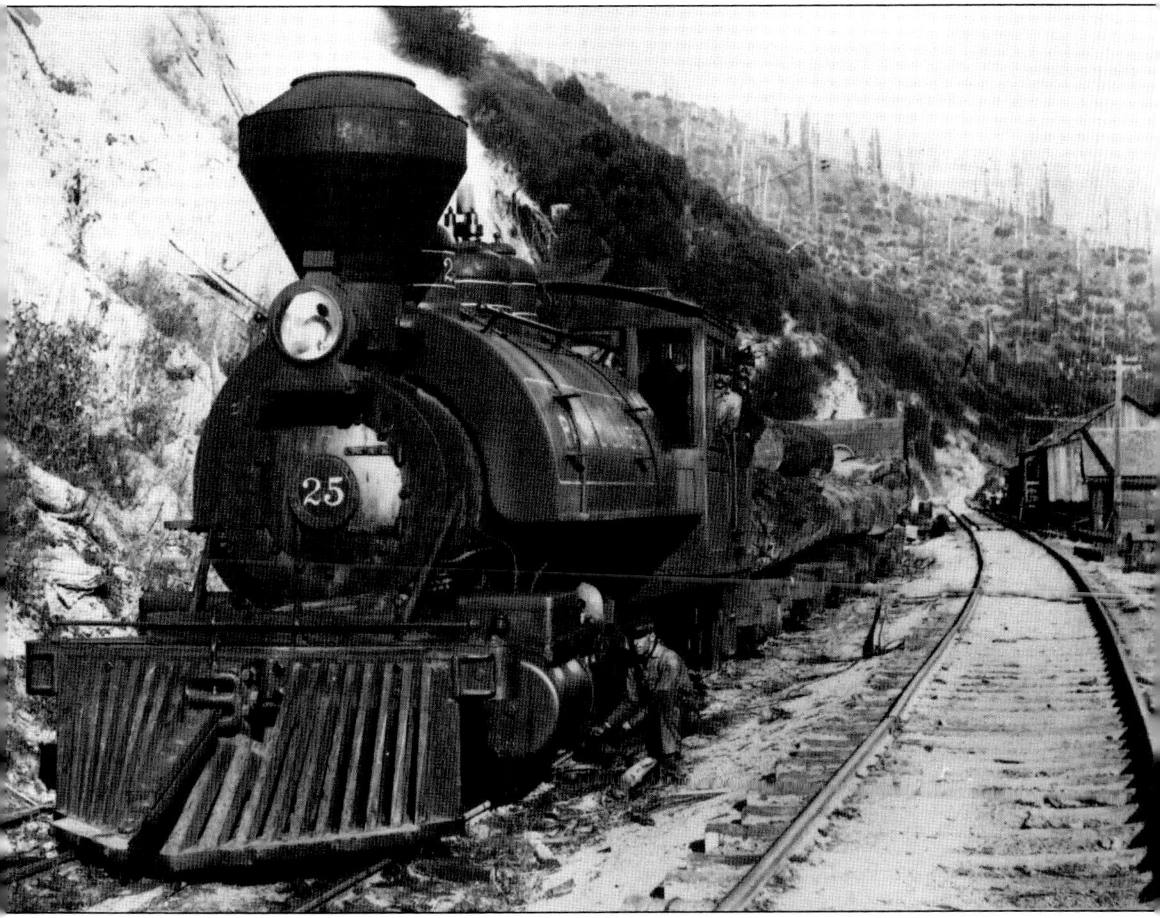

Here is TPL No. 5, a 2-4-2T (two wheels in front, four that drive, and two in the trailing position) locomotive built in 1904 by Baldwin. This style of locomotive was used by TPL since 1886. In what almost appears like a doctored photograph, the number "25" is painted right over the cast "5" on the number plate. It was a wood burner, an early style of locomotive without air brakes, link/pin couplers, and simple gas-burning lights. It was a fantastic example of a typical logging locomotive: simple, small, and fueled by the byproducts of lumber production. The engine was sold to the Holmes Eureka Lumber Company and renumbered. Still sporting the "Pacific Lumber Company" lettering, yet adorned with the new number, it had likely just been sold to its new company in this photograph. (Courtesy of the Humboldt State University Library, Humboldt Room, Swanlund-Baker Collection.)

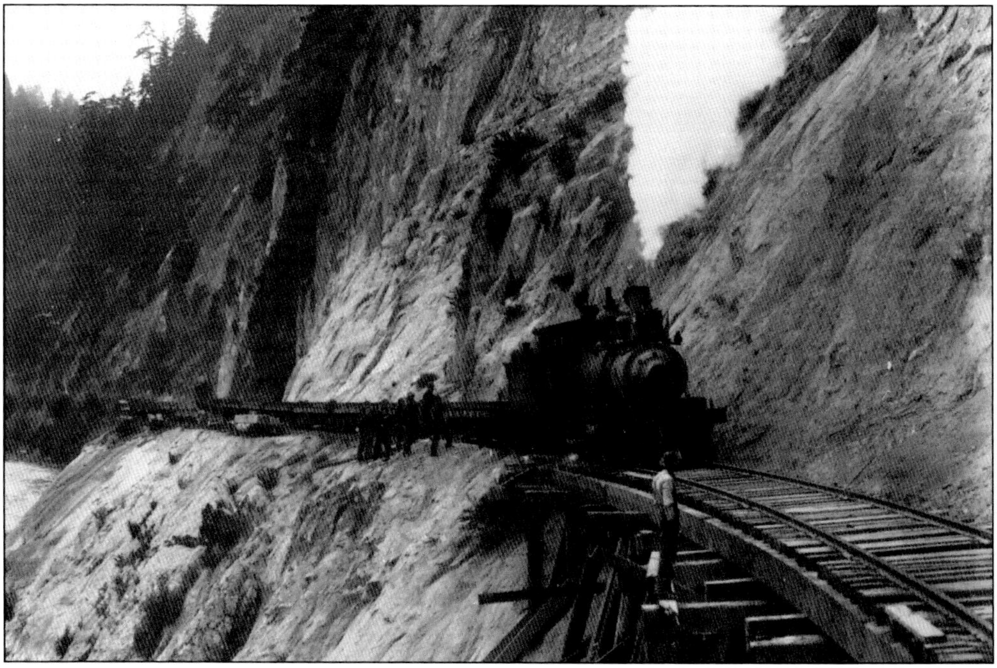

The Scotia Bluffs would prove to be the most recognizable and the most infamous feature of what would eventually become the Northwestern Pacific Railroad. As late as the 1990s, the bluffs received daily maintenance, and entire work crews were employed to keep the ever-shifting rock, dirt, and soil at bay. The bluffs contain ancient seafloor deposits, in the way of fossilized clams and other sea life, all above a railroad and the gorgeous Eel River. (What a combination!) Always beautiful, and always a headache, the Scotia Bluffs delay passengers around 1914 below. (Both, courtesy of the Humboldt State University Library, Humboldt Room. Above, Swanlund-Baker Collection; below, Palmquist Collection.)

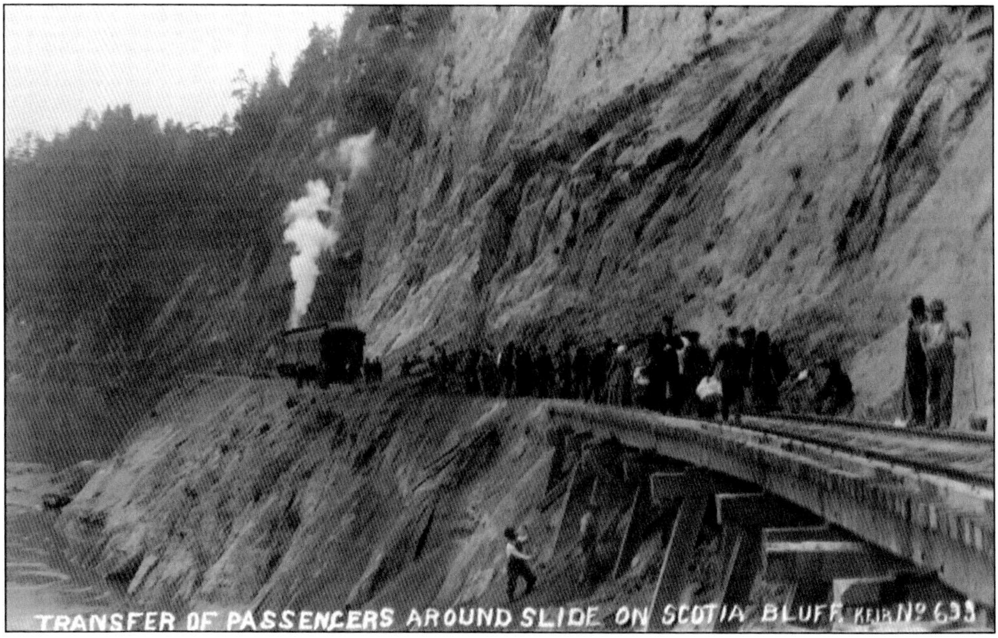

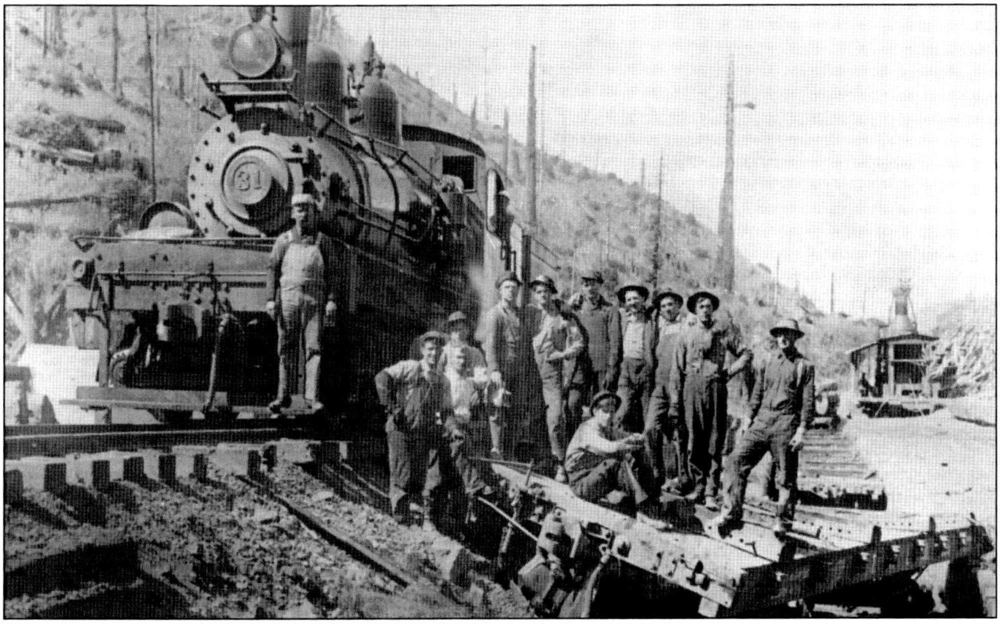

Pacific Lumber used nearly every type of logging locomotive imaginable, all unique examples of 20th-century industry. These workers pose next to TPL No. 31 at the site of a wreck near Scotia. Purchased from the California Western Railroad in 1917, this three-truck Shay served with Pacific Lumber for only three years before being sold in 1920. (Courtesy of the Fortuna Depot Museum.)

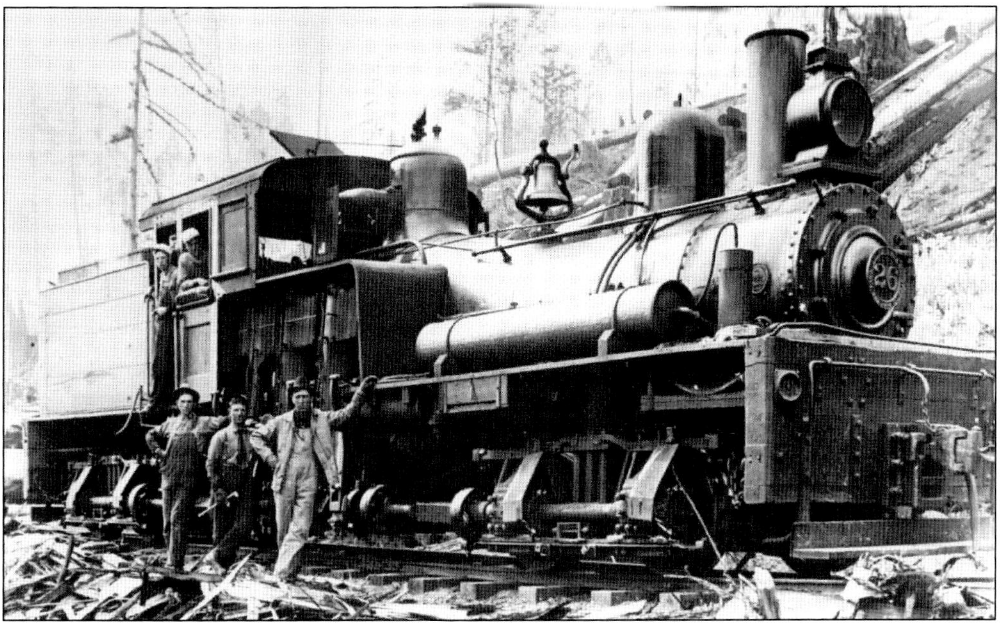

Five trainmen pose in front of TPL No. 26, a two-truck Shay, built by Lima Locomotive Works in 1906. Ephraim Shay, a Civil War veteran, designed the geared locomotive seen here with three upright steam cylinders and eight-wheel drive. Extremely powerful, yet extremely slow, Shay locomotives were perfect for the steep, crooked railroads of the redwoods. (Courtesy of the Fortuna Depot Museum.)

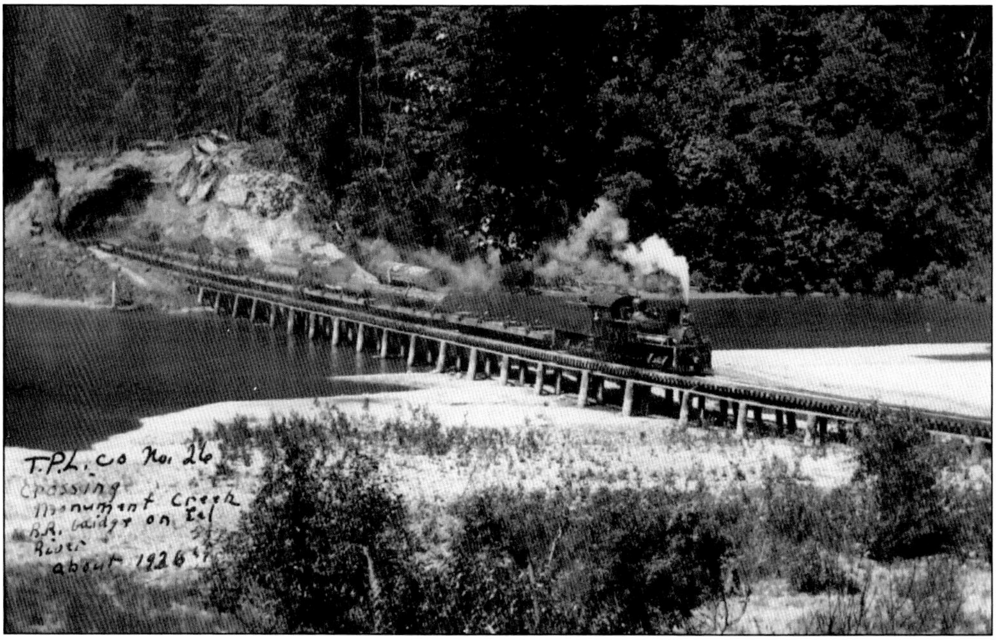

One of many branches of the railed TPL empire, the Monument Creek branch appears to be absent from historical maps. In many cases, tracks would be laid and torn up as needed, particularly if a certain stand of timber was exhausted. This makes tracing old right-of-ways difficult, especially considering these rails existed for just a short time in history. (Courtesy of the Fortuna Depot Museum.)

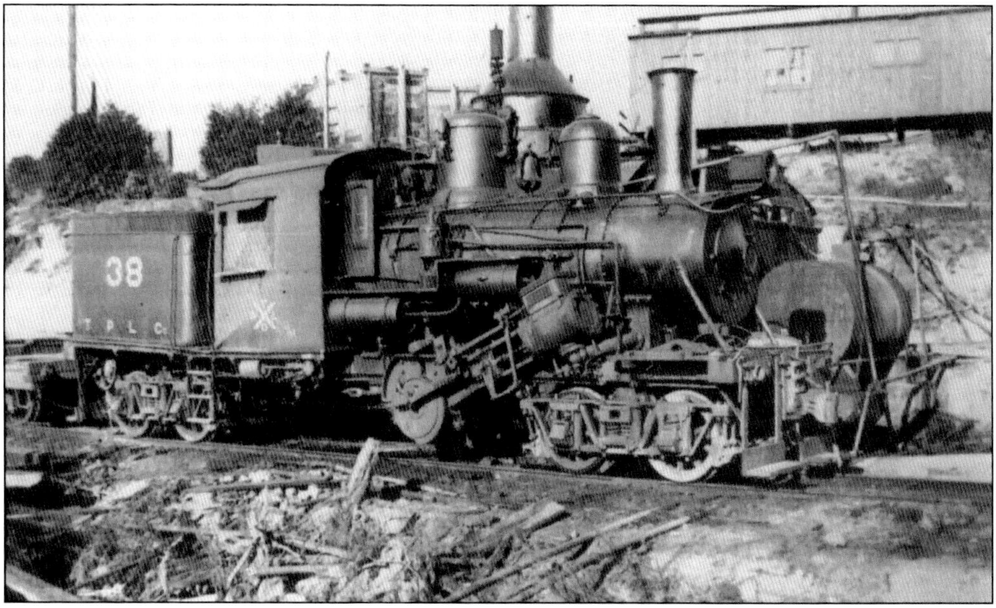

Climax engines, like TPL No. 38 shown here, were powered by geared driveshafts much like Shays. A climax engine had two steam cylinders on each side of the boiler. Each powered an opposing set of cranks. Advanced for their 1890s patent date, the climax engines had a transmission under the boiler that would translate horizontal rotation to the movement needed for the wheels. (Courtesy of the Fortuna Depot Museum.)

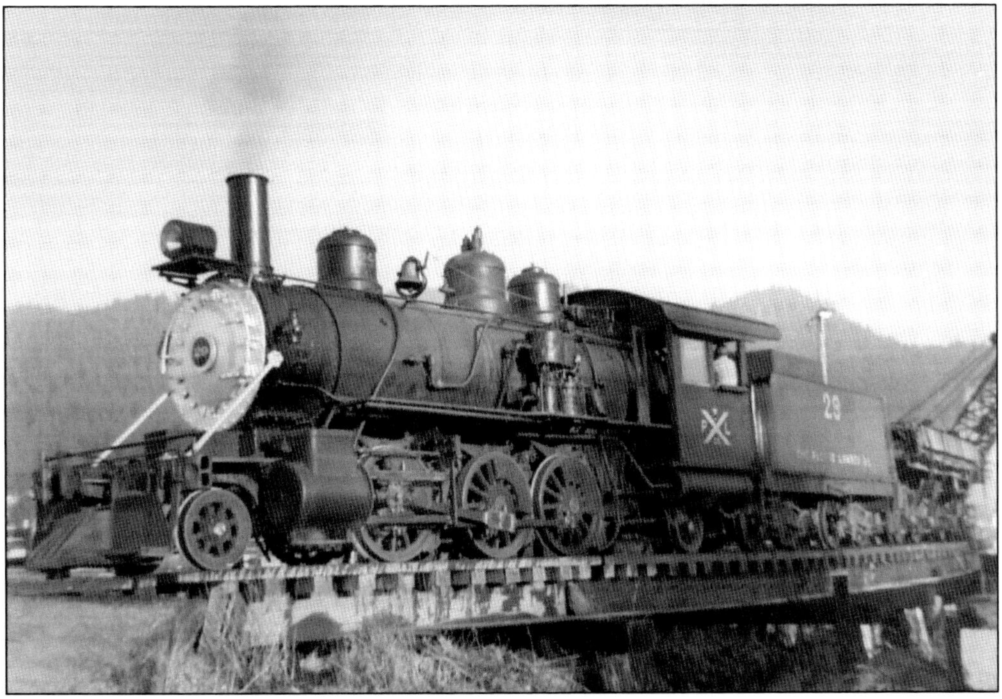

Delivered new in 1910, TPL No. 29 was one of the largest engines that operated in Scotia, and also ended up being the company's last locomotive in service. Built by Baldwin in Philadelphia as a wood burner and later converted to oil, this engine hauled loads to the shipping facilities at Fields Landing and logging trains from Shively to the mill in Scotia. Its last powered movement was in 1986 at the Eureka Southern rail yard in Eureka. Now in the care of the Timber Heritage Association, No. 29 is stored at the historic Samoa Roundhouse. (Both, courtesy of the Fortuna Depot Museum.)

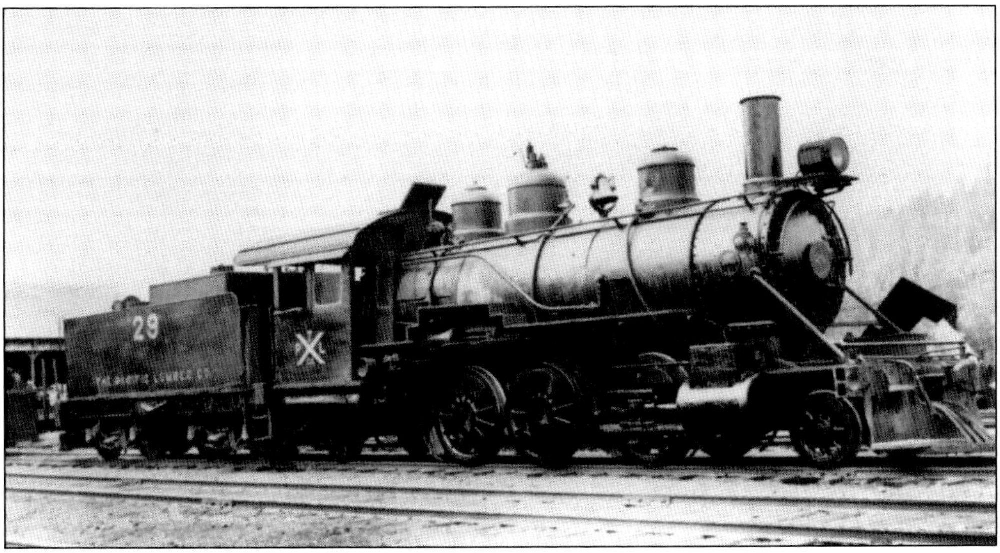

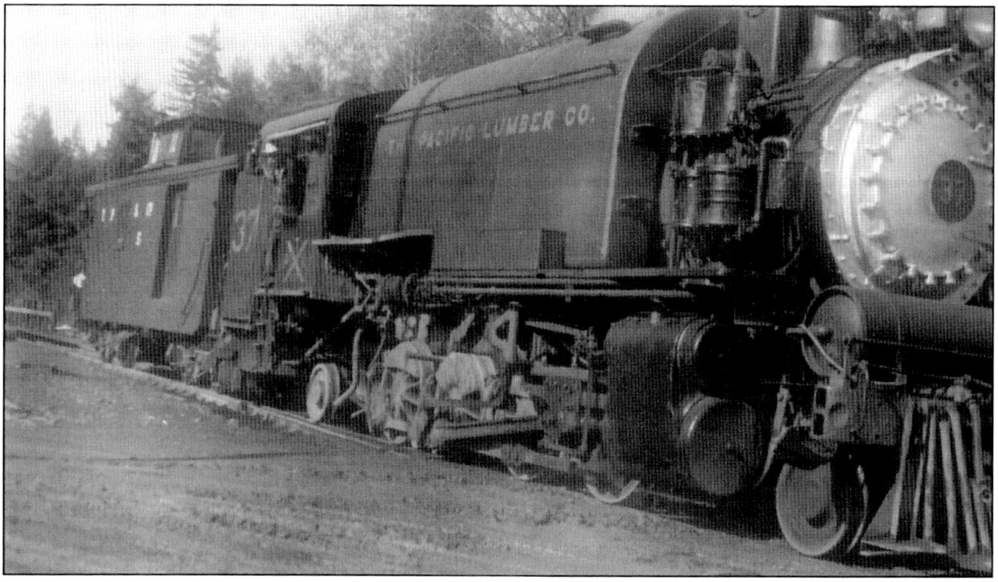

Perhaps the most exciting thing about these pictures is that both the engine and caboose still exist. TPL No. 37 is a 2-8-2T (describing its wheel arrangement, with a tank over the boiler) built by American Locomotive Works (ALCO) in 1924. Purchased from the Sugar Pine Lumber Company in 1935, it hauled lumber trains for TPL until 1966, when it left Scotia and went into excursion service in Washington. TPL No. 37 is now owned by the Timber Heritage Association and is being rebuilt by the Strasburg Shops in Pennsylvania. TPL caboose No. 5 never left Humboldt, and is currently housed at the Samoa shops, in a nearly original state. (Above, courtesy of the Fortuna Depot Museum; below, courtesy of Eldon Whitehead.)

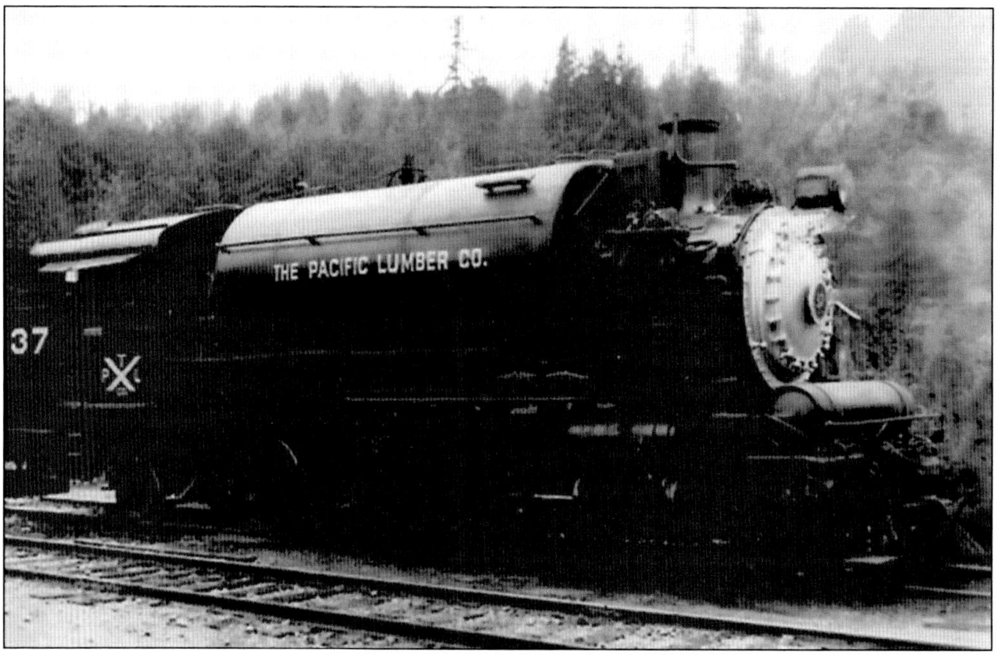

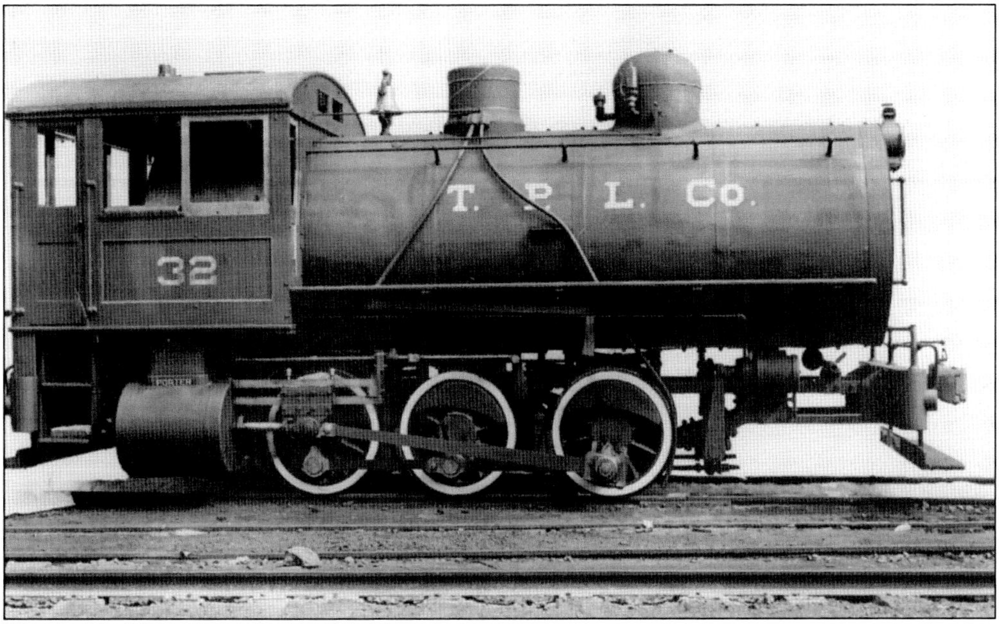

Easily the strangest of the bunch, TPL No. 32 was lacking some of the major hallmarks of the steam locomotive—no smokestack, no smoke, and no fire. Known as a "fireless"-type steam engine, No. 32 was designed to run off steam generated by the mill and was used for switching cars in the rail yard. TPL No. 32 was sold after only one year in Scotia. (Courtesy of the Fortuna Depot Museum.)

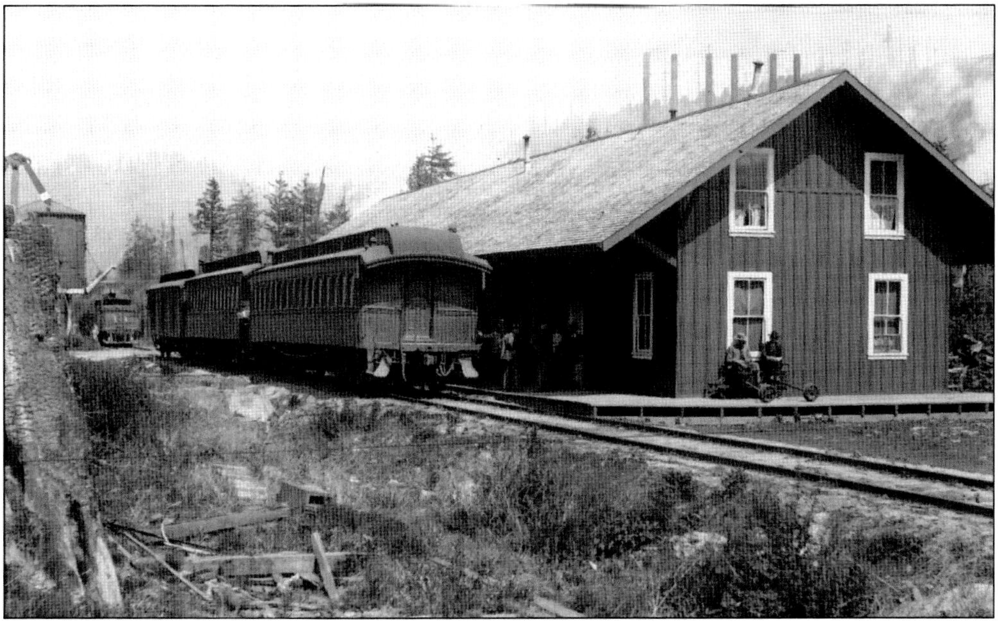
The Scotia Railroad Depot served the residents of the Scotia and Rio Dell area for many years. Before the highway came through town, people coming into the area by train would get their first glimpse of the company town from the train platform. This building was heavily damaged in the Christmas Flood of 1964 and subsequently demolished. (Courtesy of the Humboldt County Historical Society.)

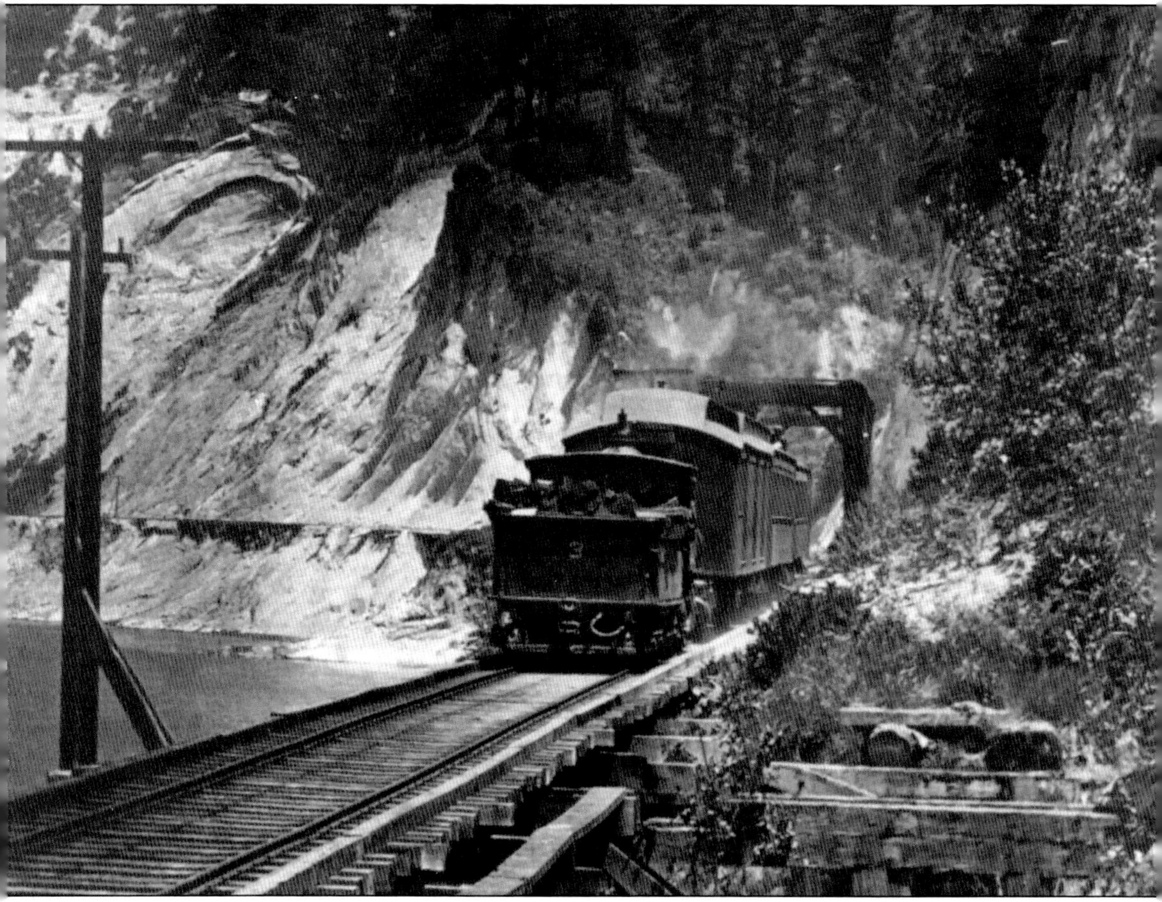

The technology of the railroad revolutionized the logging industry for the Pacific Lumber Company, but the railroad would hold influence far beyond the mill and the logging camps. The growth of the railroad made it easier to haul logs, passengers, and equipment and also encouraged the development of small towns along its tracks in places like Elinor and Shively. Facing north, Eel River & Eureka Railroad No. 3, with passenger cars in tow, traverses the notorious Scotia Bluffs. Shown here with an arched bridge structure over Nanning Creek, the appearance of the railroad trackage in this section has changed many times since this late 1800s photograph due to numerous floods, landslides, and as of 1998, the lack of a functioning railroad. The Scotia Bluffs heading north would be the gateway from Pacific Lumber to Eureka, and as of 1914, the gateway to San Francisco and the rest of the globe. (Courtesy of the Fortuna Depot Museum.)

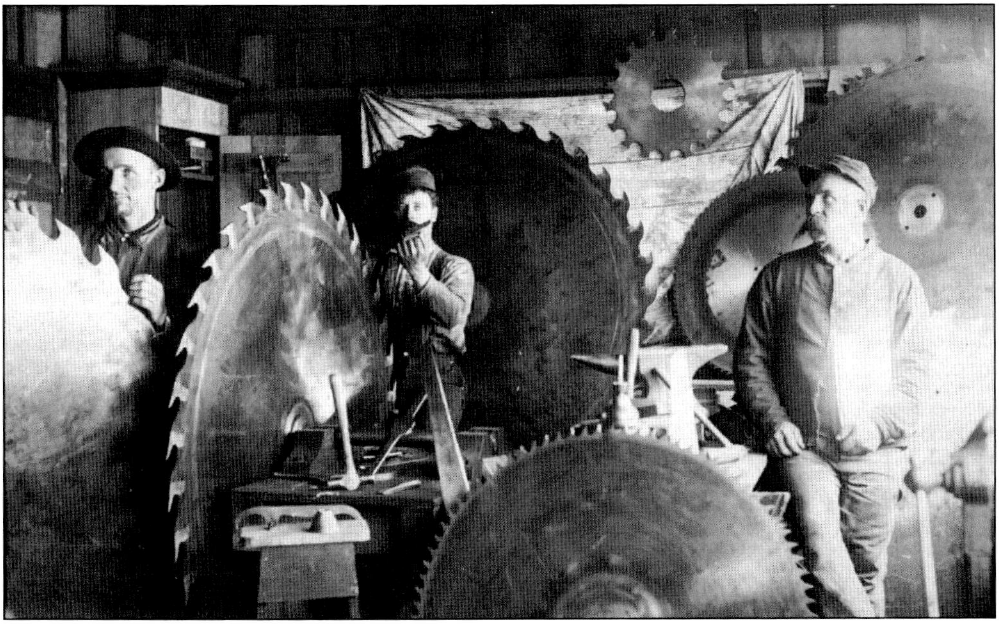

In 1891, the collapse of the Los Angeles housing boom, coupled with a tariff reduction on imported Canadian lumber, created economic hardships for Scotia and the Pacific Lumber Company. Redwood lumber prices plummeted as local companies struggled to compete against foreign producers in a dwindling market. Many local timber workers faced lay-offs, and several mills went under. (Courtesy of the Town of Scotia Company.)

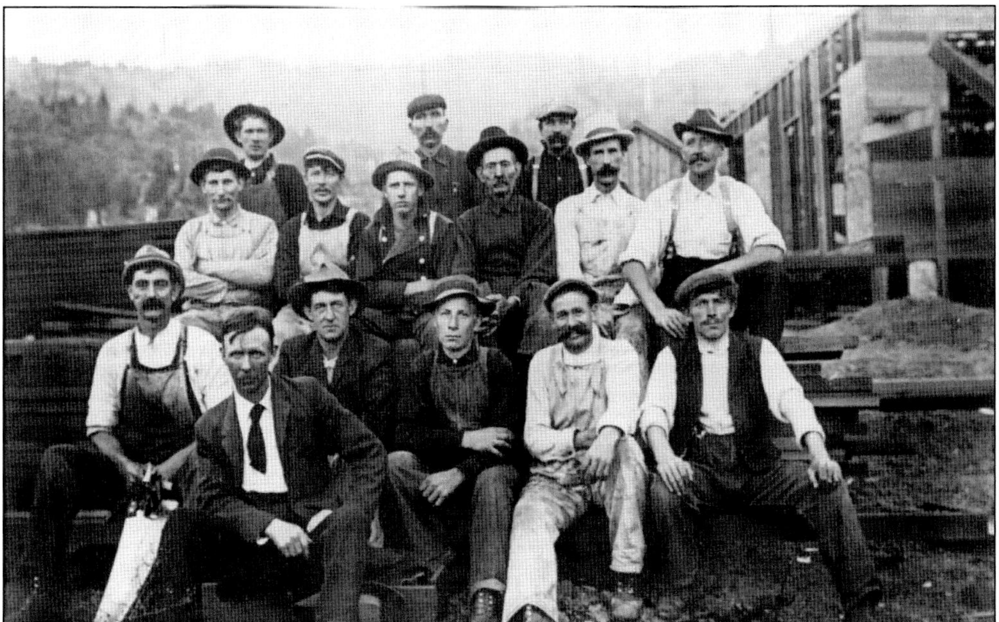

Although Pacific Lumber was forced to cut wages, the mill avoided lay-offs by working shorter shifts and sharing the available work among its employees. This benevolent approach towards its workforce during economic downturns set the tone for relations between PL management and its employees, earning it the loyalty of its workforce. (Courtesy of the Town of Scotia Company.)

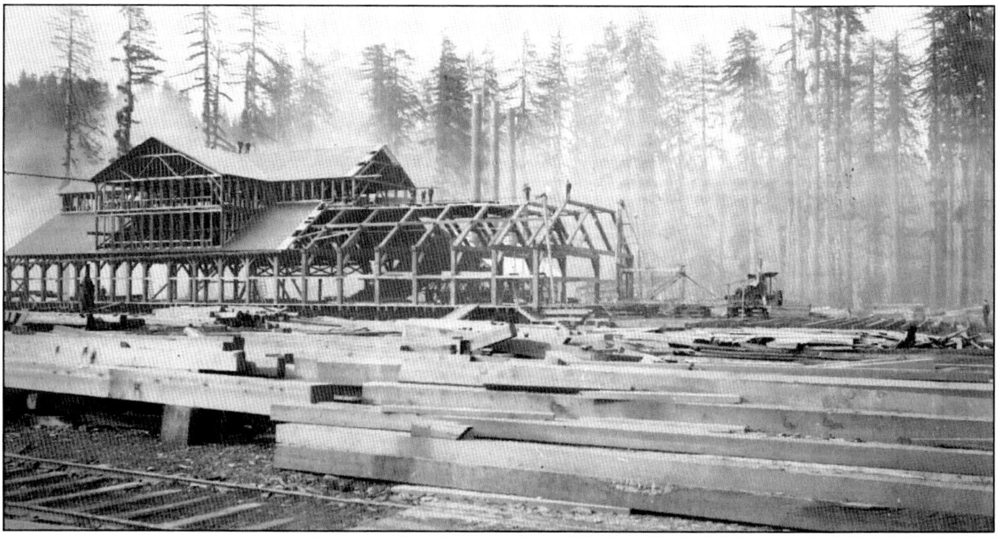

On June 6, 1895, a fire started in Pacific Lumber's sawmill. The recently organized volunteer fire department was powerless to douse the fire, and the blaze raged out of control. The fire destroyed the mill, offices, the cookhouse, a warehouse, and two stores before spreading to the lumberyard. Appeals were made to Eureka for help, but reinforcements did not arrive until early the following morning, by which time much of Scotia had been consumed by the flames. Damages exceeded $300,000, but the mill was insured for only a third of that amount. Undeterred, PL began construction of a new mill. When completed in 1896, PL's new mill was the largest, most modern, best-equipped sawmill on the West Coast. (Courtesy of the Humboldt State University Library, Humboldt Room, Palmquist Collection.)

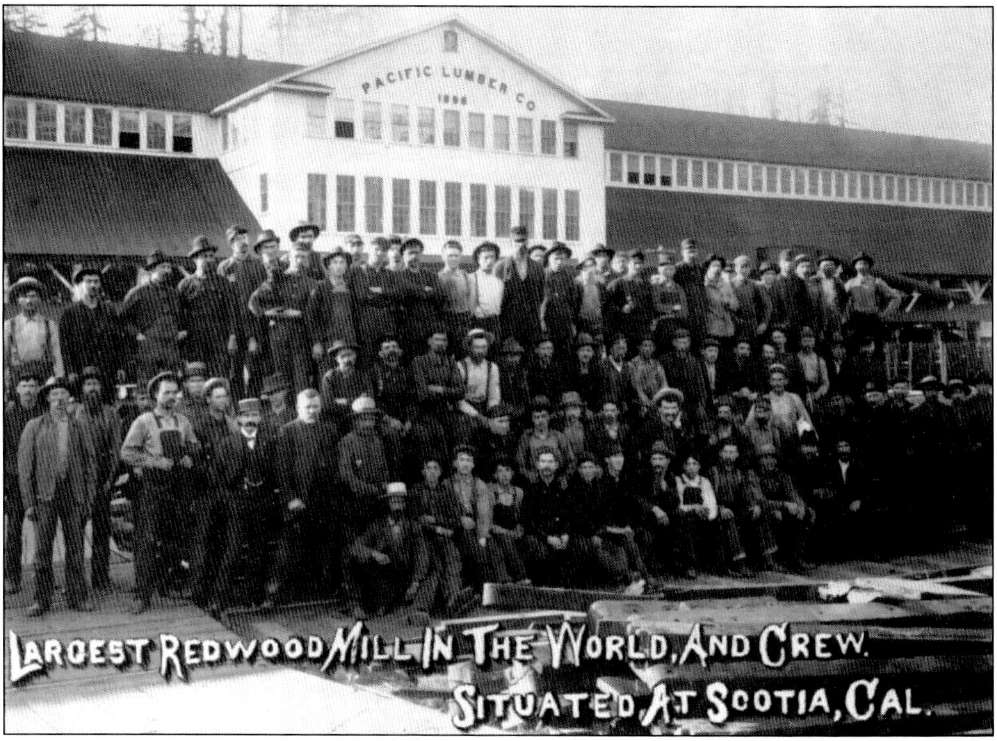

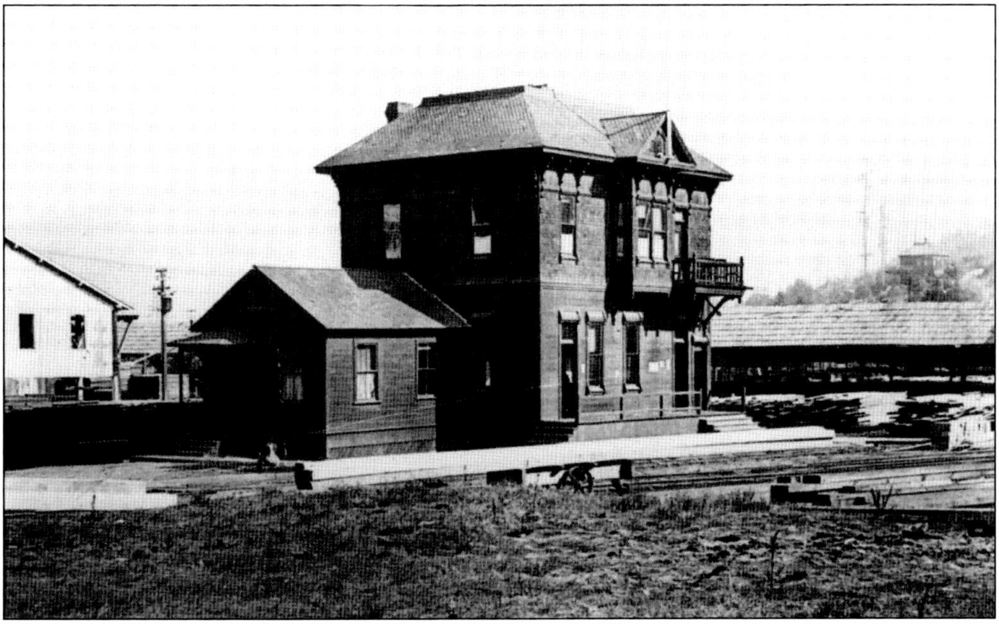

The fire gave Pacific Lumber an opportunity, albeit an expensive one, to modernize its mill and reorganize the layout of its growing town. It also forced the company to rebuild many other buildings. The new company office building, shown here at center, was built on the site of the previous office and store. (Courtesy of the Humboldt State University Library, Humboldt Room, Palmquist Collection.)

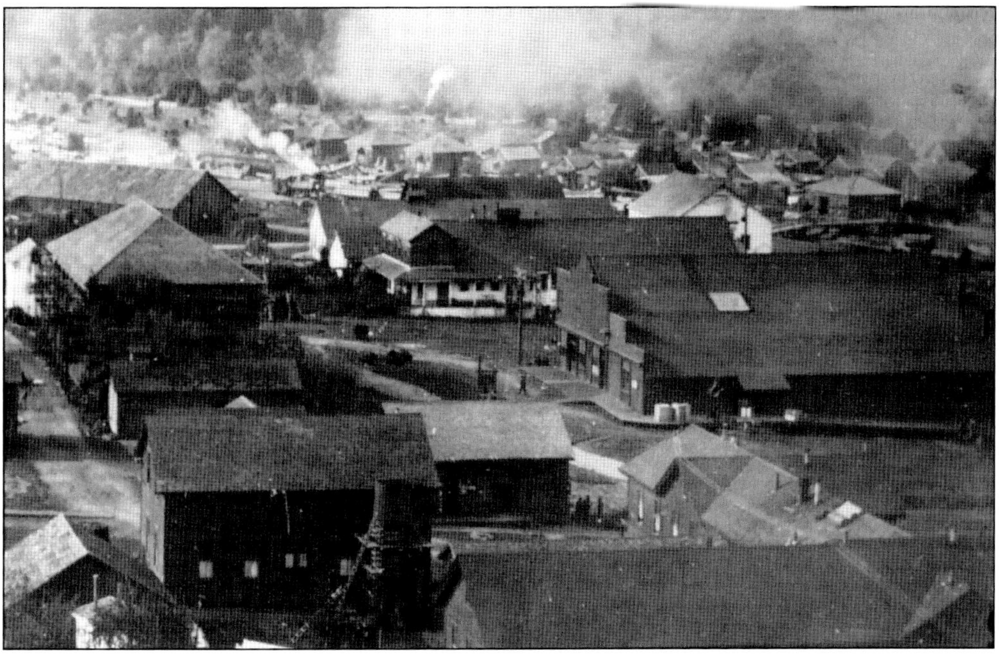

The new company store was built along what would one day become Scotia's Main Street, just west of the site of the present-day Winema Theater. Shown here (right of center), the Pacific Lumber Company's store was expanded several times in the coming years, growing to meet the demands of a growing workforce and community. (Courtesy of the Humboldt County Historical Society.)

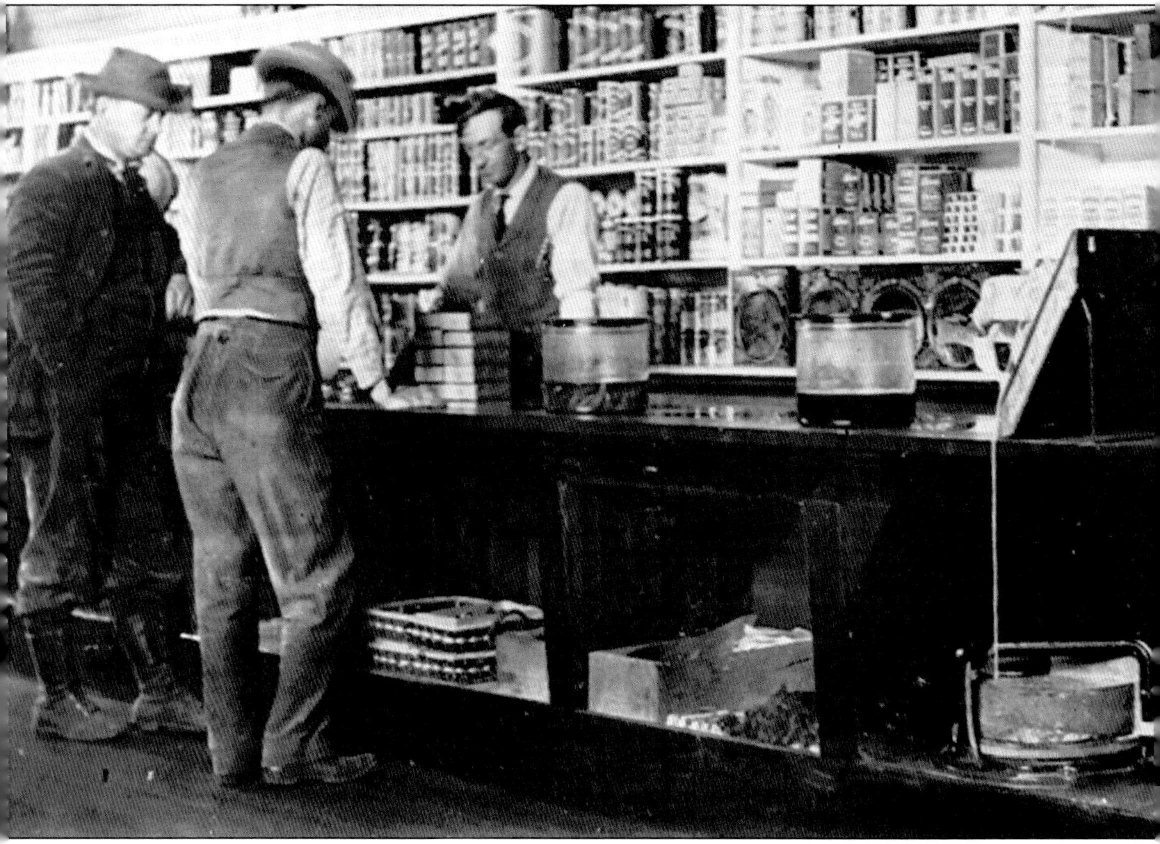

Pacific Lumber's company store provided convenient shopping to its town residents and offered credit to employees who found themselves short of money before payday. Additionally, like many companies at the time, Pacific Lumber paid its workers part of their wages in scrip. Scrip was company issued "money" that was redeemable at face value only at the over-priced company stores. Money owed to the company store was deducted from the employee's pay, and workers sometimes fell deeply into debt to the company. The practice of using scrip resulted in devaluing the wages of workers and sparked a good deal of criticism over the years, but in times of economic hardship, workers were often able to turn to the company's stores to help them get through the worst of it. (Courtesy of the Town of Scotia Company.)

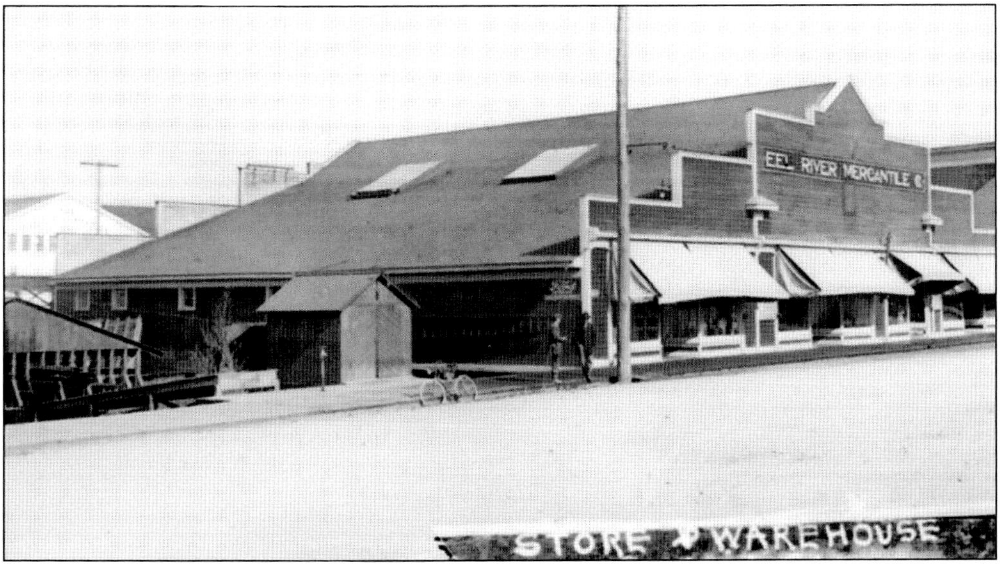

The Pacific Lumber Company continued to expand its company store in Scotia over the years. From small mercantiles providing the essentials for a mostly single workforce, these stores evolved to offer virtually everything a working man and his family could want, from groceries and furniture to new clothes and automobiles. (Courtesy of the Town of Scotia Company.)

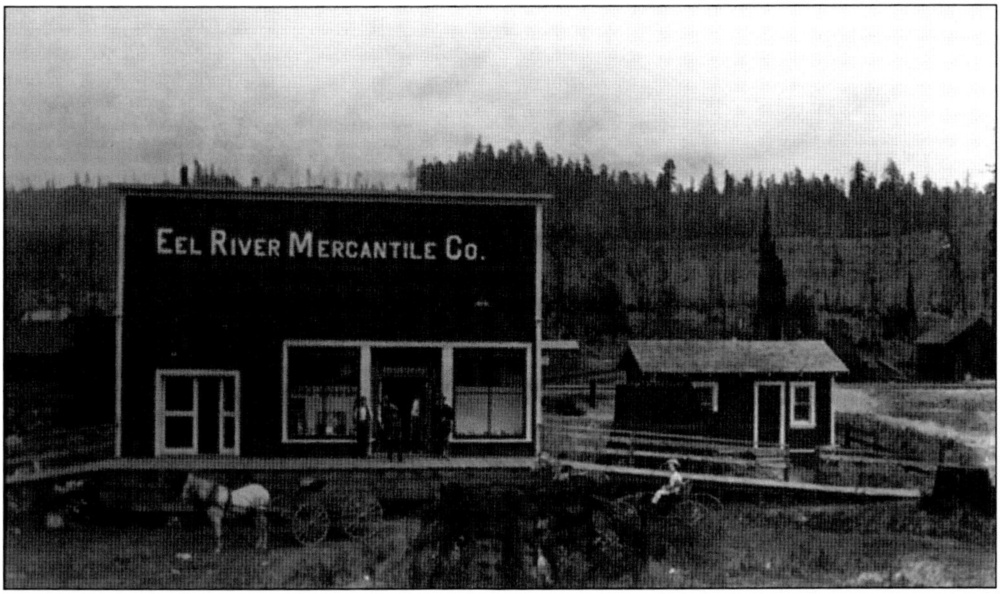

As Pacific Lumber's railroad and logging operations moved south into the more remote areas of the county, the company built stores to serve its workers in communities like Shively and Dyerville. PL's Eel River mercantile stores were sold off after the work was done, but the company continued to operate the store in Scotia until the 1950s. (Courtesy of the Humboldt State University Library, Humboldt Room, Neill Collection.)

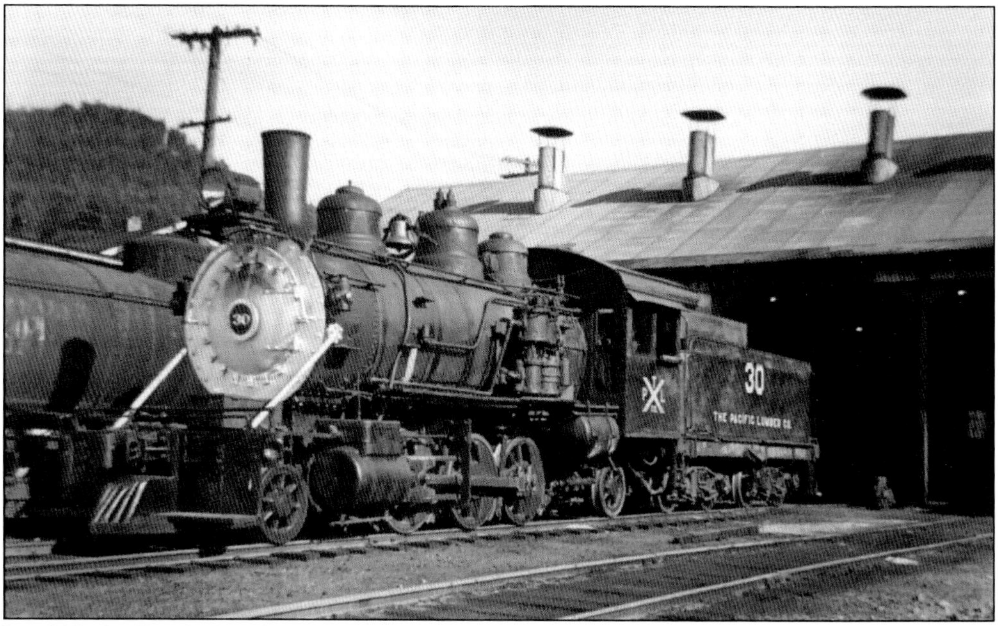

In 1903, the Pacific Lumber Company came under the ownership of Simon Jones Murphy and the Santa Fe Railroad. By 1905, Murphy had control of Pacific Lumber, while Santa Fe retained the railroad. Consolidating the Pacific Lumber Company with the Freshwater Lumber Company, Murphy incorporated his interests as the Pacific Lumber Company of Maine. (Courtesy of the Fortuna Depot Museum.)

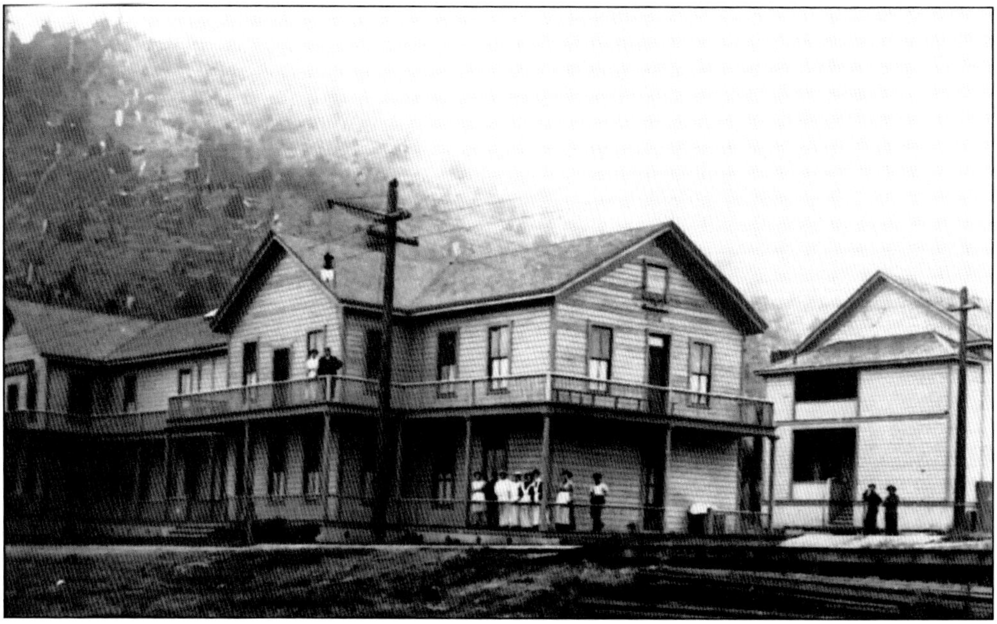

The first Scotia Inn, originally christened the Mowatoc, was built by Pacific Lumber in 1903 to replace its aging Scotia Hotel. "Mowatoc" was an early spelling for Modoc, an Indian tribe in the northeastern part of the state. A popular stage and rail stop, the new hotel was equipped with electric lighting, along with the rest of the buildings in town that year. (Courtesy of the Humboldt County Historical Society.)

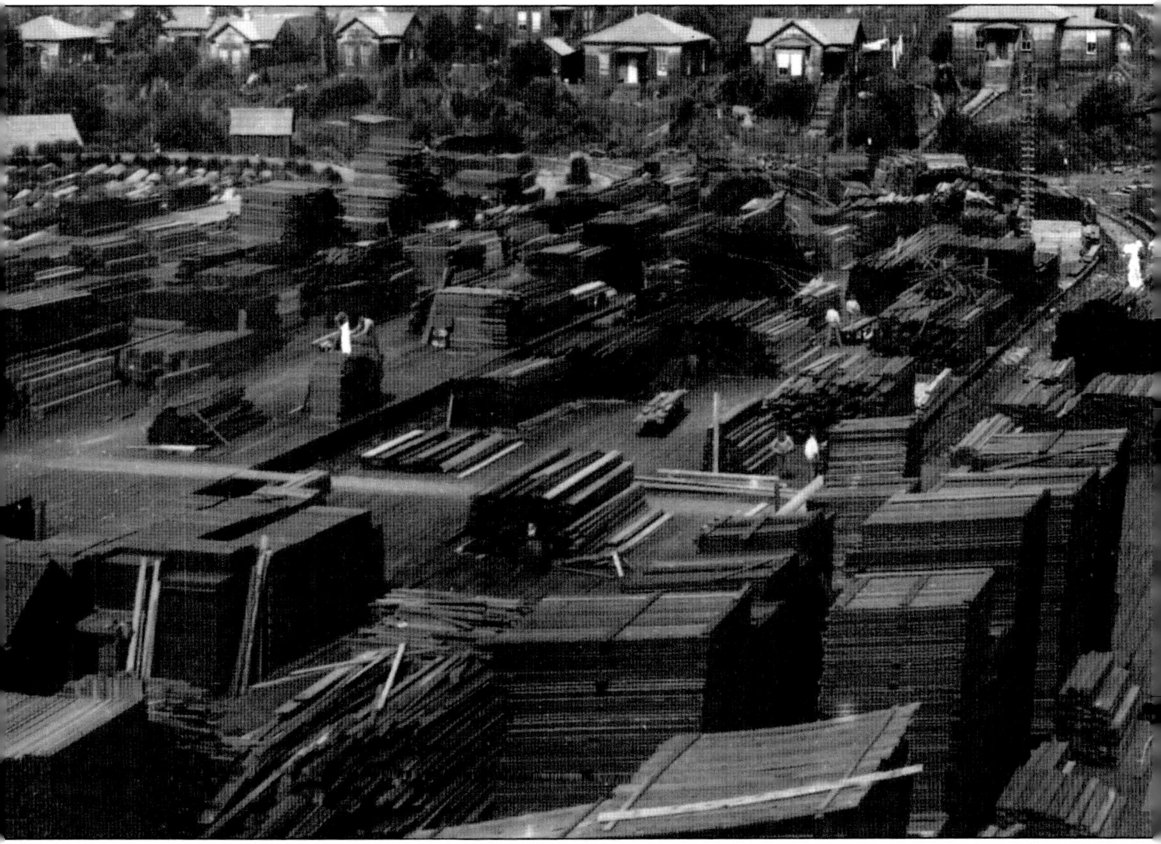

Earthquakes have rocked Scotia many times during its history, as shown in this picture of Pacific Lumber's mill yard after a quake in the early 1890s. One of the most eventful tremors to ever impact this logging community was centered not in Humboldt County but hundreds of miles away. In 1906, a catastrophic earthquake and subsequent fire destroyed much of San Francisco and was reportedly powerful enough to crumble chimneys and knock over stacked lumber in the Scotia mill yard. The Pacific Lumber Company's offices in San Francisco burned in the fire following the quake, but its lumberyards and docks were spared. The survival of Pacific Lumber's assets in the city proved particularly profitable when redwood, with its reputation for fire resistance, was deemed the only wood authorized for temporary reconstruction without a permit in the suddenly fire-conscious city of San Francisco. (Courtesy of the Humboldt State University Library, Humboldt Room, Ericson Collection.)

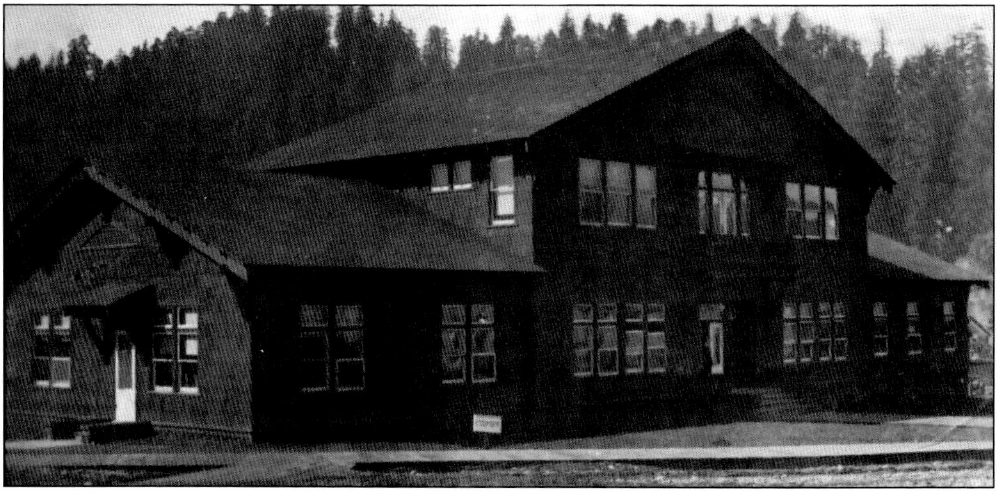

A new office was constructed in 1909 at the west end of Scotia's town center. This building, which was substantially remodeled in 1948, served as the nerve center for Pacific Lumber's operations for nearly a century. Shown here with its original redwood finish, the Pacific Lumber Company's headquarters now serve as the offices of the Humboldt Redwood Company. (Courtesy of the Humboldt State University Library, Humboldt Room, Neill Collection.)

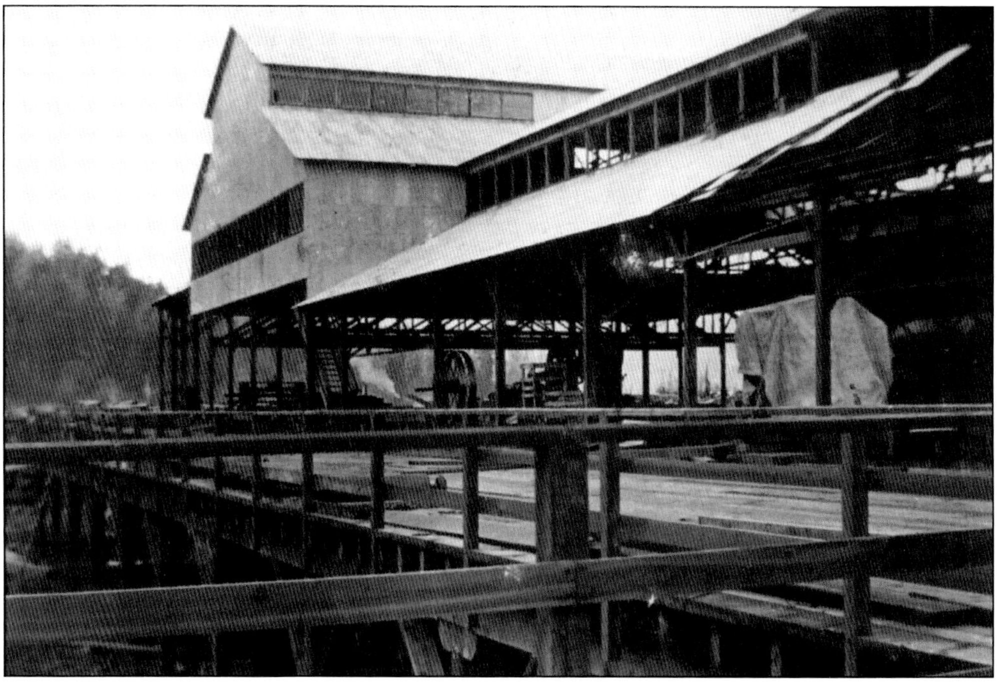

The millpond was expanded and the foundations were laid for Pacific Lumber's new mill beginning in 1908. In full production by 1910, the new mill added three headrig saws and more than doubled the company's production. It also increased the company town's population when a flood of immigrants came to the area to work in the new mill. (Courtesy of the Humboldt State University Library, Humboldt Room, Neill Collection.)

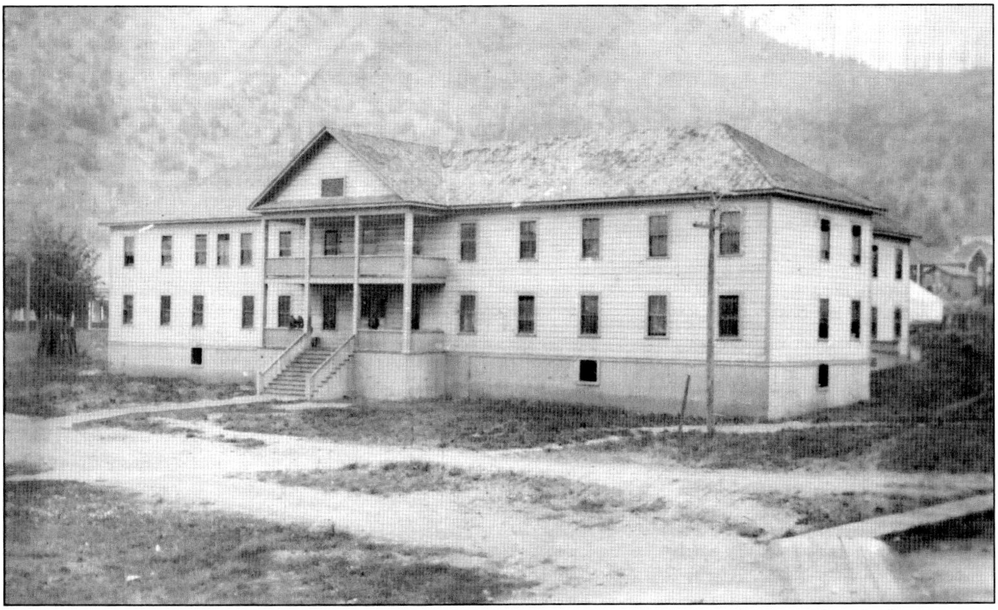

To accommodate its increasing workforce, Pacific Lumber constructed more family housing at the south end of town near the new mill, and a second cookhouse and bunkhouse were built to meet the needs of the company town's growing population. Despite these additions, many PL workers were forced to find housing outside of Scotia. (Courtesy of the Humboldt State University Library, Humboldt Room, Neill Collection.)

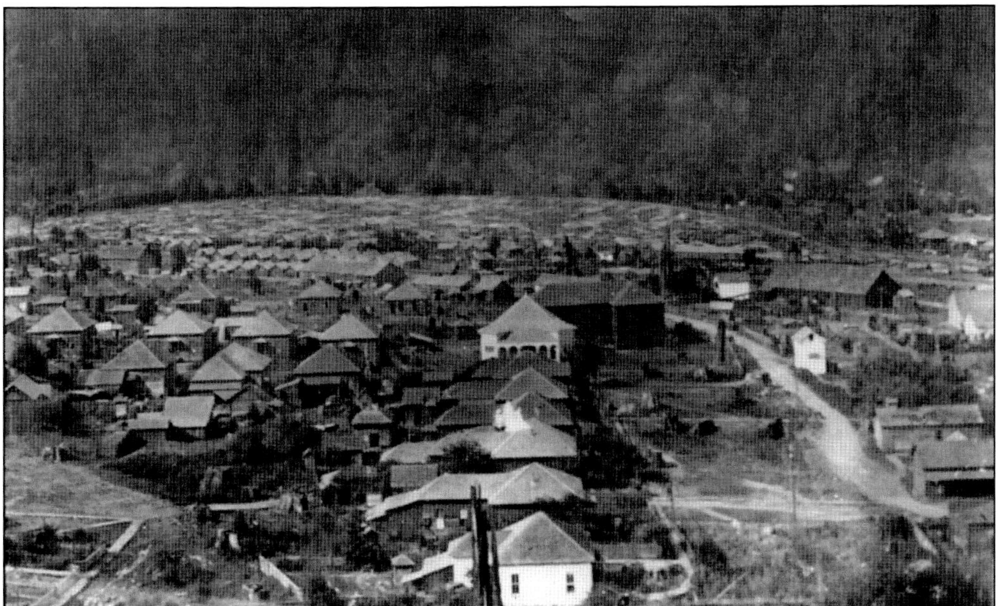

As Pacific Lumber's workforce grew, the town of Scotia slowly started to take on something of its present-day shape. Streets were laid out and houses were built to lodge the company's growing population. Mill, Church, Eddy, and First Streets soon hosted tidy cottages built in the National Folk style and connected by wooden plank sidewalks. (Courtesy of the Town of Scotia Company.)

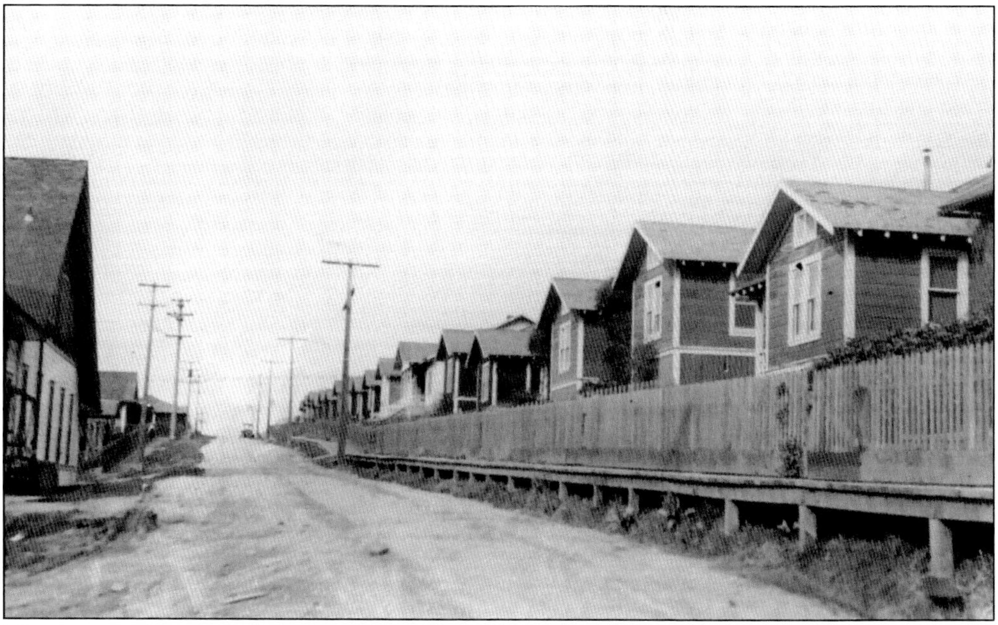

The company's town, once centered entirely around the mill, was finally beginning to transform from a logging camp and mill yard with houses scattered around randomly into a well-organized and pleasant community. The neat rows of tidy cottages in Scotia contrasted sharply with the roughneck environment of Wildwood and Rio Dell, just across the bridge and beyond the control of the company. (Courtesy of the Town of Scotia Company.)

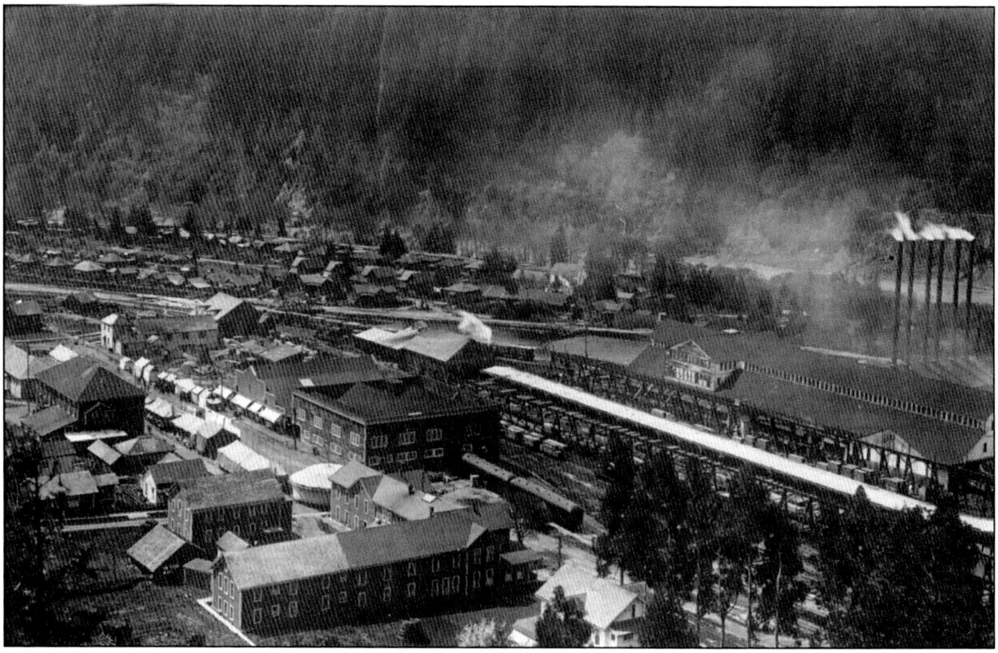

By 1910, Pacific Lumber had cut a main thoroughfare through the congested mill town, creating a town center and making room for the Redwood Highway, a motor route from San Francisco to the Oregon border that would eventually pass directly through Scotia and Rio Dell. (Courtesy of the Town of Scotia Company.)

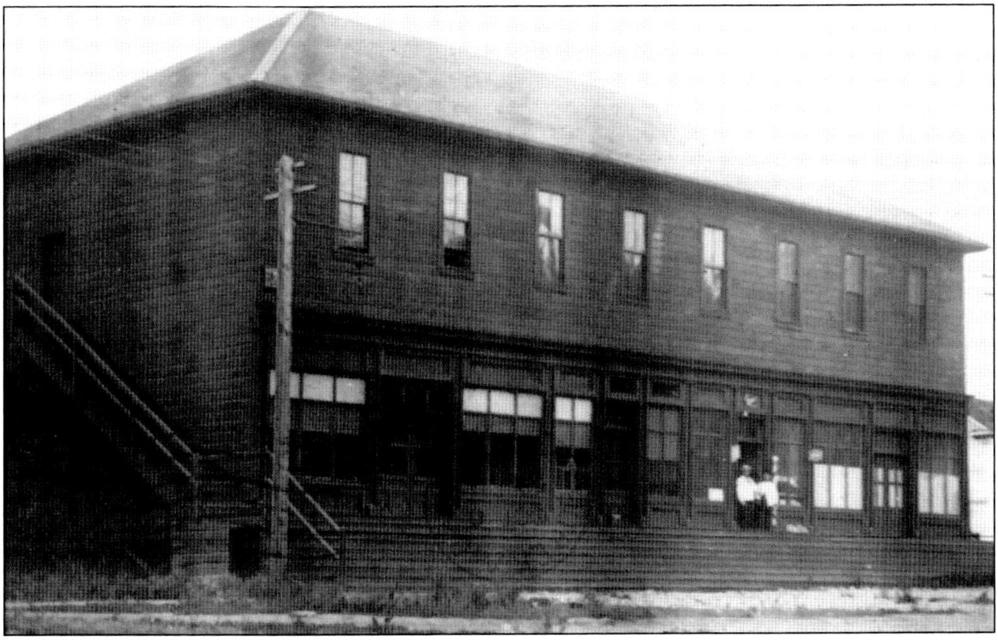

Pacific Lumber management started cleaning up the town in an attempt to also clean up its image. It wanted to transform the rough lumber town, populated by rowdy loggers, and develop the town, and its workforce, into a respectable community. Tearing down the company saloon and replacing it with a men's club sent a clear message as to what activities were approved of in the town. Firm but fair, Pacific Lumber Company management did not forbid workers from drinking, it just did not allow them to do it in Scotia. It was, after all, the company's town, and the company made the rules. (Above, courtesy of the Humboldt County Historical Society; below, courtesy of the Fortuna Depot Museum.)

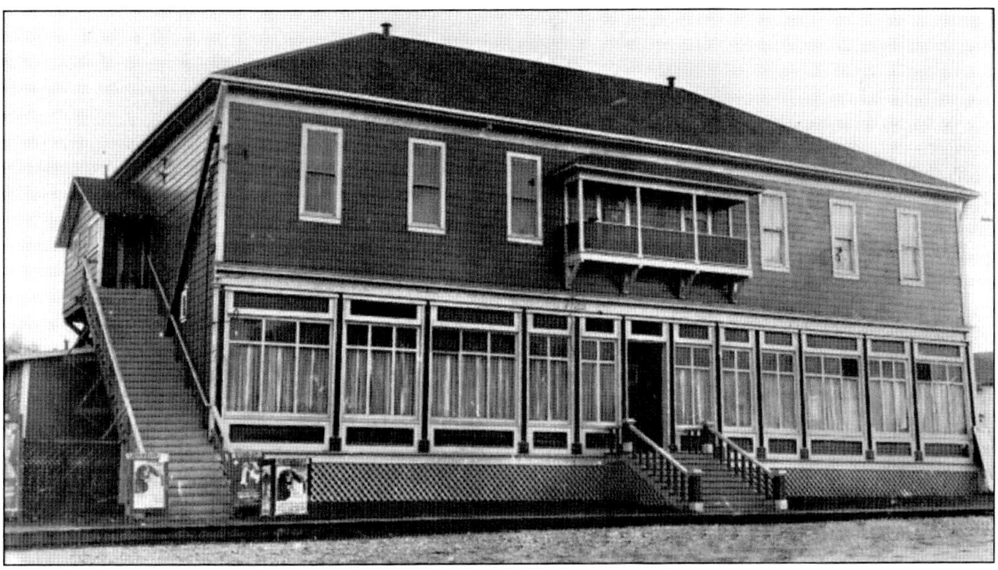

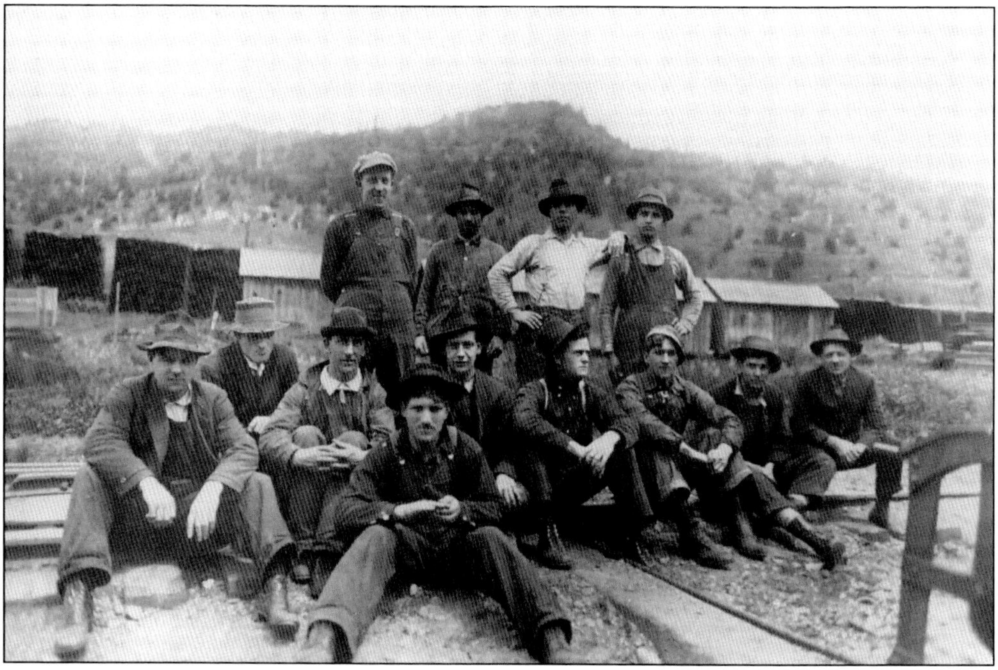

Long hours and low wages continued to prevail in the timber industry, often leading to worker unrest and the rise of unions amongst the Pacific Northwest's loggers and millworkers. The Pacific Lumber Company and its town of Scotia, however, remained relatively unscathed during this era of strikes and picket lines, largely owing to the company's benevolent, albeit paternalistic, relationship with its employees. (Courtesy of the Town of Scotia Company.)

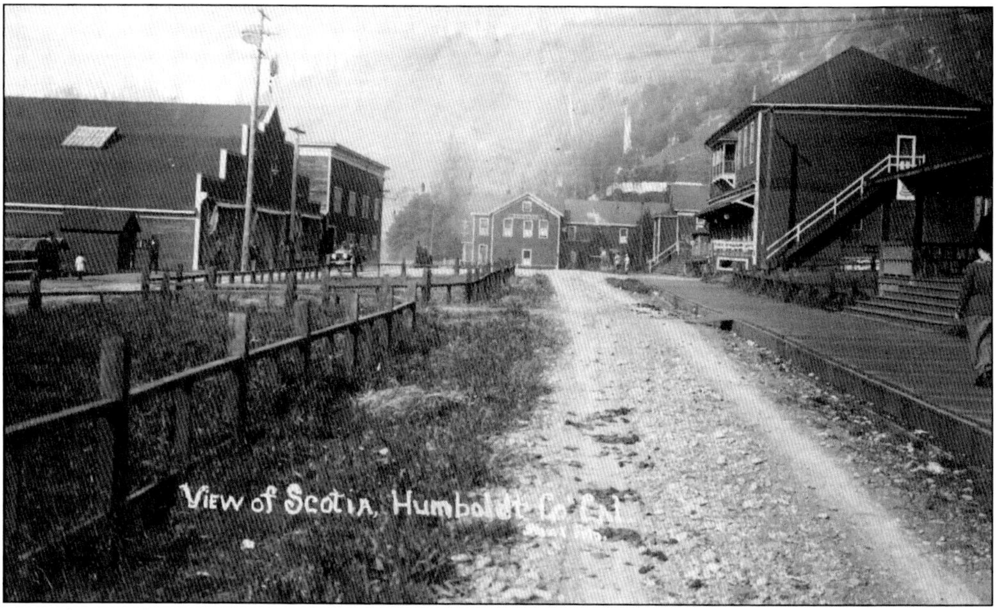

PL took care of its workers, treating them well and offering incentives for working for the company and living in the community. The company's outlook was explained by general manager E.A. Blockinger in a 1911 newspaper article: "Make your mill town beautiful. Get your men loyal, and keep them so. Let this replace loyalty to a union." (Courtesy of the Humboldt County Historical Society.)

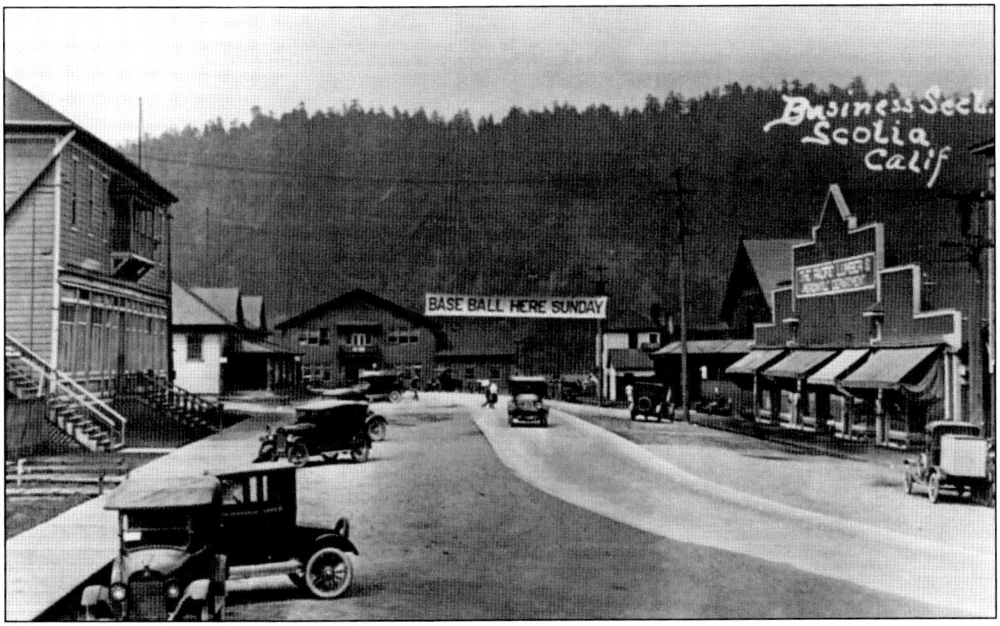

The incentives offered by PL included health care and pension plans, college scholarships for workers' children, and access to company-owned recreation facilities. The company also hosted many special events in order to gather with employees and promote a sense of community. Ball games, company picnics, and Christmas parties became traditions that lasted for decades in Scotia. (Courtesy of the Town of Scotia Company.)

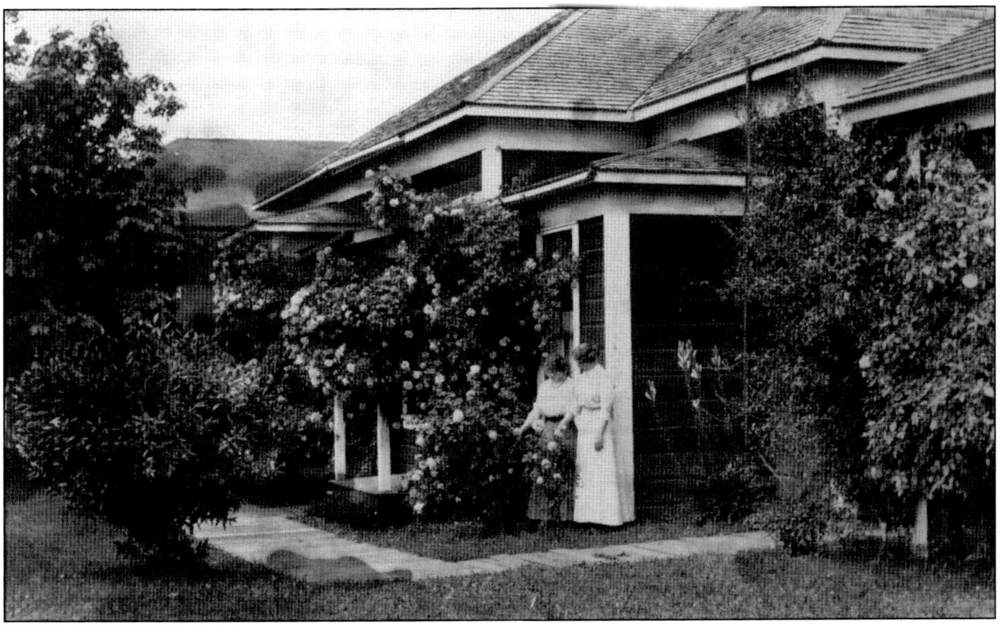

Pacific Lumber maintained a crew of workers to keep its houses in good repair and the town looking respectable. Workers living in Scotia were expected to maintain their lawns, and to this effect, a cash prize was given out each month for the best-looking yard. Neglected lawns were mowed by the town crew, and the worker was charged. (Courtesy of the Humboldt State University Library, Humboldt Room, Neill Collection.)

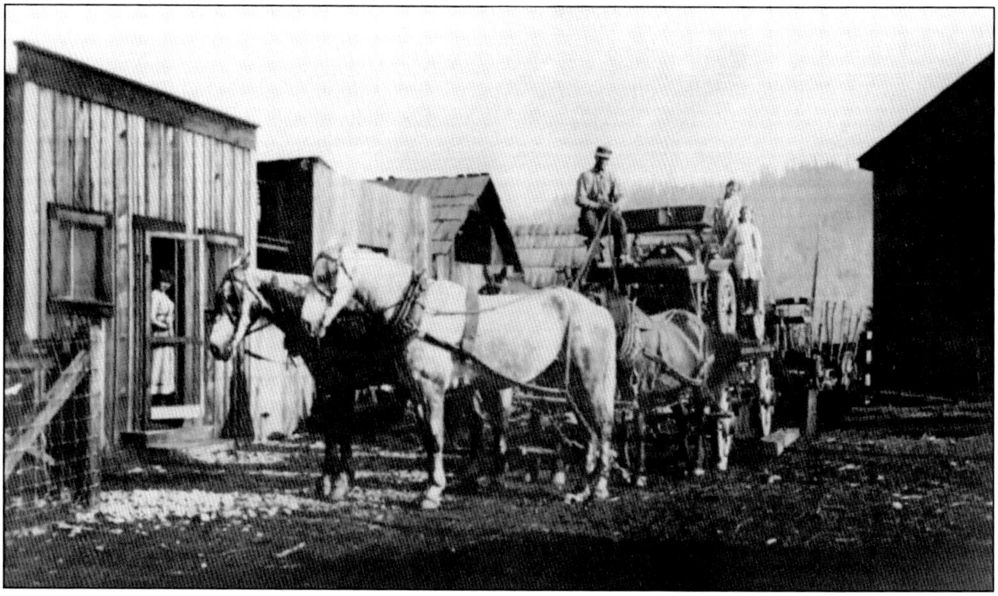

The automobile was a growing fascination for people in Humboldt County just as it was for the rest of the nation. Cars arrived in Humboldt even before there were roads, or a railroad, to bring them into the area. After a lengthy journey by rail and ship, the 1912 REO Roadster shown here is being delivered to its final destination by a horse-drawn wagon. (Courtesy of the Fortuna Depot Museum.)

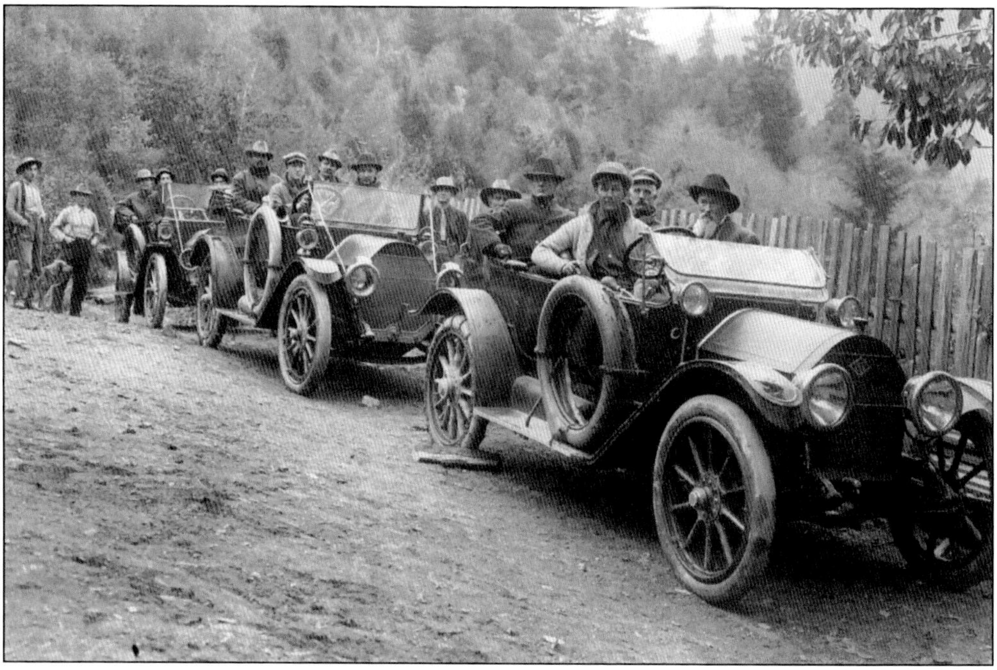

By the 1920s, the automobile was well on its way to replacing the horse-drawn carriage as the primary means of getting around in the county. The roads were far from good, however, and many motorists chained up for more traction to avoid becoming stuck on the old wagon trails. (Courtesy of the Humboldt County Historical Society.)

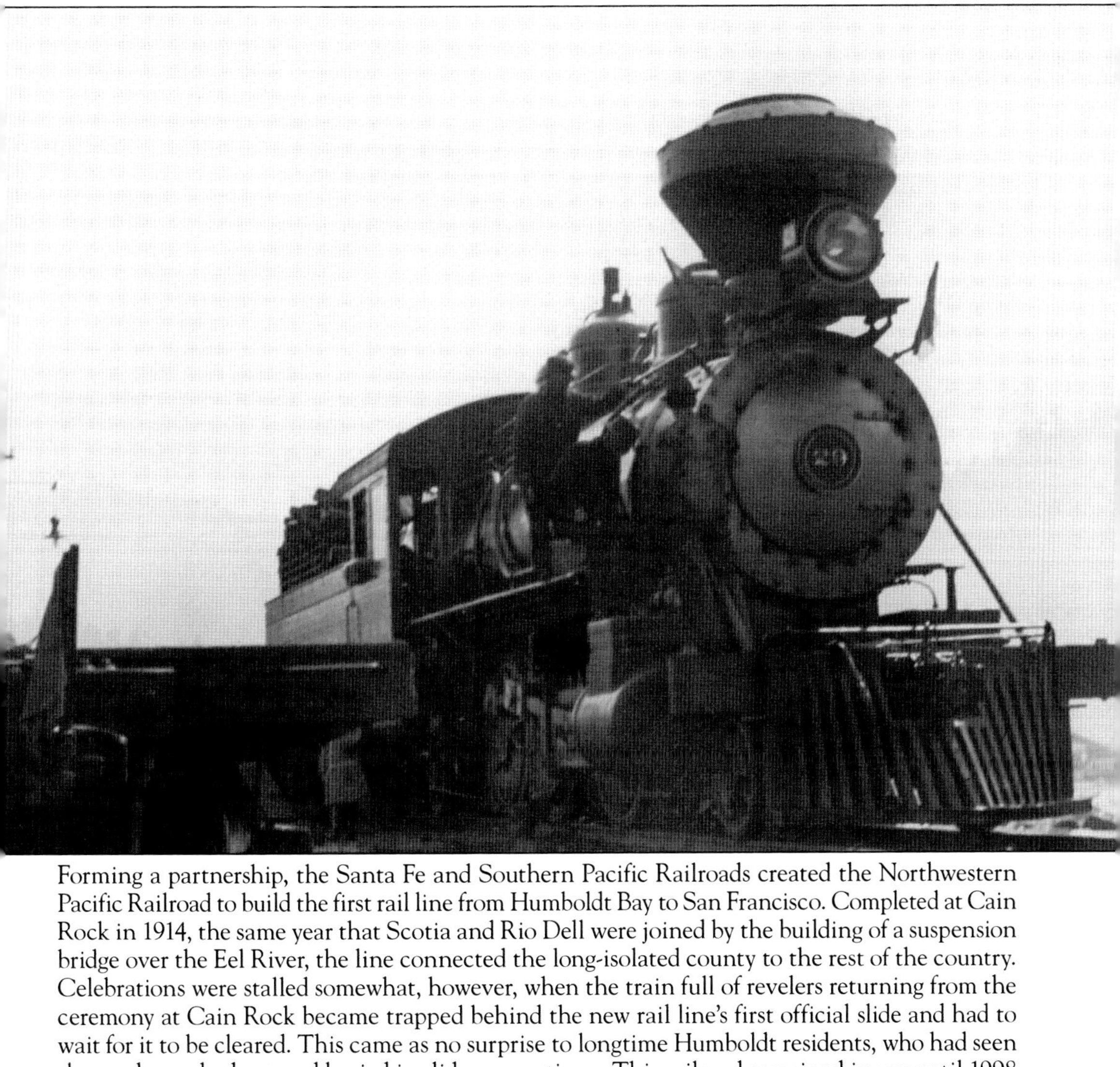

Forming a partnership, the Santa Fe and Southern Pacific Railroads created the Northwestern Pacific Railroad to build the first rail line from Humboldt Bay to San Francisco. Completed at Cain Rock in 1914, the same year that Scotia and Rio Dell were joined by the building of a suspension bridge over the Eel River, the line connected the long-isolated county to the rest of the country. Celebrations were stalled somewhat, however, when the train full of revelers returning from the ceremony at Cain Rock became trapped behind the new rail line's first official slide and had to wait for it to be cleared. This came as no surprise to longtime Humboldt residents, who had seen the tracks washed out and buried in slides many times. This railroad remained in use until 1998 and was plagued with difficulties throughout its existence. (Courtesy of the Humboldt State University Library, Humboldt Room, HCC Collection.)

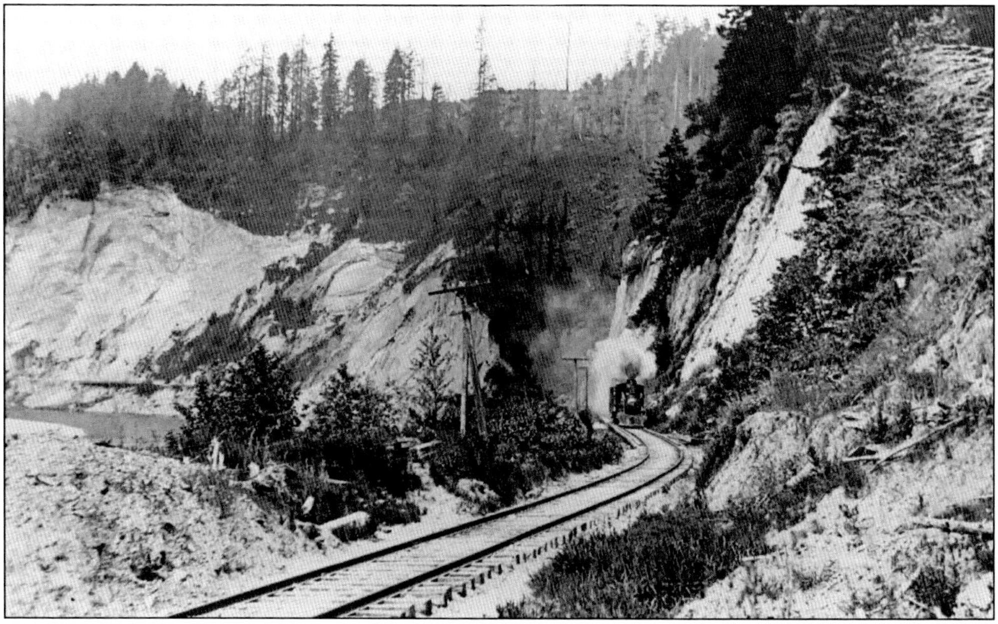

The completion of the railroad was a momentous event for the citizens of Humboldt County. The railroad connected the long-isolated region to the rest of the state, making travel and shipping much cheaper and safer than by sea. By 1915, most of Pacific Lumber's transport needs were being met by the railroad, and the company's shipping fleet was sold. (Courtesy of the Humboldt County Office of Public Works, Tuttle Collection.)

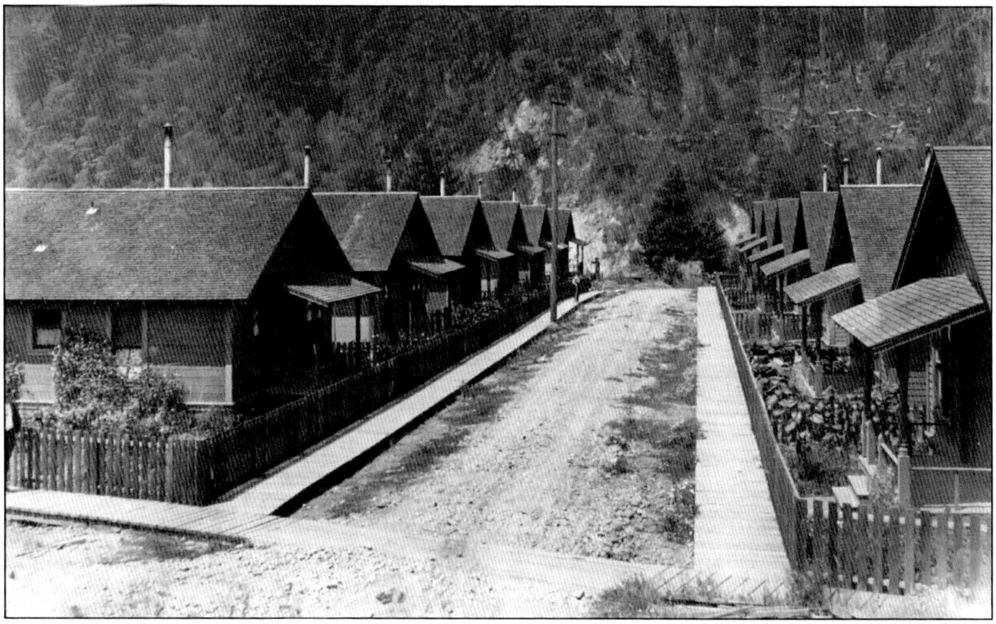

The company's yards in the San Francisco area were closed in 1915, and all equipment and operations were relocated to Scotia, which became the second-largest town in Humboldt County for a time. Construction of new housing went on virtually nonstop in Scotia as PL struggled to keep up with the needs of its expanding operations and workforce. (Courtesy of the Town of Scotia Company.)

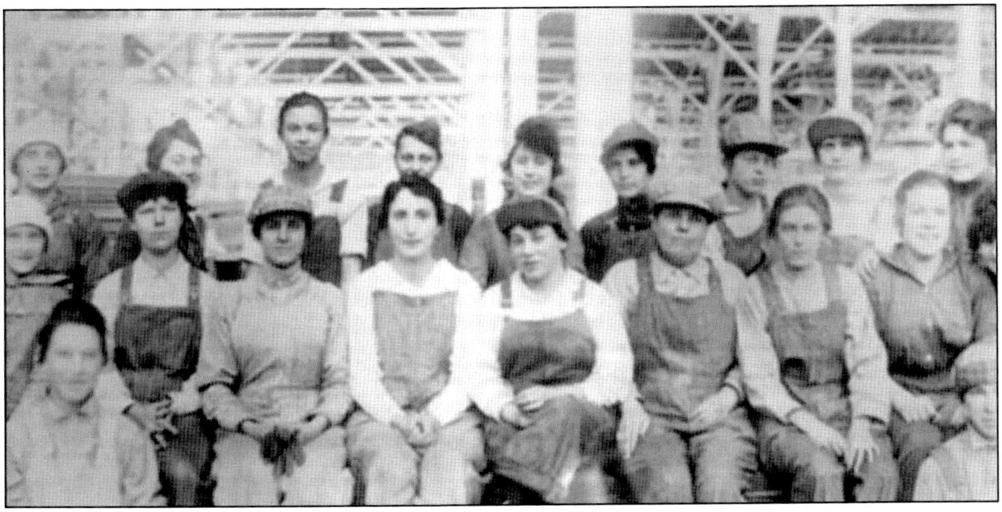

The demand for lumber spiked again as the nation geared up for World War I and Pacific Lumber once again stepped up production. However, while demand was at an all-time high, the labor force was at an all-time low. PL addressed the labor shortage by employing women to work in its factory in 1917. By the end of the war, over 200 women worked at Pacific Lumber. (Courtesy of Eldon Whitehead.)

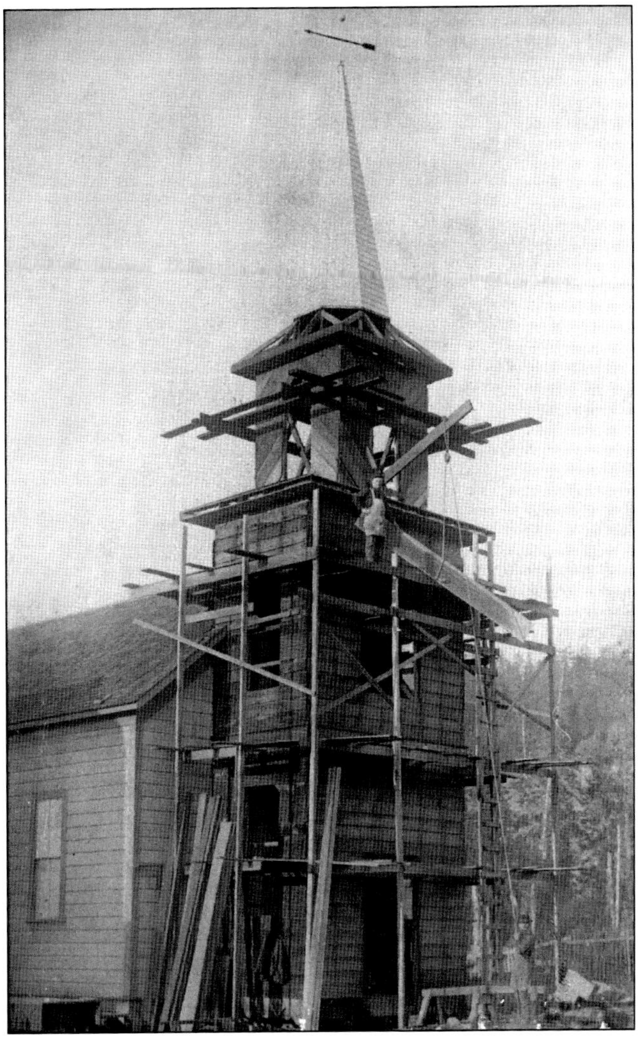

Scotia continued to grow, with houses going up virtually nonstop until 1925. The company also built two new churches, the Scotia Union Church in 1924 and St. Patrick's Catholic Church in 1925. Seen here is St. Patrick's with its steeple still under construction. (Courtesy of the Humboldt State University Library, Humboldt Room, Palmquist Collection.)

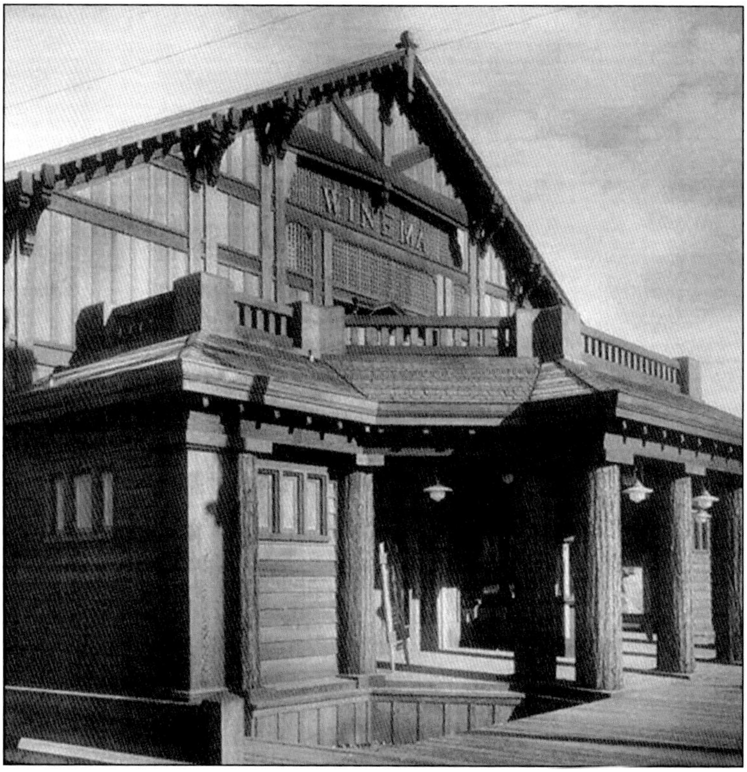

The Winema Theater was built in 1920 and named for a Modoc Indian woman, Toby "Winema" Riddle, who served as an interpreter in negotiations between the Modoc tribe and federal troops during the Modoc War. Constructed of redwood and resembling a traditional Swiss chalet, Scotia's theater was a very popular attraction. (Courtesy of the Town of Scotia Company.)

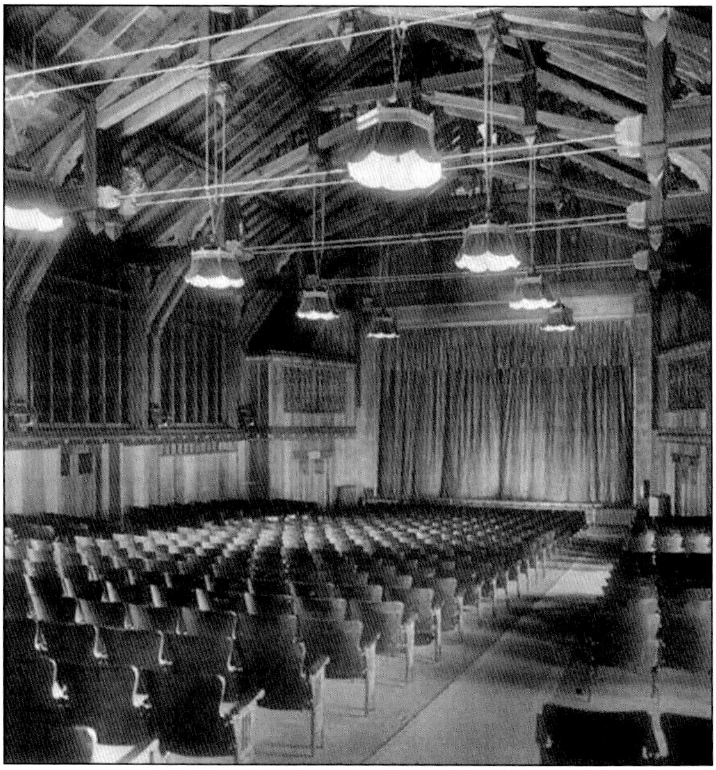

Featuring films and live entertainment until the 1950s, the theater had a traditional ticket booth outside and seated more than 250 moviegoers. The theater was enthusiastically attended by both Scotia and Rio Dell residents, although they reportedly sat on opposite sides of the theater and threw things at each other. Some things never change. (Courtesy of the Town of Scotia Company.)

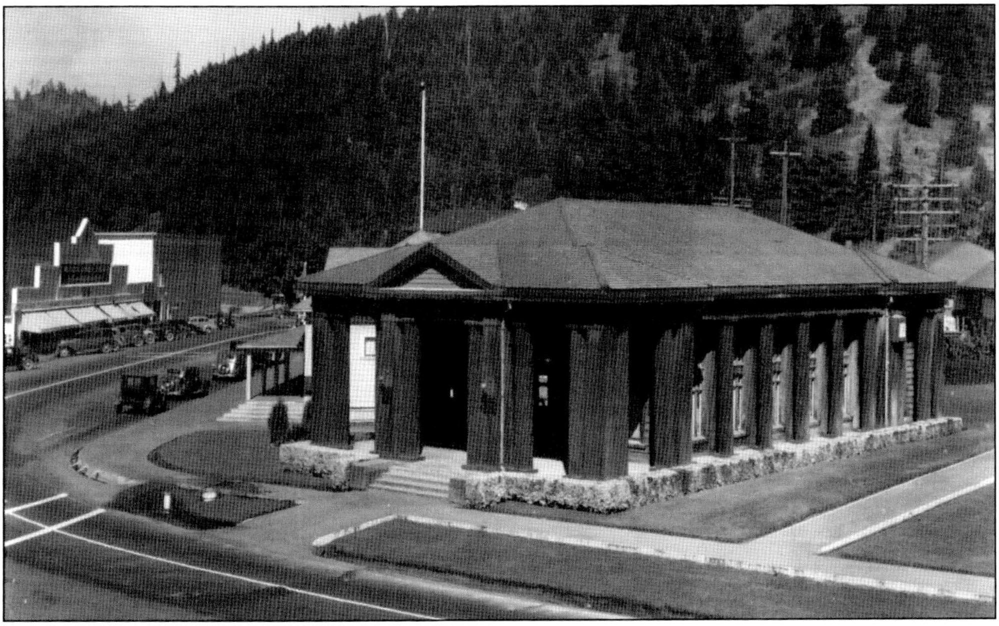

In 1921, construction was completed on the First National Bank of Scotia. The bank was designed in Greek Revival style using all redwood. The columns, complete with bark to simulate a grooved appearance, finish off the classic design. This immaculately maintained building currently serves as the town's museum and features artifacts and displays of Pacific Lumber Company's rich logging heritage. (Courtesy of the Town of Scotia Company.)

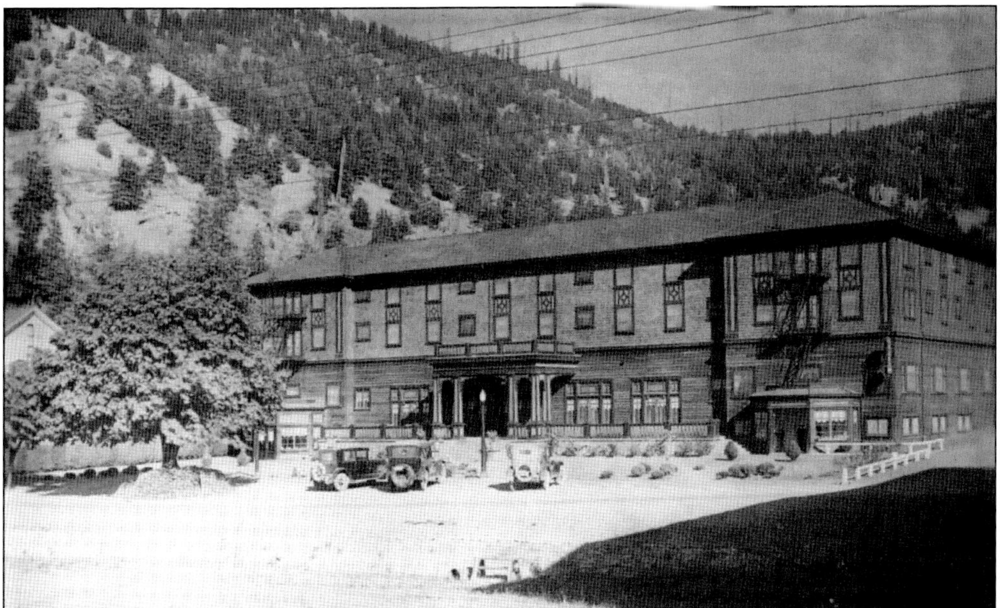

That same year, a fire destroyed the original Scotia Inn. It did not take the town long to begin reconstruction, and in 1923, the first wing of the new hotel was completed. By 1924, the second wing was added, and the hotel sported 135 rooms. A popular place for weddings, this iconic building stands as a tribute to Scotia's resilience and ability to continually rise from the ashes. (Courtesy of the Town of Scotia Company.)

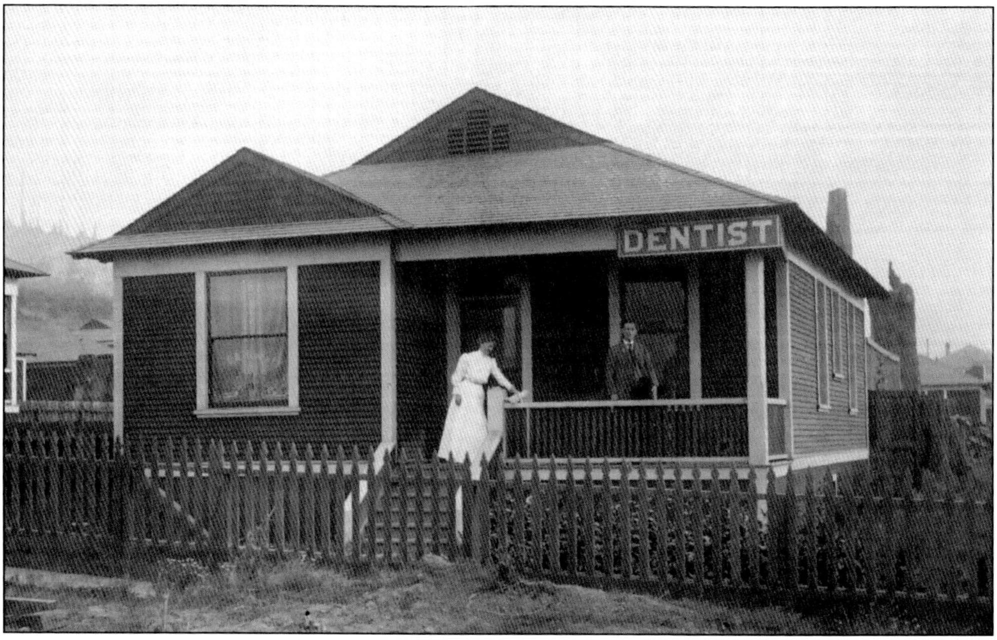

Dental care was provided by Scotia's dentist, Dr. Gilbert A. Howatt. The dentist's office was located in the house shown here. Dental care for Pacific Lumber workers and their families was paid for by a payroll deduction, along with medical care. Dr. Howatt's bicycle-powered dental drill can be seen at the Scotia Museum. (Courtesy of the Humboldt County Historical Society.)

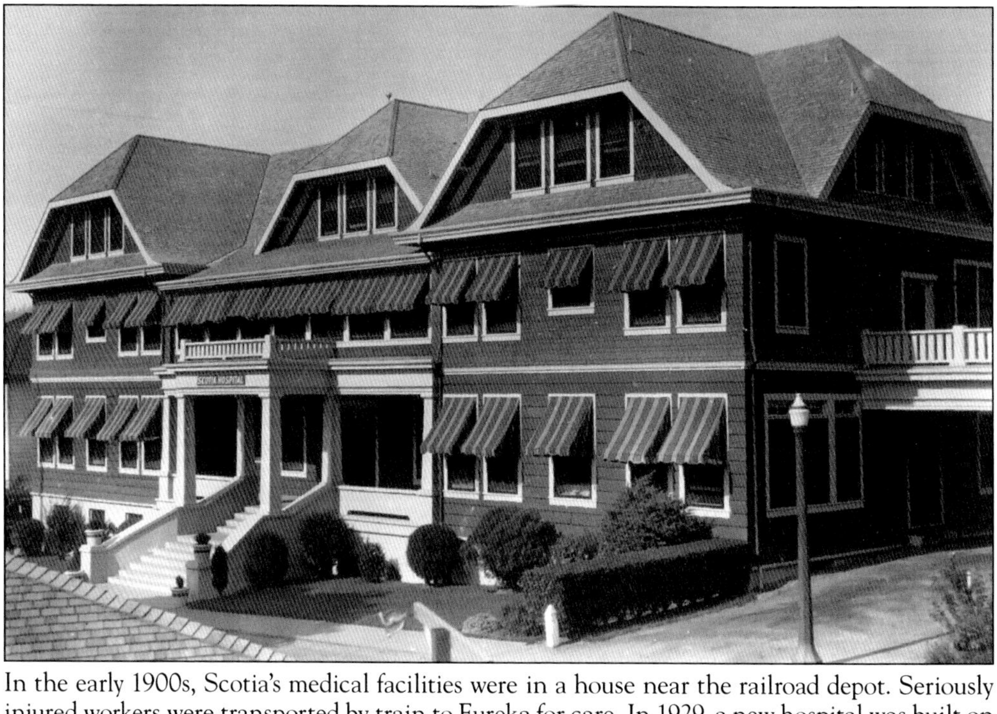

In the early 1900s, Scotia's medical facilities were in a house near the railroad depot. Seriously injured workers were transported by train to Eureka for care. In 1929, a new hospital was built on the site of the old Rigby house. The hospital provided complete medical care for Pacific Lumber's workers for $1 a month. (Courtesy of the Humboldt County Historical Society.)

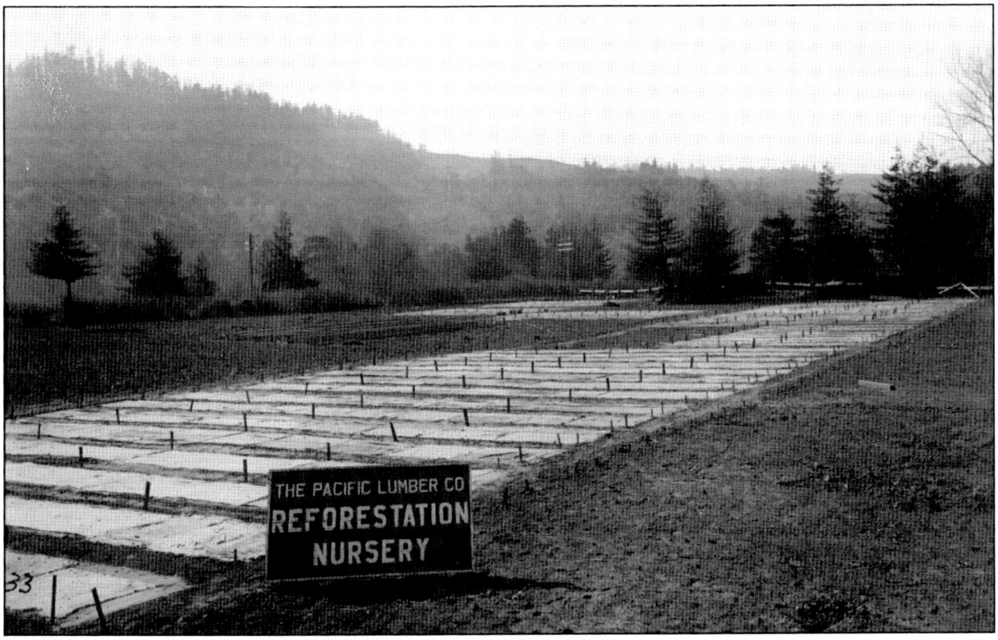

In 1923, Pacific Lumber established a seedling nursery in Scotia to facilitate the reforestation of cut-over lands. Over a million redwood, spruce, cedar, and fir seedlings were grown there each year. This nursery was closed down during the Depression and converted to pasture for the company's large herd of beef cows, used to help feed the company's workforce and its families. (Courtesy of the Town of Scotia Company.)

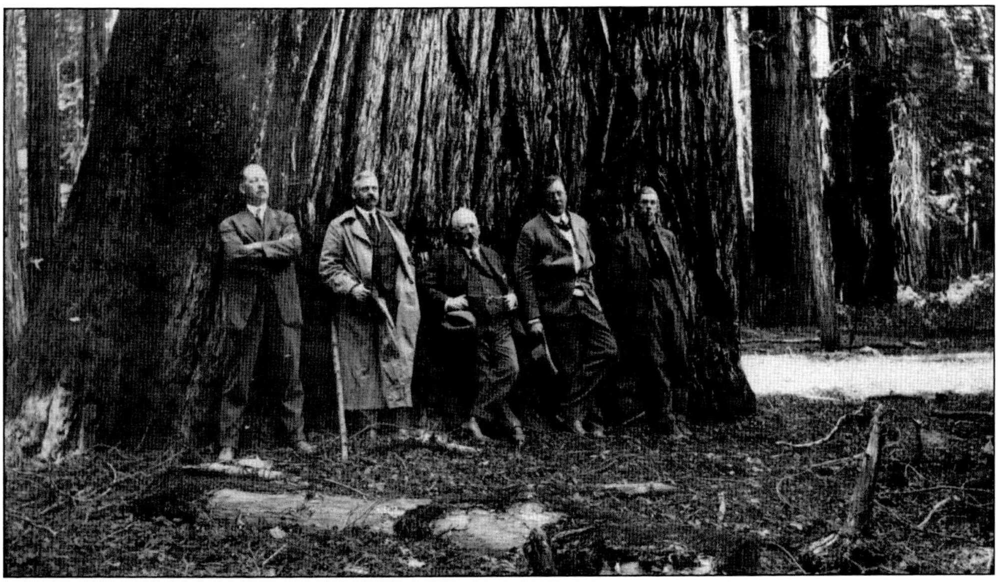

In 1928, a revolutionary agreement was reached between the Pacific Lumber Company and the Save-the-Redwoods League to preserve and protect old-growth redwood groves along the Eel River. Nearly 20,000 acres of Pacific Lumber Company land went into creating Humboldt Redwoods State Park and the Avenue of the Giants. These men pose in front of a giant redwood at Bull Creek in 1910. (Courtesy of the Humboldt State University Library, Humboldt Room, Neill Collection.)

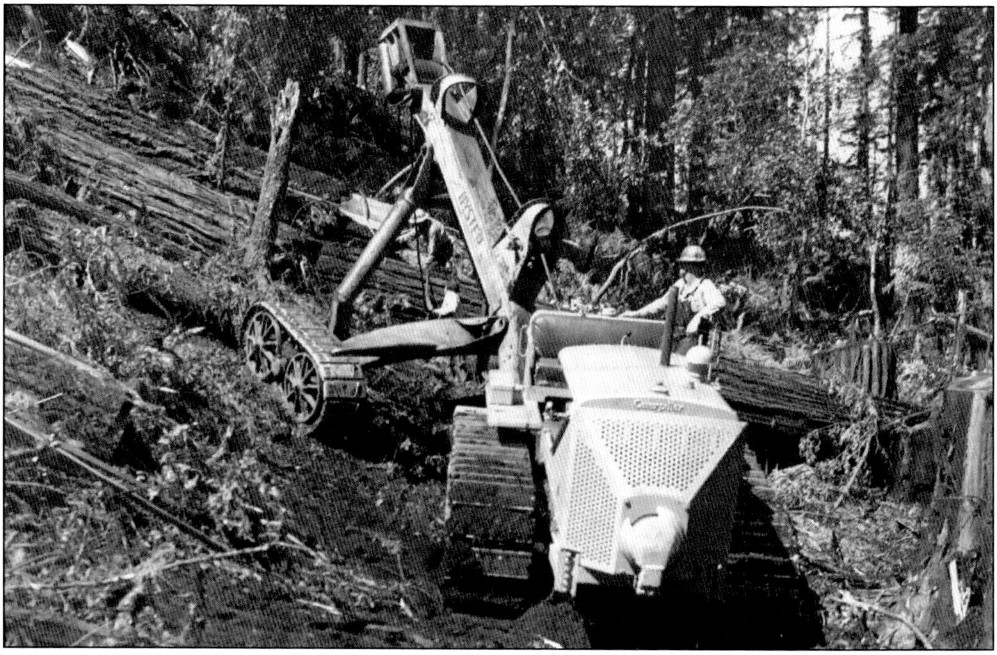

Albert S. Murphy became president of the Pacific Lumber Company in 1931. Under his leadership, Pacific Lumber continued to look to the future and adopted more sustainable logging practices. Advances in logging technology, such as the crawler tractor, made it possible for Pacific Lumber to return to selective logging practices. Like the oxen that had provided the pulling power in the woods before Dolbeer's steam engine, the tractor's cleated steel tracks and powerful winch enabled it to maneuver loads better through the woods, allowing immature trees to remain uncut and undamaged during logging operations. These versatile machines were put to use in the woods and in the fields and continue to be used on logging and construction sites worldwide. In 1934, Pacific Lumber began using the tractors in its Monument Creek operations, across the Eel River from Scotia. (Both, courtesy of the Town of Scotia Company.)

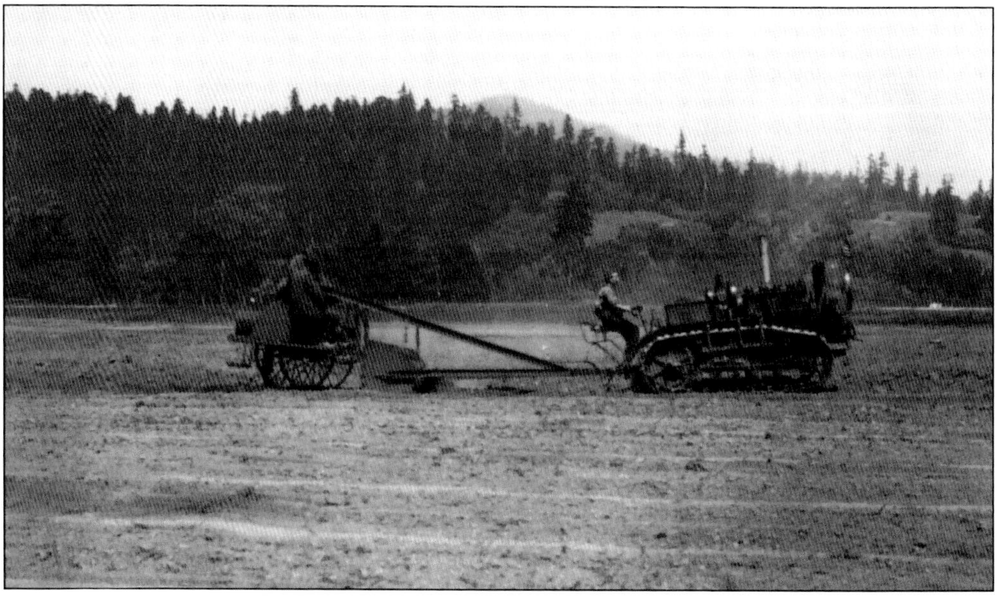

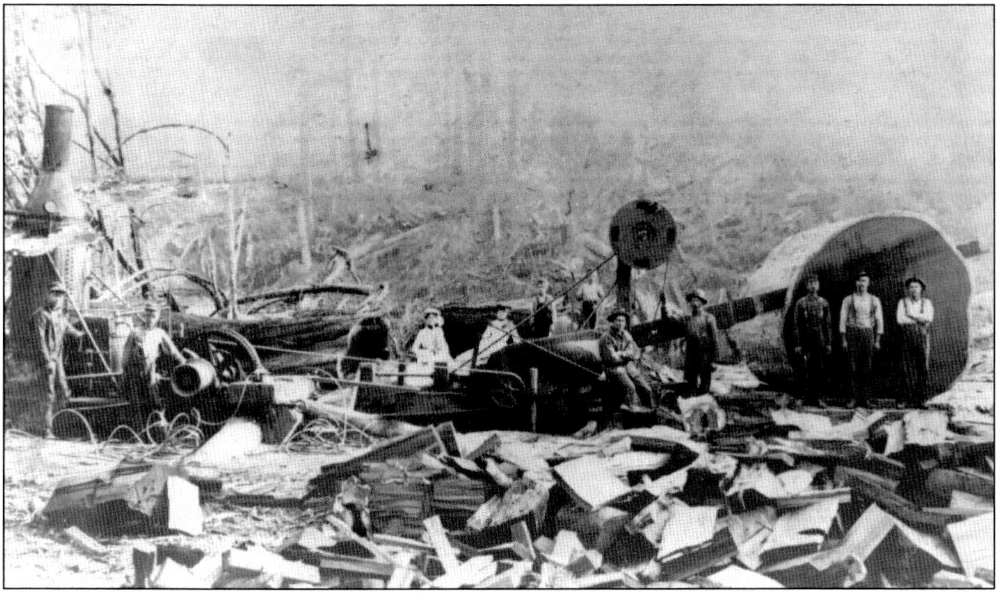

The Pacific Lumber Company kept pace with advancements in both railroading and logging technologies, making the job of processing and transporting its products easier, cheaper, and more efficient. The job of felling the redwood giants, however, remained the domain of the axe and saw for many years. Attempts had been made as early as the 1870s to mechanize the felling of the big trees, but with little success. Too cumbersome and too difficult to maintain for use in felling, early drag saws saw a good deal of use in bucking up fallen trees. Gas-powered drag saws continued to improve over the years, however, and by the mid-1930s were widely used. Below, Dick Beach fuels up a portable drag saw for a demonstration in 1968. (Above, courtesy of the Town of Scotia Company; below, courtesy of the Humboldt State University Library, Humboldt Room, Boyle Collection.)

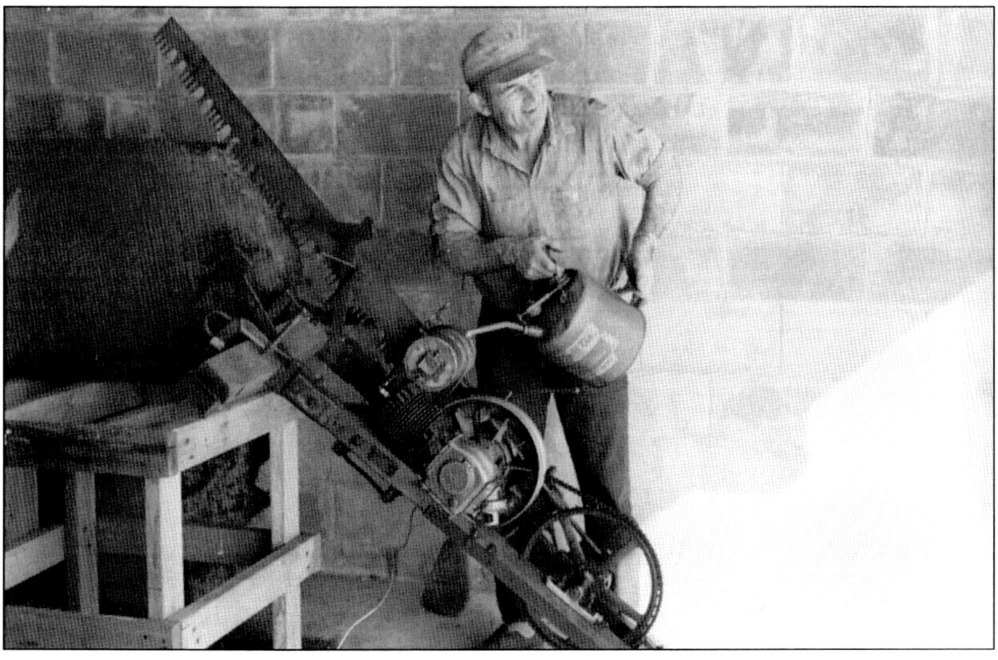

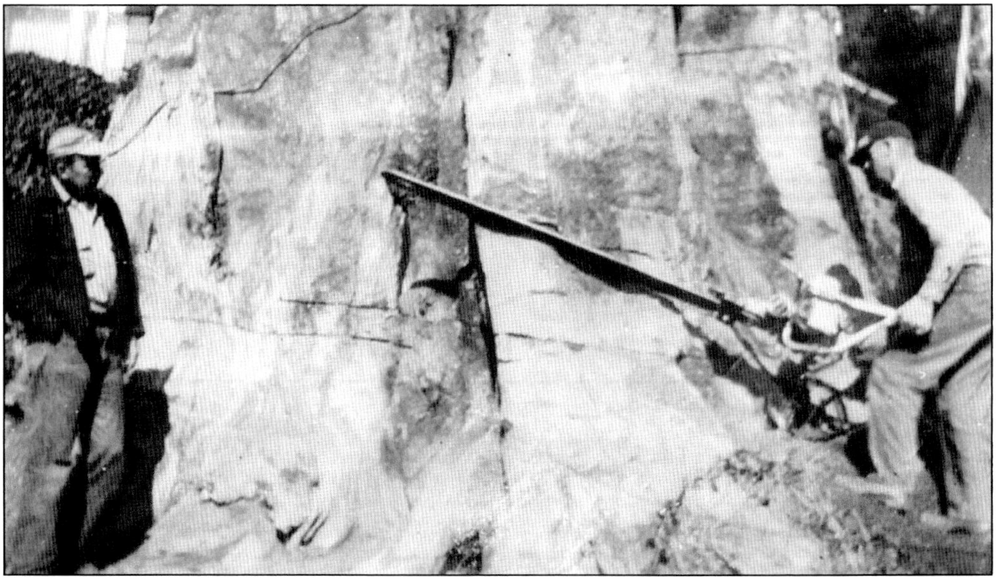

About the time the drag saw was being refined into a lightweight and efficient machine, the first chainsaws were beginning to appear in the redwoods. However, like the drag saws, these machines needed many improvements before they could be considered a viable replacement for their predecessors. Early hand-held, gas-powered chainsaws had a stinger and pulley at the tip of the blade, limiting the diameter of tree they could cut. The chainsaw would not come into widespread use in felling until the invention of the bucking bar in the late 1940s, which eliminated the pulley and stinger, allowing the feller to take down much larger trees. (Above, courtesy of the Humboldt State University Library, Humboldt Room, Boyle Collection; below, courtesy of the Town of Scotia Company.)

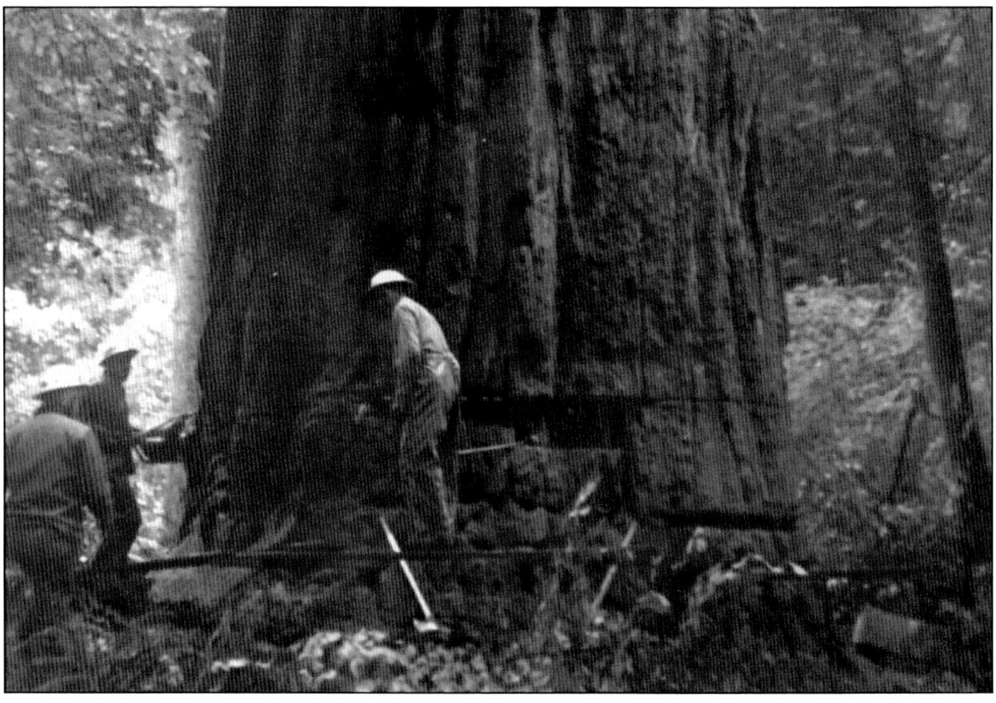

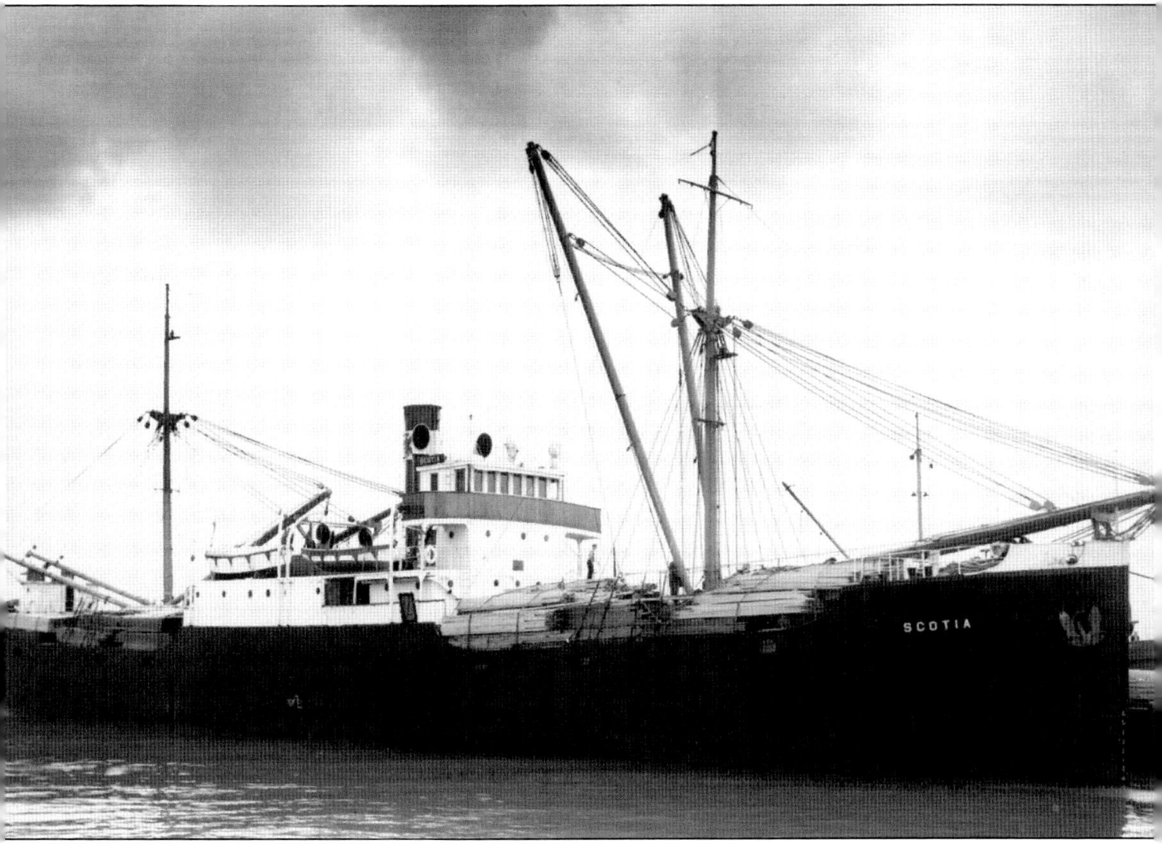

In 1935, Pacific Lumber reentered the timber shipping business with its purchase of the *Scotia.* Built in 1919 and originally christened the *Lake Galewood*, Pacific Lumber's new steamship was capable of transoceanic travel and delivered lumber and cargo to ports throughout the Pacific. *Scotia* went down in a gale off Alaska's Aleutian Islands in 1943. The lumber strike of 1946 brought things screeching to a halt at Pacific Lumber for the first time in the company's history. The costly strike closed the mill for six months before it resumed operations in October of that year. While the strike was ultimately unsuccessful in unionizing the timber industry, it did bring awareness to the plight of many West Coast loggers and forced mill operators to negotiate with their employees. Pacific Lumber had worked for years to maintain good relations with its employees and reaped the benefits of these efforts. (Courtesy of the Town of Scotia Company.)

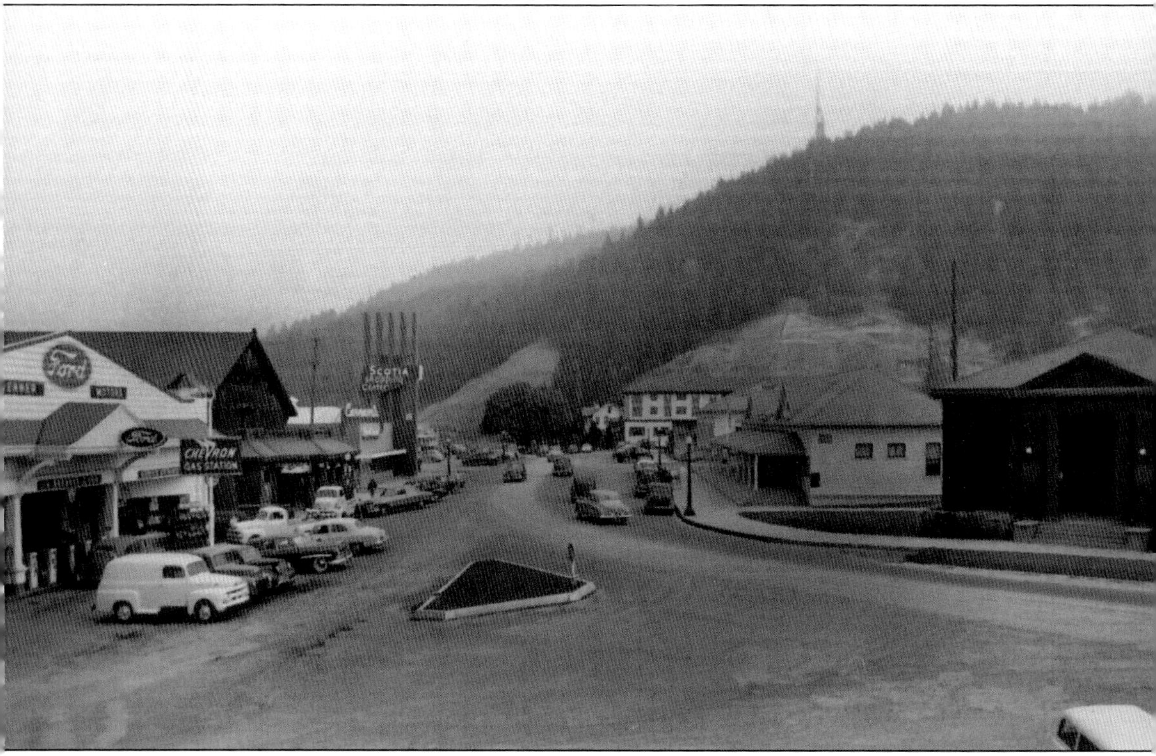

For decades, the Pacific Lumber Company had been the backbone of the communities of Scotia, Rio Dell, and Wildwood, providing not only jobs but also many services and recreational programs throughout the region. The company sponsored ball teams and youth athletic programs in Scotia and throughout the county and constructed gymnasiums, swimming pools, recreation centers, parks, and movie theaters. It also provided many other services and activities for the communities it supported. After the tumultuous opening decades of the 20th century, having endured World War I, the Great Depression, World War II, and years of intermittent labor disputes, the Pacific Lumber Company and its workers were ready to face the future. (Courtesy of the Todd-Schuler/Bartleson family.)

Three

WILDWOOD

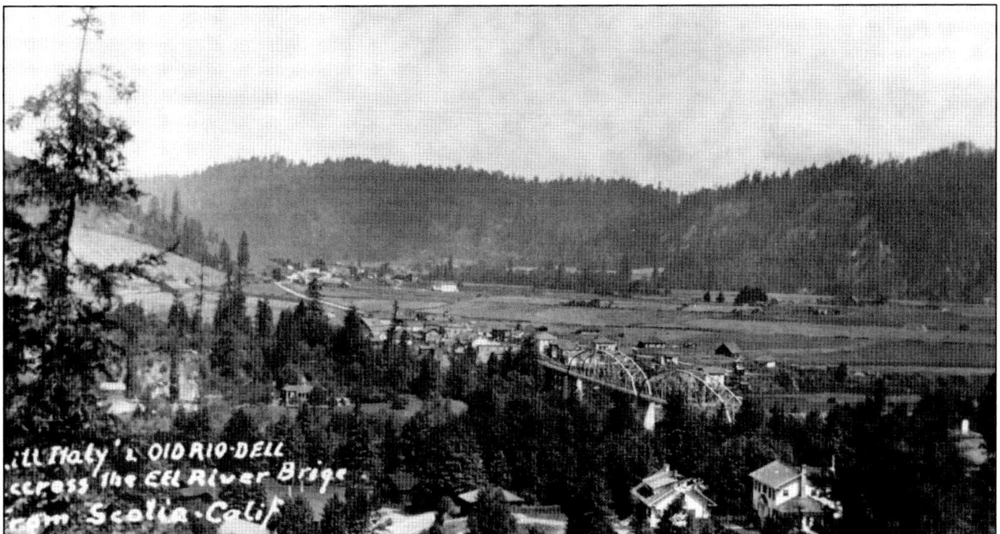

Italian families came to the area seeking work after the construction of the Pacific Lumber Company's second mill in 1910. Housing for these new immigrants was limited in the company's town, and most were compelled to settle across the river at the south end of Eagle Prairie. (Courtesy of the Todd-Schuler/Bartleson family.)

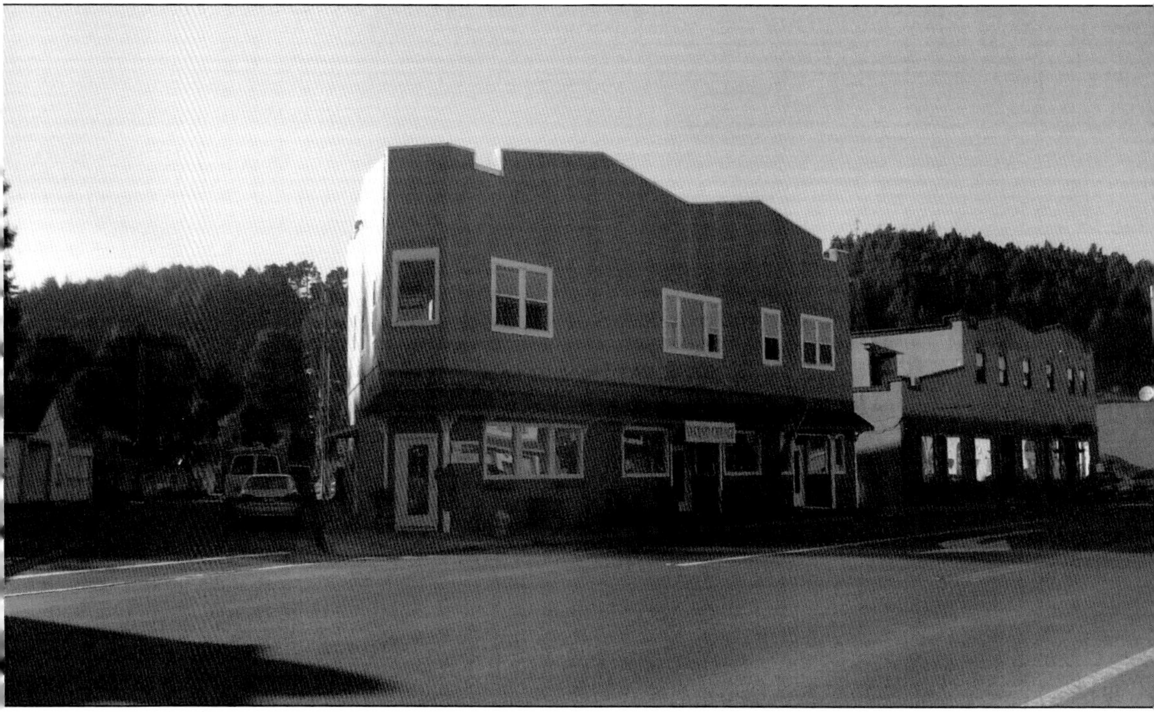

Unlike the earlier settlers in Rio Dell, who came to the area to pioneer new country and stake their claim to a piece of land, many of these later arrivals largely came as wage-laborers seeking an opportunity for employment. Italian immigrants were frequently confronted with language barriers and faced discrimination and racism. Many Italians found work in the woods or at the Pacific Lumber Company's mills in Scotia, but most of them lived in Wildwood. In those days, family housing for Italian workers in Scotia was limited to 18 houses situated on the "wrong side of the tracks." Some of these Italians purchased land from Thomas H. Selvage and John Kelly and laid out a townsite that later became known as Wildwood or "Little Italy." Arthur Scatena and his wife, Zermira, built a 12-room hotel in the new community that same year. The Scatena Hotel, shown here, housed many of the local loggers and featured its own saloon and card room. Scatena also ran the ferry between Wildwood and Scotia for a time. (Author's collection.)

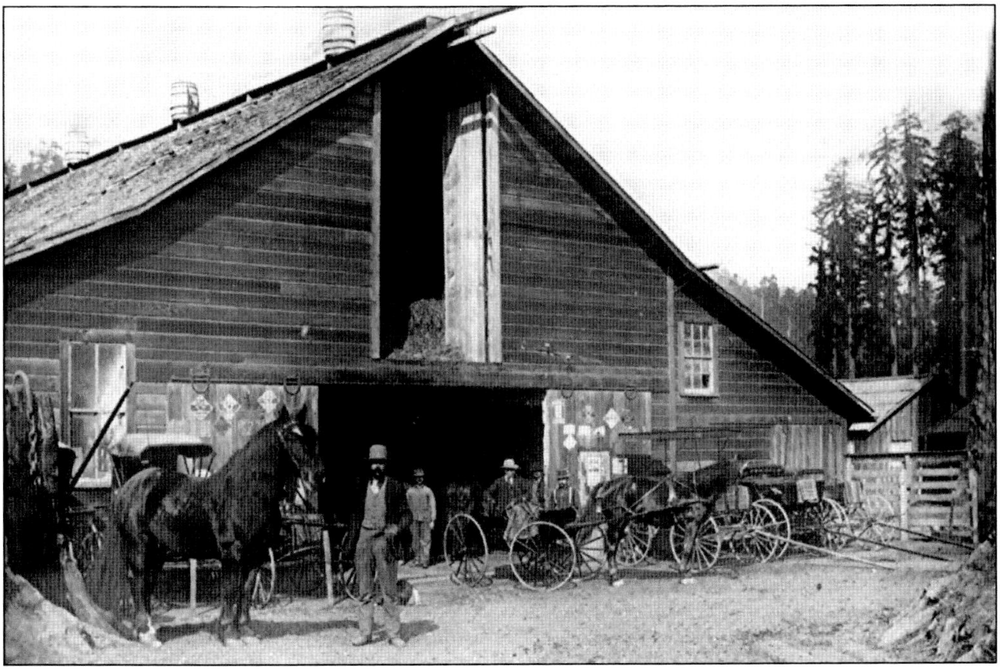

Some of the Italian residents operated businesses in Wildwood, many of them while working at other jobs as well. Wildwood soon hosted Frank Nicoletti's bakery, the first in town. It was joined by cobbler Frank Corsetti, Mr. and Mrs. Capana's grocery, and Guido Mengali's barbershop. A livery, blacksmith, and general store were also located in Wildwood. (Courtesy of Greg Rumney.)

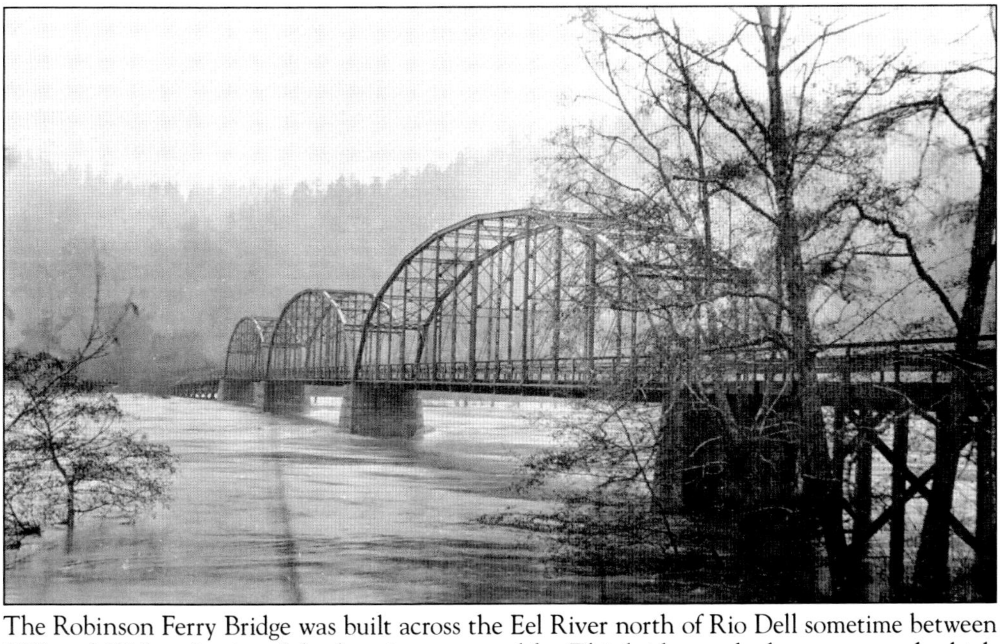

The Robinson Ferry Bridge was built across the Eel River north of Rio Dell sometime between 1912 and 1915 at the site of the ferry it was named for. This bridge made the county road, which had been dependent on the ferry, more reliable and convenient for travel. This bridge was replaced in 1941 with the Paul Mudgett Memorial Bridge. (Courtesy of the Humboldt State University Library, Humboldt Room, Palmquist Collection.)

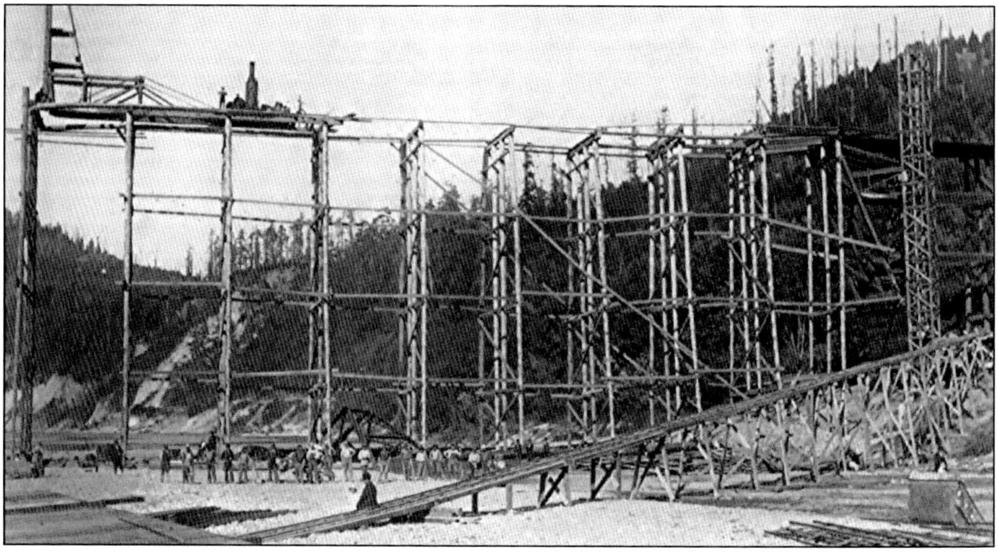

As the population expanded in the area, demands for a bridge between Eagle Prairie and Scotia grew loud enough for the county to respond. The Pacific Lumber Company offered to donate materials and help fund the bridge, and construction began in 1913. The bridge was completed in 1914, and citizens on both sides of the river rejoiced. (Courtesy of Greg Rumney.)

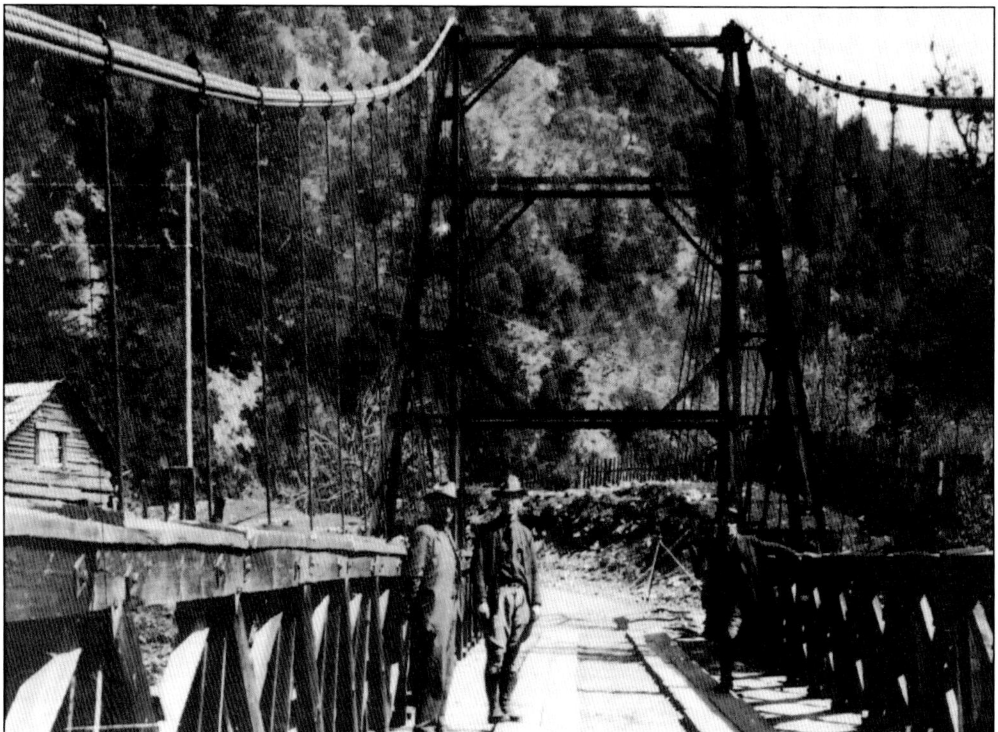

The bridge brought the communities closer together, making it much easier for residents of Wildwood and Rio Dell to reach the mill and railroad station in Scotia and for people in Scotia to shop in the stores and enjoy the restaurants, bars, and other services found across the river. (Courtesy of the Humboldt County Historical Society.)

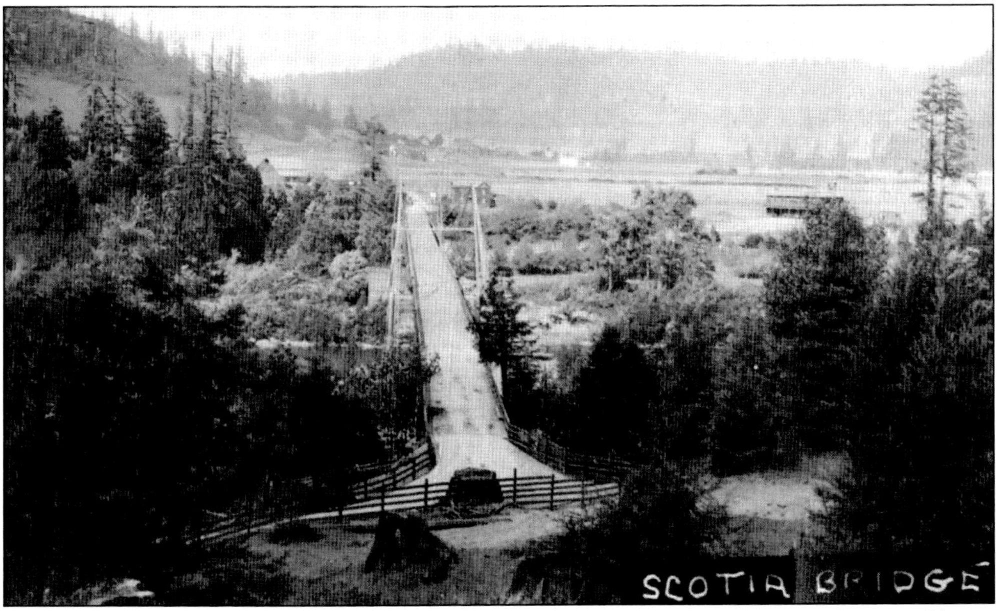

Businesses on both sides of the river benefitted from the easier access between towns. In addition to shopping and entertainment, many Pacific Lumber workers and retirees looked to Rio Dell as a place to buy property and build homes, something they could not do in Scotia, where the company owned all of the land. (Courtesy of the Humboldt County Historical Society.)

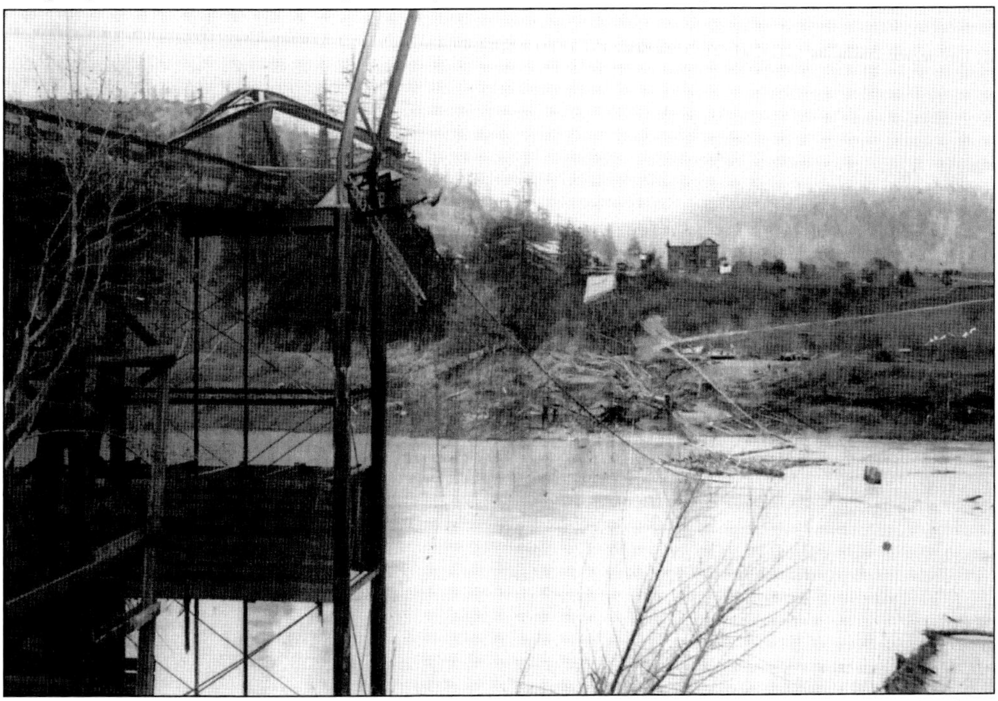

The celebrations were short-lived, as the first Rio Dell–Scotia bridge was wiped out by flooding in February 1915. After 17 inches of rain fell in just 36 hours, a huge tree was washed against the bridge supports on the Wildwood side. The tremendous pressure and weight of the resultant debris jam toppled the supports, and the bridge collapsed into the river. (Courtesy of Greg Rumney.)

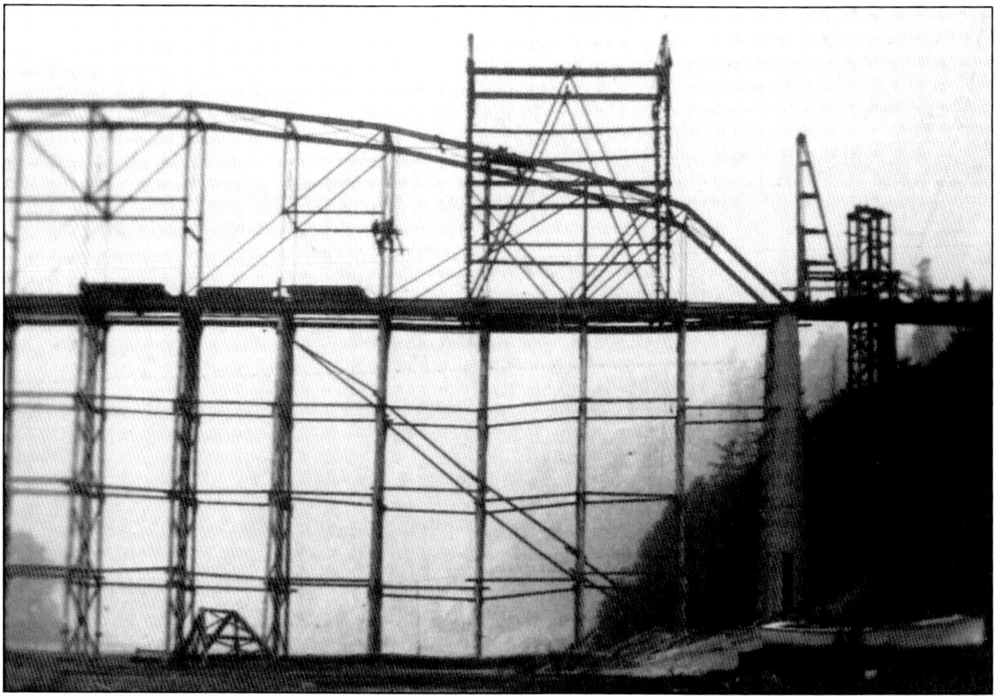

This was a tremendous disappointment but came as little surprise to many area residents, who had seen the destructive power of the Eel River in past floods. Despite this calamity, the residents were determined to rebuild, and by 1917, another bridge stood over the Eel, uniting the two communities once again. (Courtesy of the Todd-Schuler/Bartleson family.)

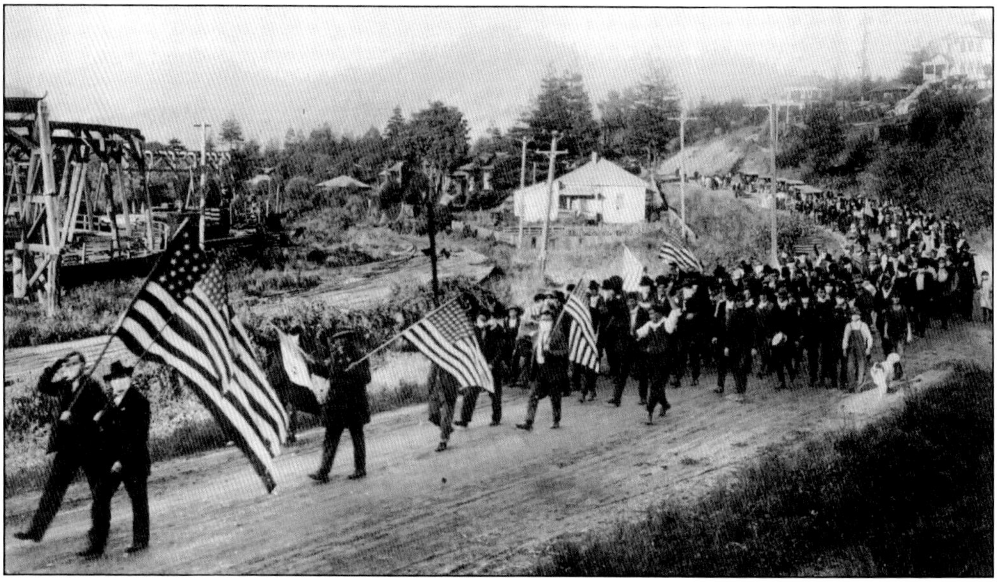

In 1918, an influenza pandemic swept the globe, claiming the lives of an estimated 20 million people worldwide. Over 200 lost their lives in Humboldt County, and an ordinance was passed requiring school children to wear masks to class. In the midst of this scare, the people of Rio Dell, Wildwood, and Scotia still came together to hold a parade celebrating the end of World War I. (Courtesy of the Town of Scotia Company.)

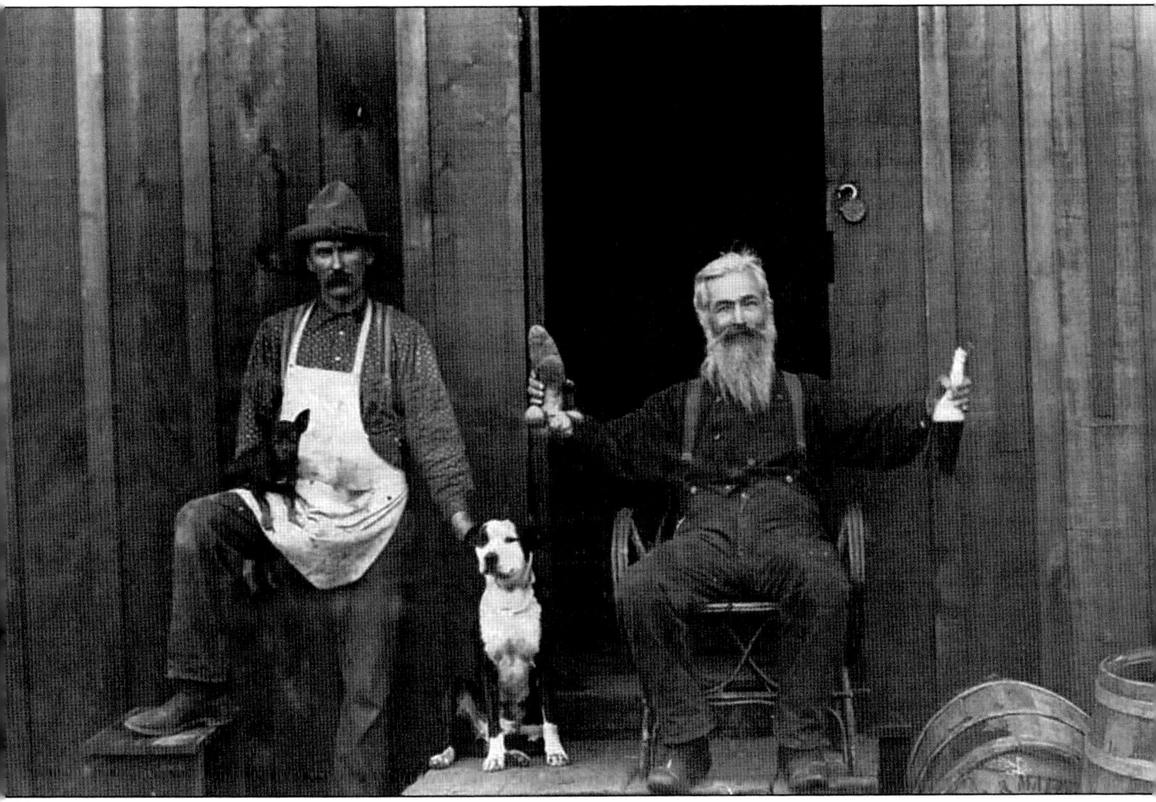

Before Prohibition, Eureka was declared the wettest city in the state, but during the dry years, Wildwood was definitely in the running. Wildwood really came into its own and earned its name during the Prohibition years. If Pacific Lumber Company management thought the saloons of Rio Dell were a bad influence in the 1880s, one can only guess how it felt about Wildwood in the 1920s. Gambling, prostitution, and speakeasies became the town's primary attractions, livened up with an occasional fistfight, stabbing, or shooting. While the nation struggled to give up drink and vice, people in Wildwood found ways to conceal the production and distribution of alcohol in the small town and keep their nighttime businesses profitable. Humboldt County was full of rowdy, hard-working lumbermen and pioneers, among whom the Temperance Movement had never been very popular. This was especially true in Little Italy, where many of the residents hailed from countries where wine was considered a staple and was often made at home. (Courtesy of the Todd-Schuler/Bartleson family.)

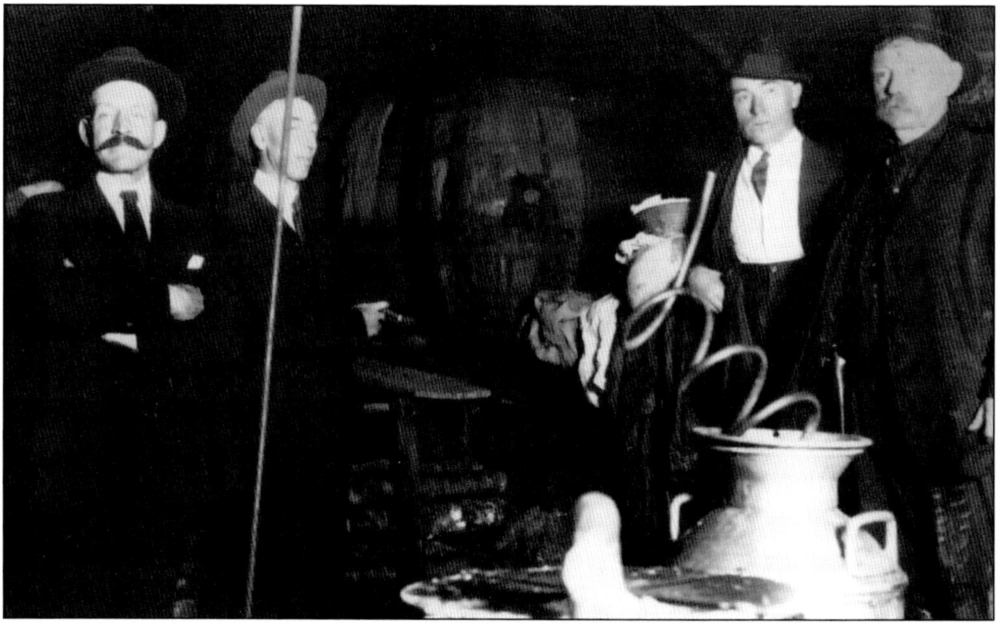

Wine, beer, and spirits had long been produced and distributed in the county, and Prohibition simply drove these operations underground and made them far more profitable. Stills were hidden in sheds and in the woods, and false walls containing holding tanks for liquor were cleverly crafted in buildings throughout town. (Courtesy of the Humboldt State University Library, Humboldt Room, HCC Collection.)

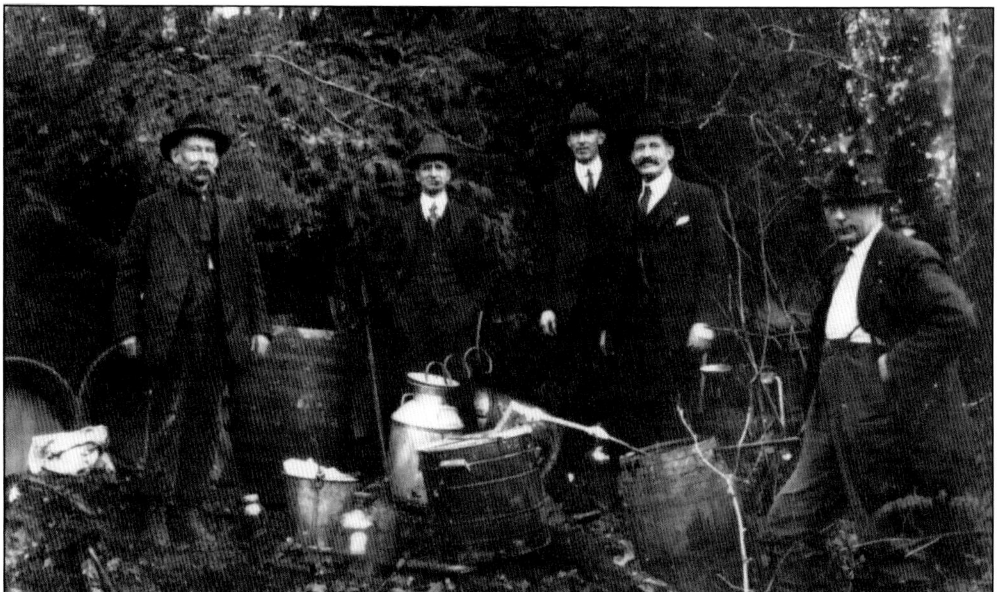

The county dry squad conducted surprise raids on places suspected of manufacturing or selling alcohol. Eureka and Wildwood were the most commonly raided locations, and several arrests were made over the years. While the county profited handsomely from fines, the efforts of these men did little to stem the flow of illegal liquor. (Courtesy of the Humboldt State University Library, Humboldt Room, HCC Collection.)

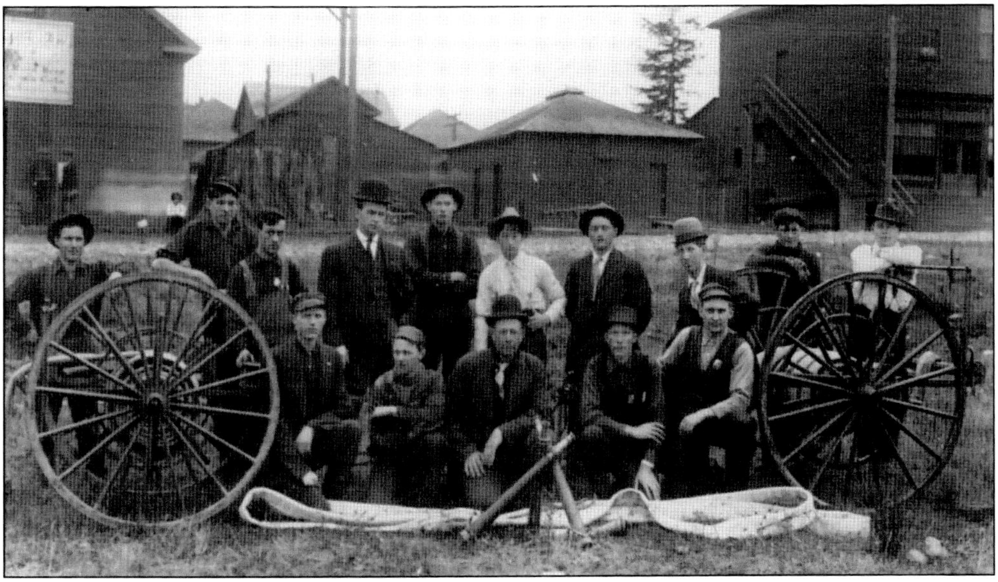

The thirst for liquor and profit nearly spelled the end of Wildwood in 1928 when a still exploded in the back room of a restaurant. The resulting fire almost destroyed the entire town. The Scatena Hotel was spared destruction by hanging wine-soaked burlap on its exterior. Fire departments from Scotia, Fortuna, and Ferndale arrived too late to save many of the early downtown buildings. With the end of Prohibition in 1933, the bootleggers became legitimate businessmen once again. Licenses were purchased, bars were opened, and hotels and restaurants resumed legally selling beer and wine to their customers. People in the area celebrated their renewed freedom to do what they had never stopped doing in the first place, and Wildwood continued to be wild. (Above, courtesy of the Fortuna Depot Museum; below, courtesy of the Humboldt State University Library, Humboldt Room, HCC Collection.)

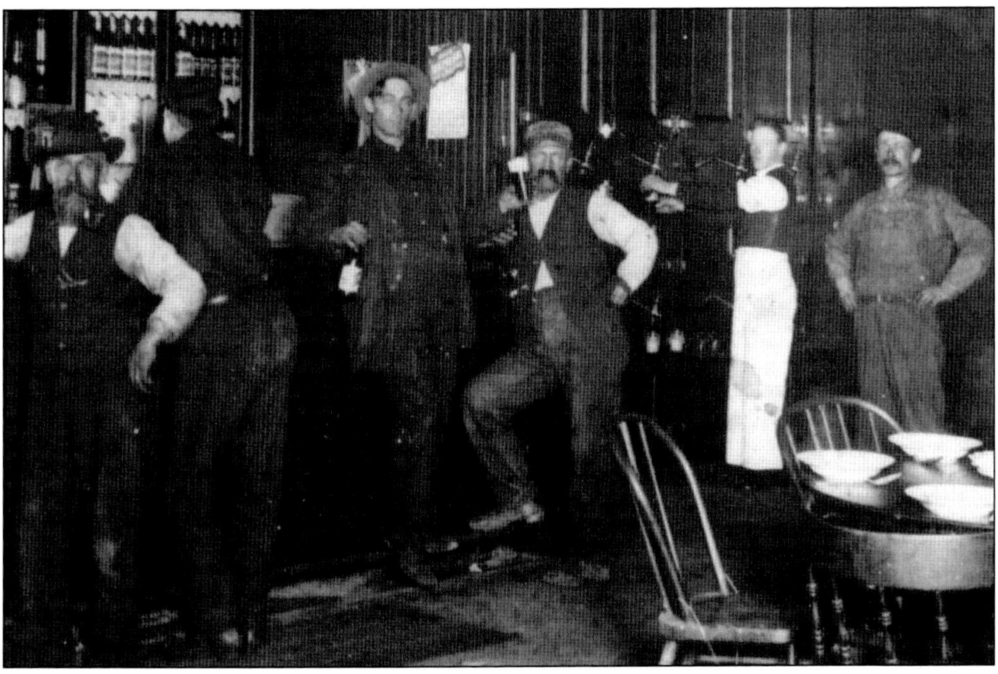

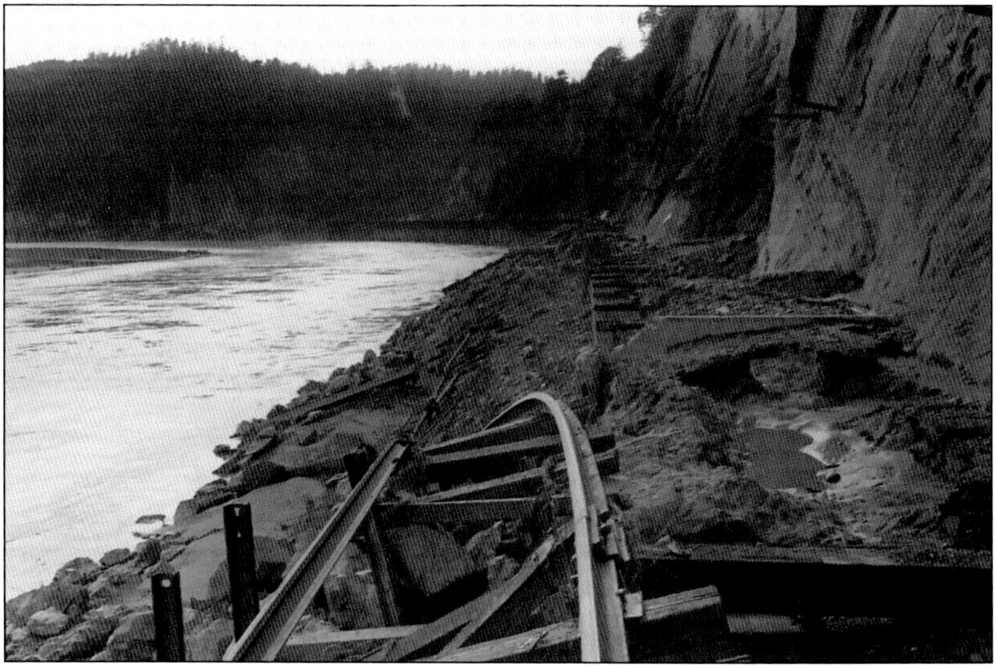

Major floods had struck the area many times since settlers first arrived in the county, causing significant damage in 1913, 1914, and 1915. Rio Dell and Scotia were at the heart of the disastrous floods, yet avoided the worst of the damage due to their higher elevation from the floodplain. Communities farther upriver were not always so lucky, and low-lying homes and settlements were periodically swept away by the rising water. In 1937, the waters rose again, consuming homes, fields, and railroad tracks and damaging the bridge between Scotia and Rio Dell. The bridge was repaired and continued to see use until it was replaced in the 1940s. The flood of 1937 would serve as a reminder to locals of the power and ferocity of the Eel River and foreshadow even bigger floods to come. (Both, courtesy of Greg Rumney.)

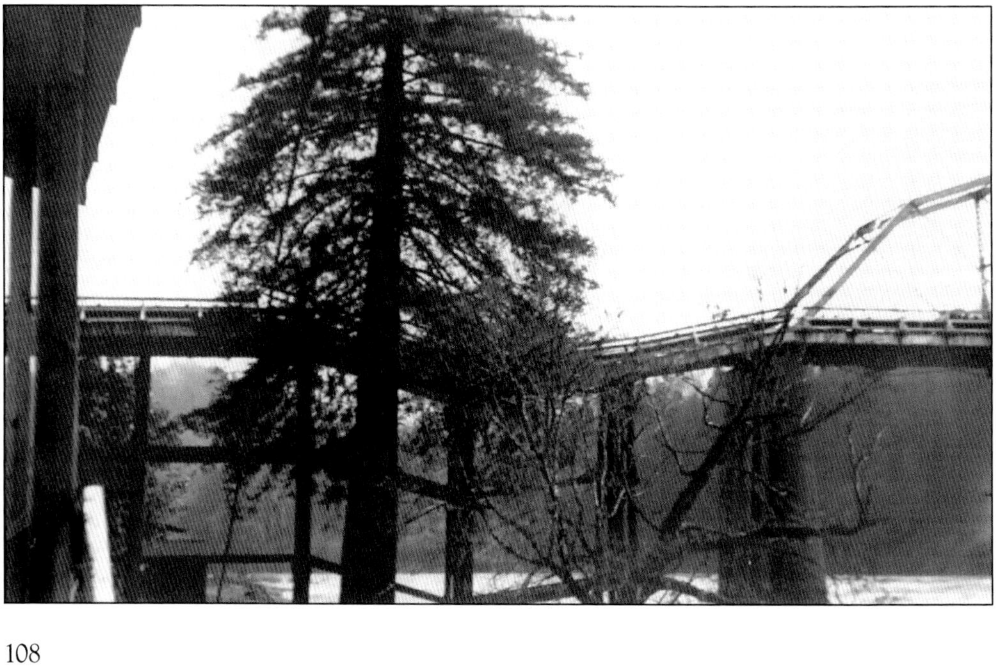

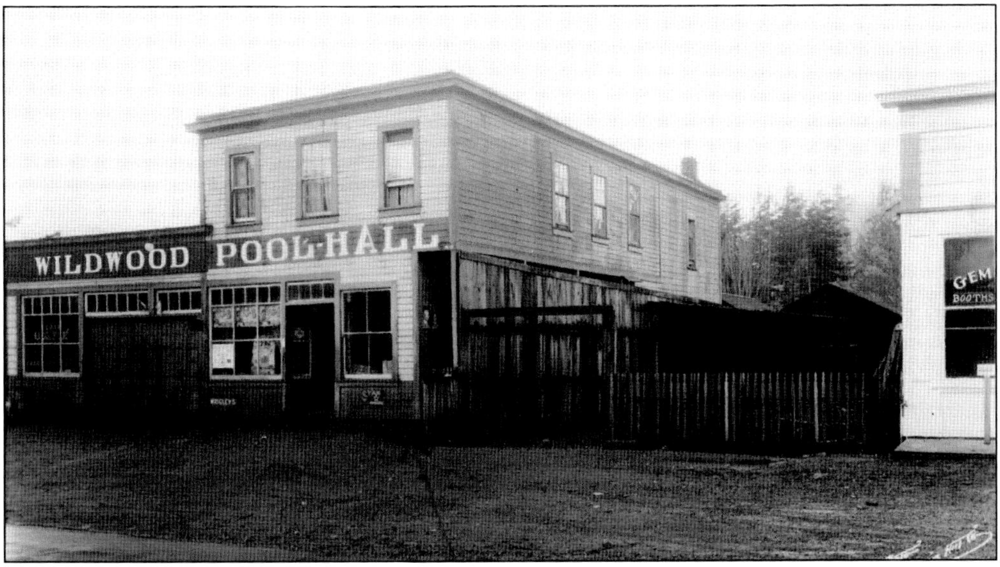

During the Depression and World War II, bars and gambling halls were some of the few profitable businesses remaining. Saloons, card rooms, and pool halls flourished in Wildwood and Rio Dell for many years, unlike the town's other attraction, prostitution, which would come to an end in the 1940s. Wildwood's ladies of the evening were faced with settling down or moving on. (Courtesy of the Humboldt State University Library, Humboldt Room, HCC Collection.)

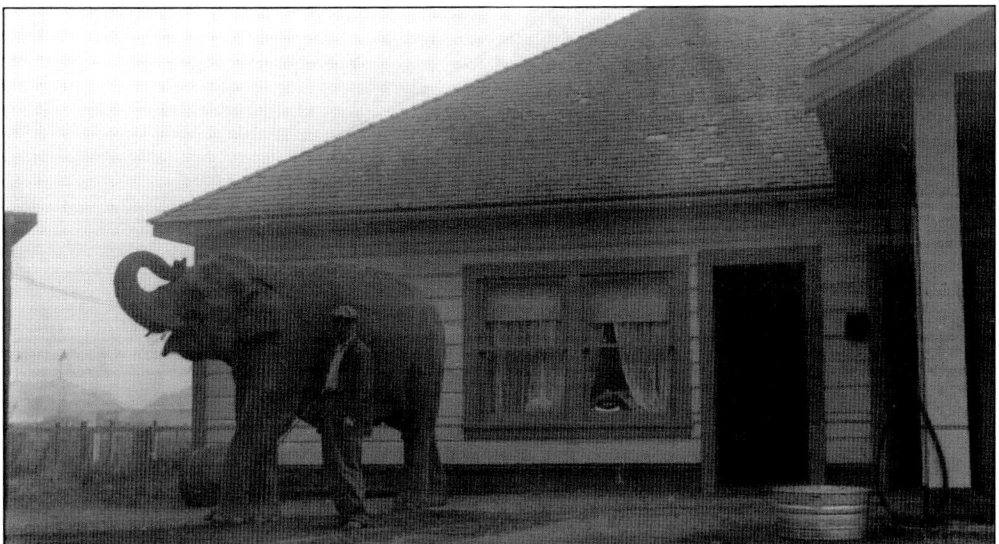

Besides adult entertainments, Wildwood had many other more socially accepted businesses as well. Filling stations began popping up on the prairie soon after the arrival of the automobile. This station belonged to Harry Jenson, who clearly demonstrated that he operated a full-service station. The elephant belonged to a circus visiting the area in the 1930s. (Courtesy of Deborah Baskette.)

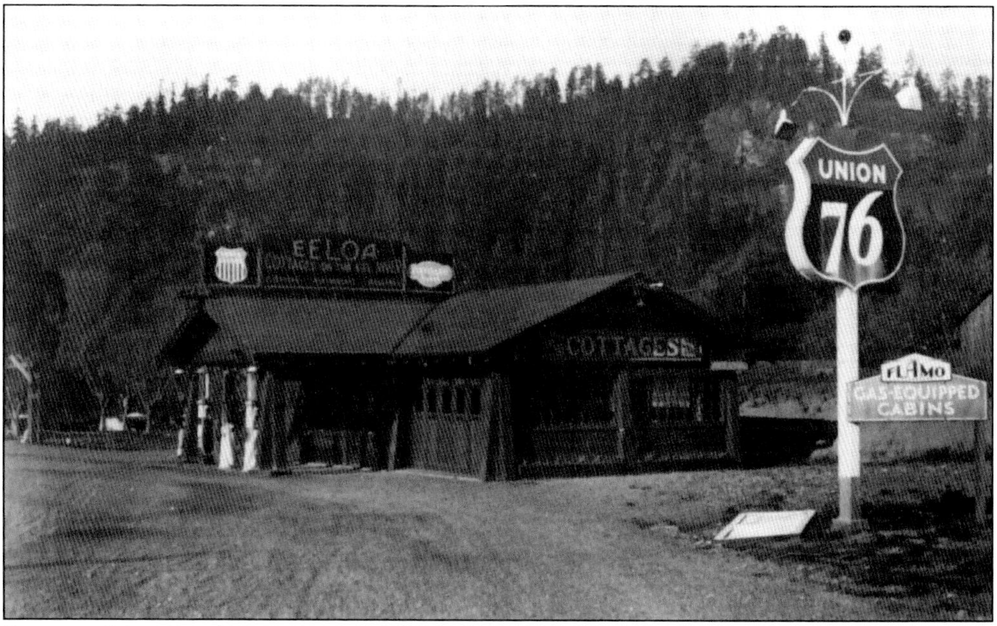

Hunting, fishing, and enjoying nature have continued to be a part of life for many in Humboldt County. Founded in 1937, Grundman's Sporting Goods remains a fixture in Rio Dell, providing equipment for outdoor enthusiasts for generations. In commemoration of the community's pioneer roots, a mural of Seth Kinman is displayed on the storefront. In the 1950s, another vacation spot opened up in Rio Dell near where the Whetstone mill had once stood catering to the outdoorsmen. The Eeloa Cottages were operated by Mr. and Mrs. Francis G. Epperson and offered vacation cottages for rent near the Eel River, still seen as a premier spot for fishing and swimming. Epperson's cabins were advertised as "fully modern" with kitchenettes, carports, free heat, and electric radios. (Above, courtesy of the Humboldt State University Library, Humboldt Room, Swanlund-Baker Collection; below, author's collection.)

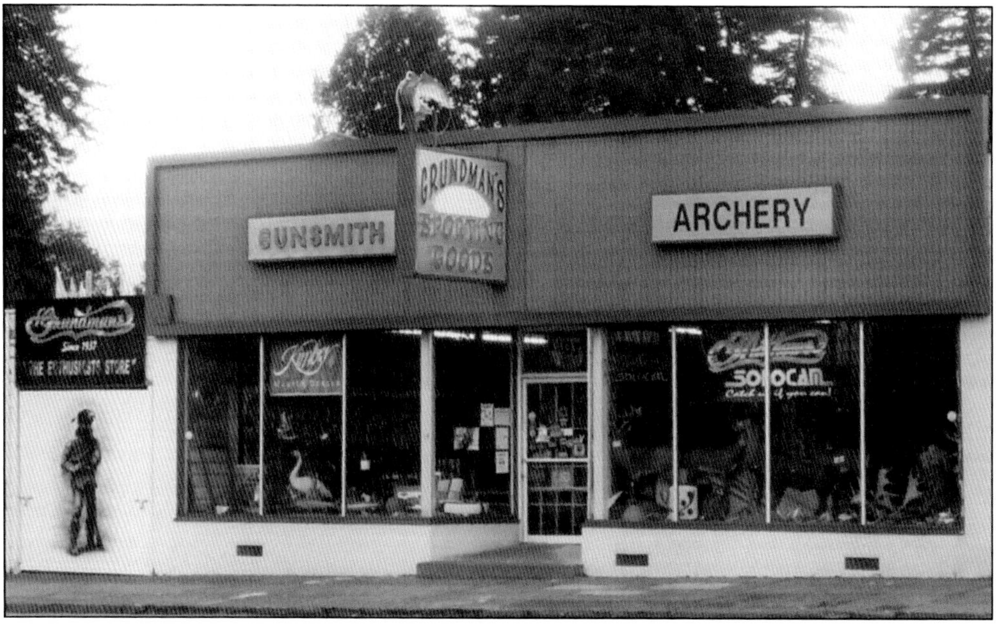

Four

Both Sides of the River

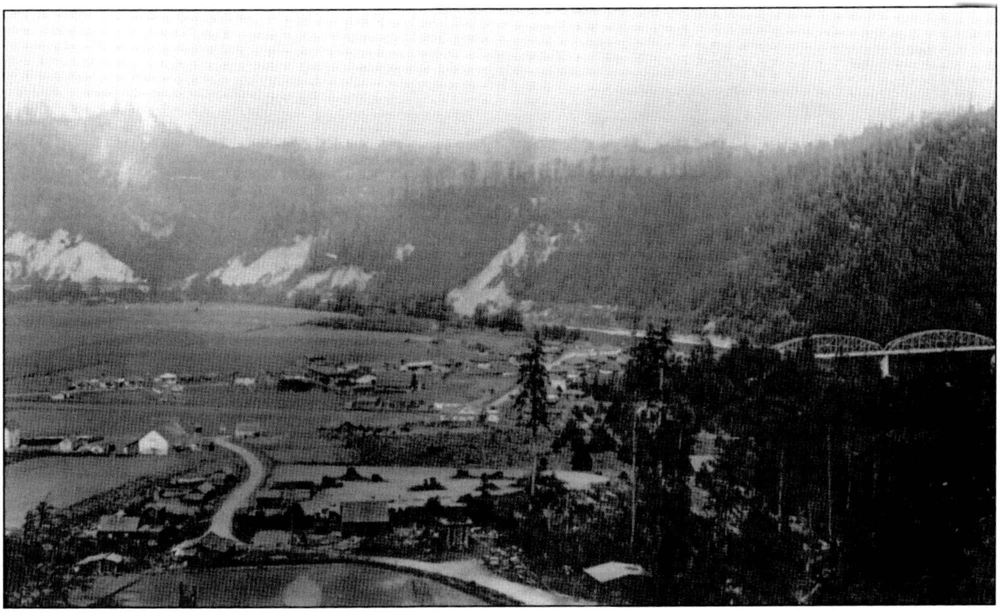

Scotia, Rio Dell, and Wildwood had developed into separate, distinctive communities yet were closely tied together. Residents of all three towns shared the same workplaces, attended the same community functions, and socialized with the same people. As the years stretched on, these ties grew stronger, and the lines separating the communities began to blur. (Courtesy of the Humboldt County Historical Society.)

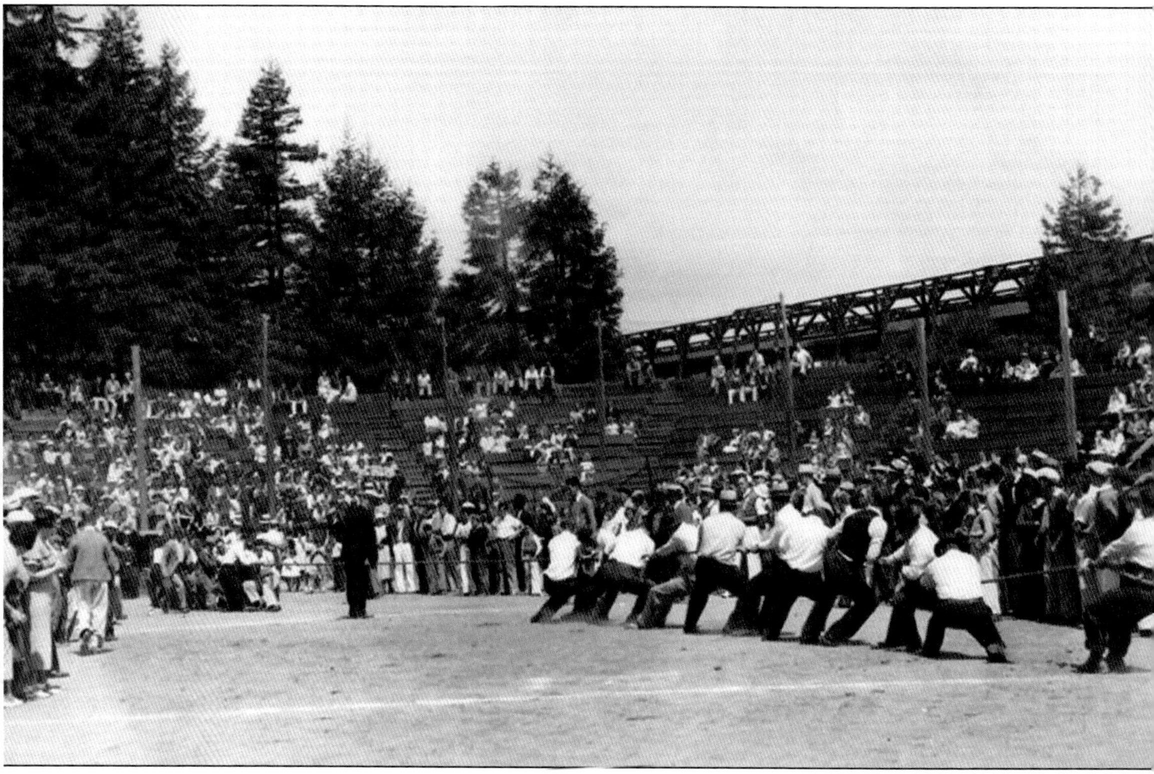

With Rio Dell and Wildwood serving as a bedroom community for many Pacific Lumber Company workers and their families, picnics, athletic events, and social gatherings included people from both sides of the bridge. Pacific Lumber built hospitals and stores to serve the needs of these communities and also constructed parks, ball fields, skating rinks, swimming pools, movie theaters, and gymnasiums for its workers. The company also sponsored baseball teams and youth athletic programs in addition to starting a company band, which is still going strong today, welcoming musicians of all ages from throughout the county to join its ranks. The workers shown here compete in a tug-of-war at the company picnic, held annually at the Scotia Park. (Courtesy of the Town of Scotia Company.)

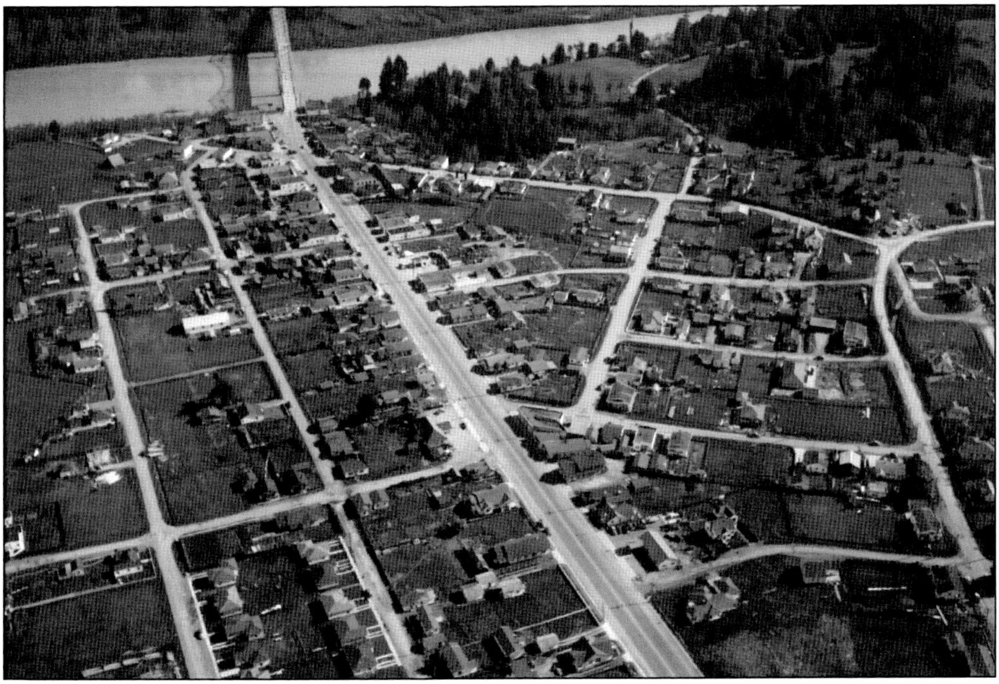

The 1940s brought another surge of growth to the prairie, and not just at night. New housing went up as the population swelled to 2,000 by 1950. The aged Rio Dell School was pressed to its limits and a new school had to be built in the early 1950s to serve the needs of the growing town. (Courtesy of the Humboldt State University Library, Humboldt Room, Schuster Collection.)

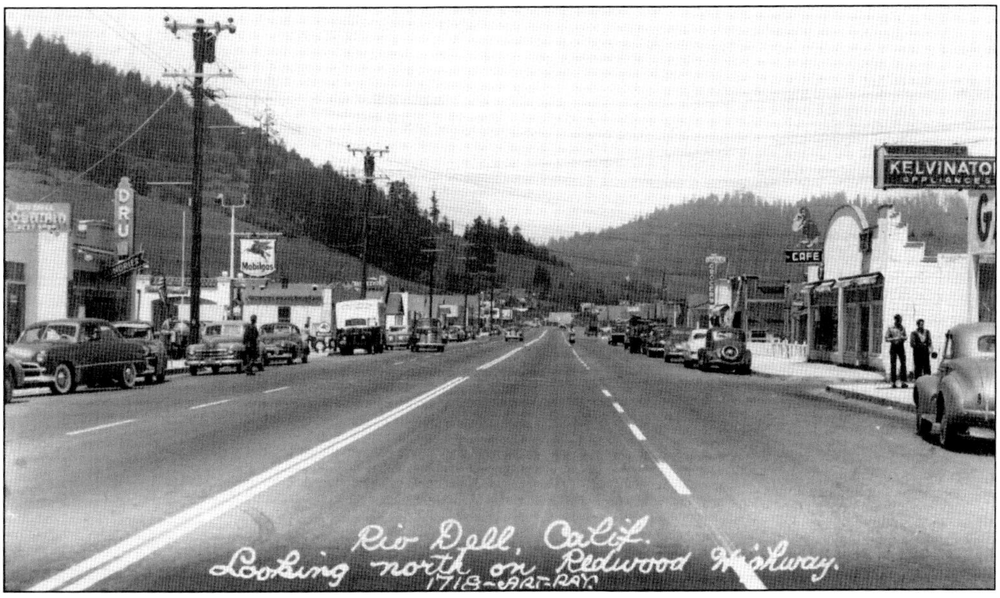

The biggest strike in Humboldt's logging history took place in 1946, shutting down most of the mills in the area for months. Businesses closed their doors and houses went up for sale as locals struggled to make ends meet. The Jayhawk Café served as union headquarters during this time, much to the distaste of the "Scotia-lites" across the river. (Courtesy of the Todd-Schuler/Bartleson family.)

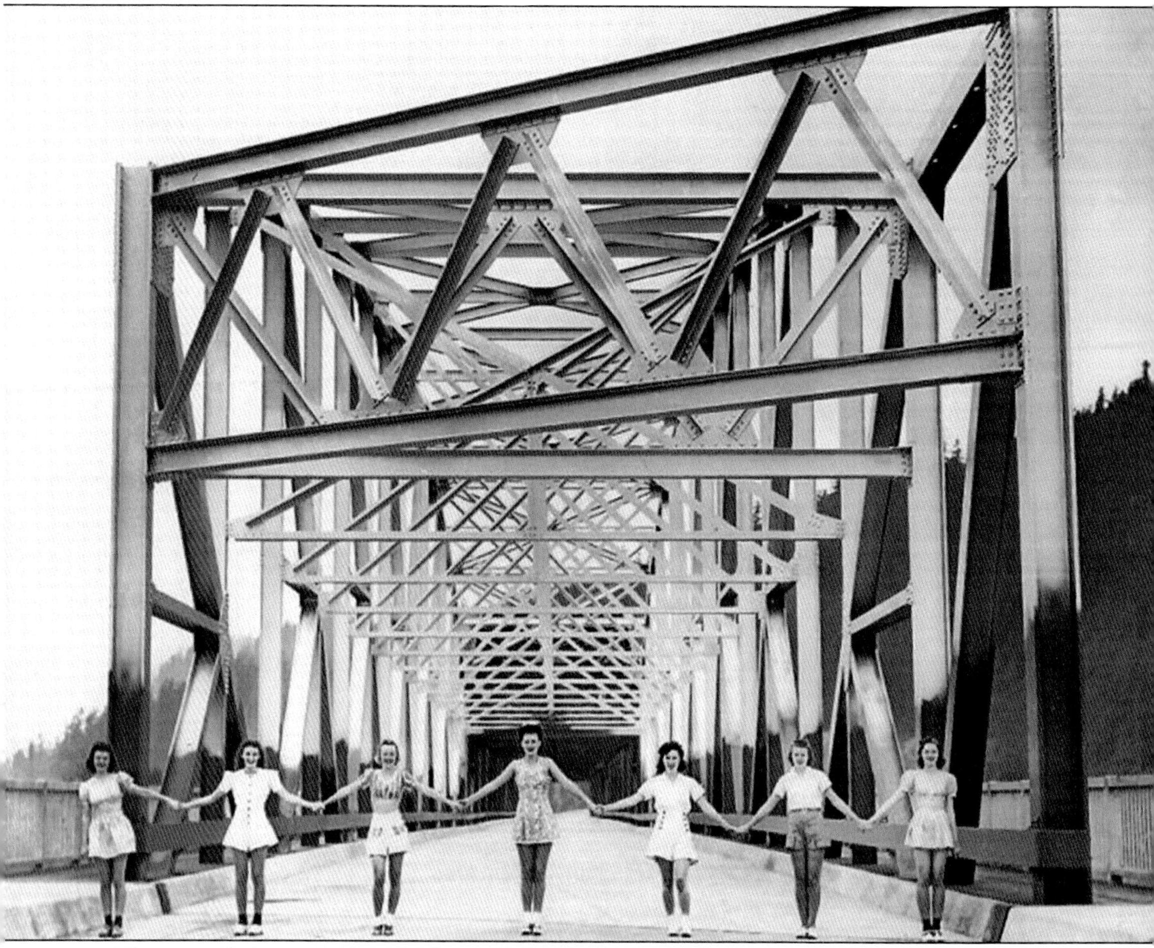

The aging Robinson's Ferry Bridge over the Eel River north of Rio Dell was replaced with the Paul Mudgett Memorial Bridge in 1941 as part of ongoing improvements to the Redwood Highway. Opened with much fanfare, the Mudgett Bridge still serves as the northbound freeway bridge over the Eel. (Courtesy of the Todd-Schuler/Bartleson family.)

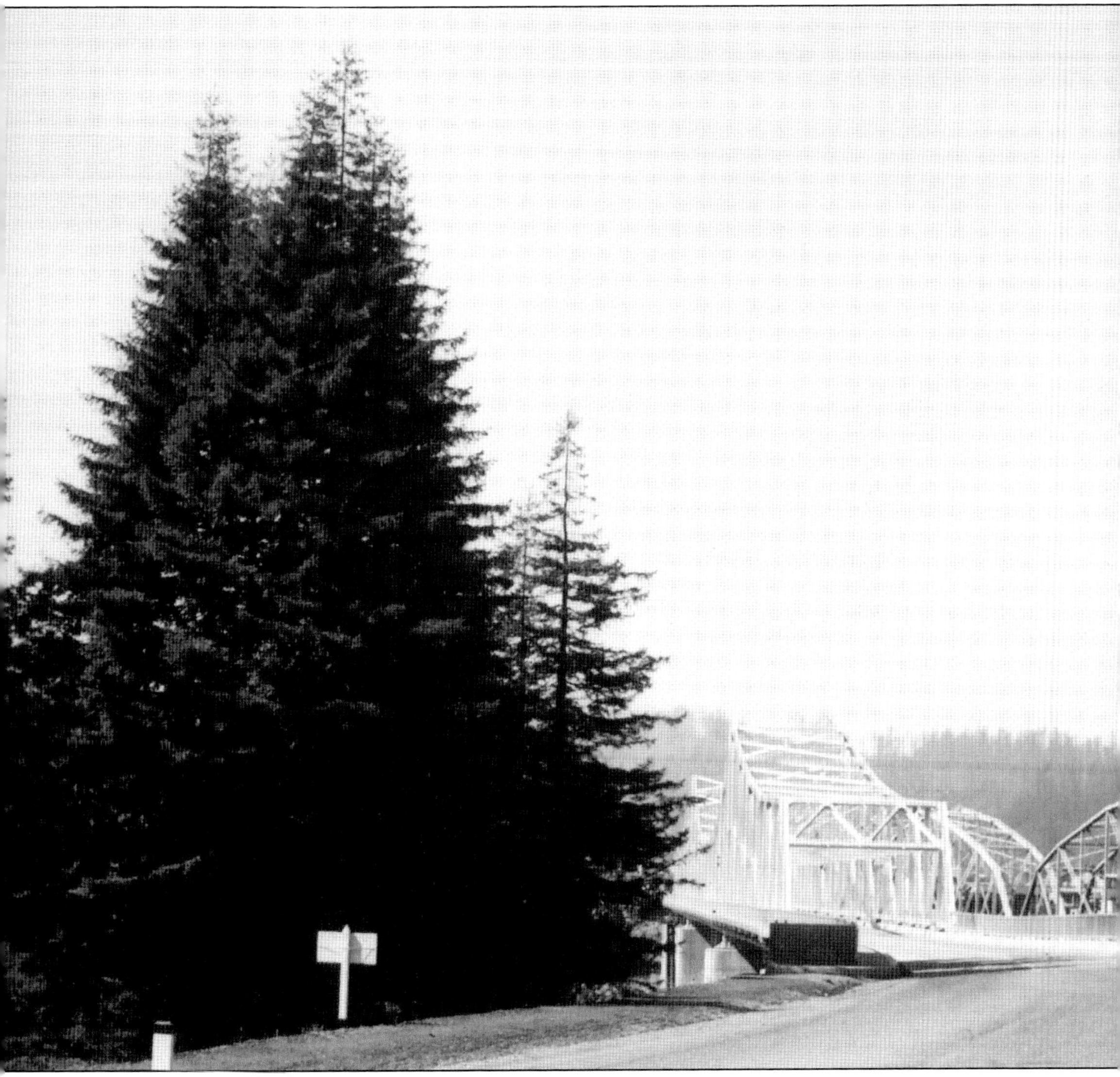

The 1941 highway improvements also included a new bridge between Scotia and Rio Dell. Renamed the Stanwood A. Murphy Bridge in 1977, the bridge was bypassed by the new freeway bridges that were built across the river in the early 1970s. Designated now as State Highway 283, the bridge is one of the shortest highways in the nation at only one-third of a mile in length. (Author's collection.)

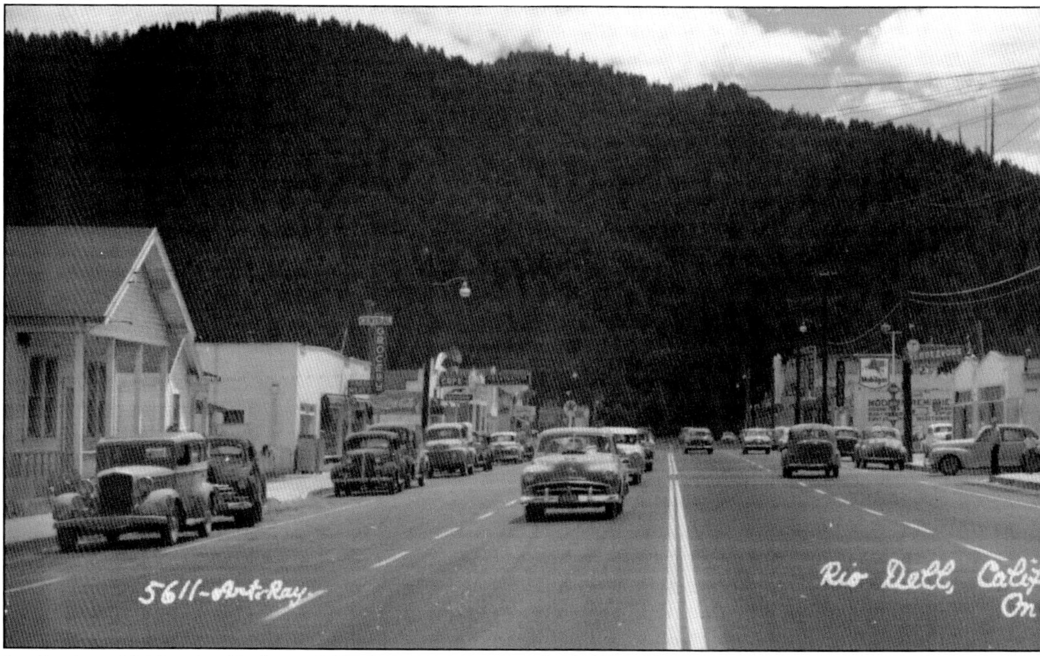

In the late 1940s, the Redwood Highway was expanded through Rio Dell, with four lanes going down Wildwood Avenue. In 1947, the Rio Dell Post Office moved from its previous location in old Rio Dell to the building it currently resides in on Wildwood Avenue. Once the capitol of vice in the county, Wildwood soon became Rio Dell's new town center as businesses packed

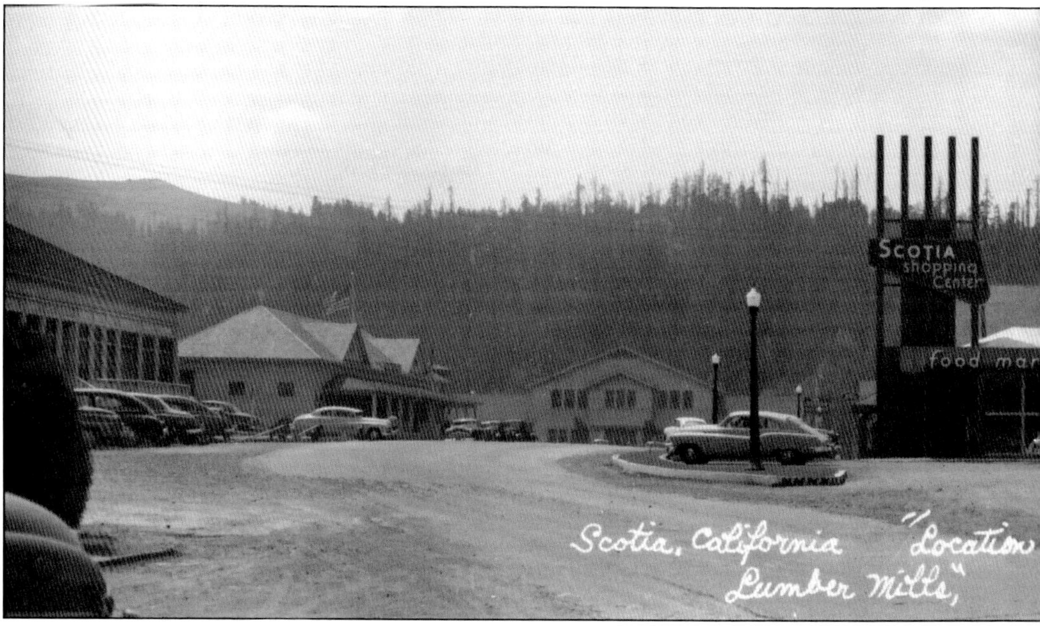

Scotia had been tightly organized and controlled by the Pacific Lumber Company since its inception. This iron grip began to relax a bit in the 1950s, when PL closed its company store and allowed private business owners to begin opening stores in town. The company built a shopping center and rented space for many different stores over the years, including grocery and hardware stores, coffee shops, and the Palco Pharmacy, which is still in business today. Herb Colby, who

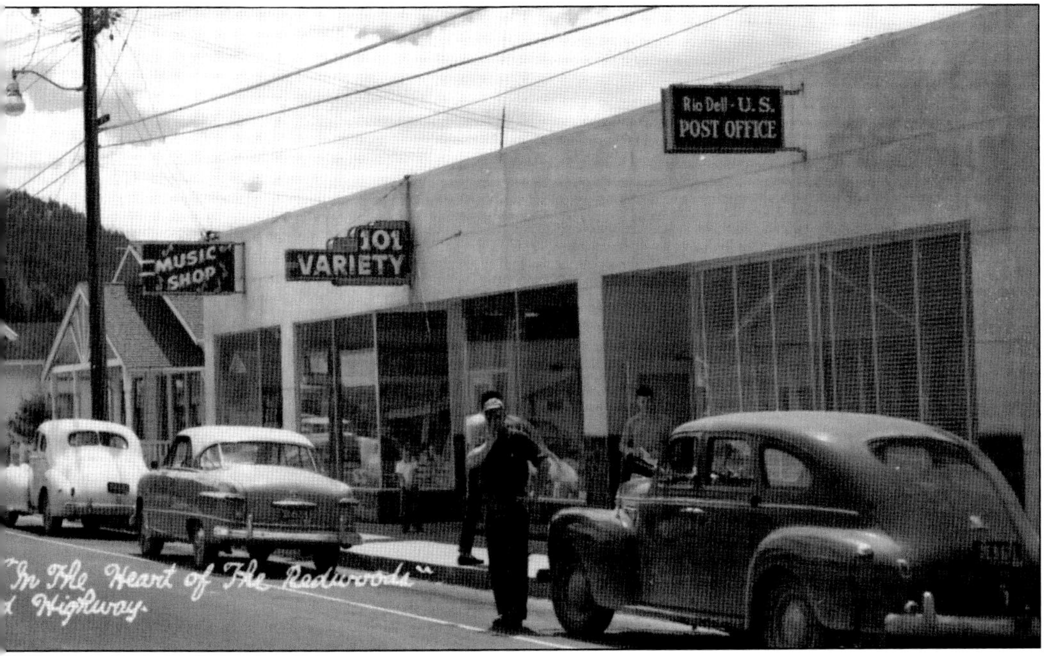

both sides of the highway. As Wildwood took over the prominent position once held by Rio Dell, talks soon began concerning incorporating the communities as a single town. While talks may have continued, little action was taken towards this proposal until the 1960s. (Courtesy of the Humboldt County Office of Public Works, Tuttle Collection.)

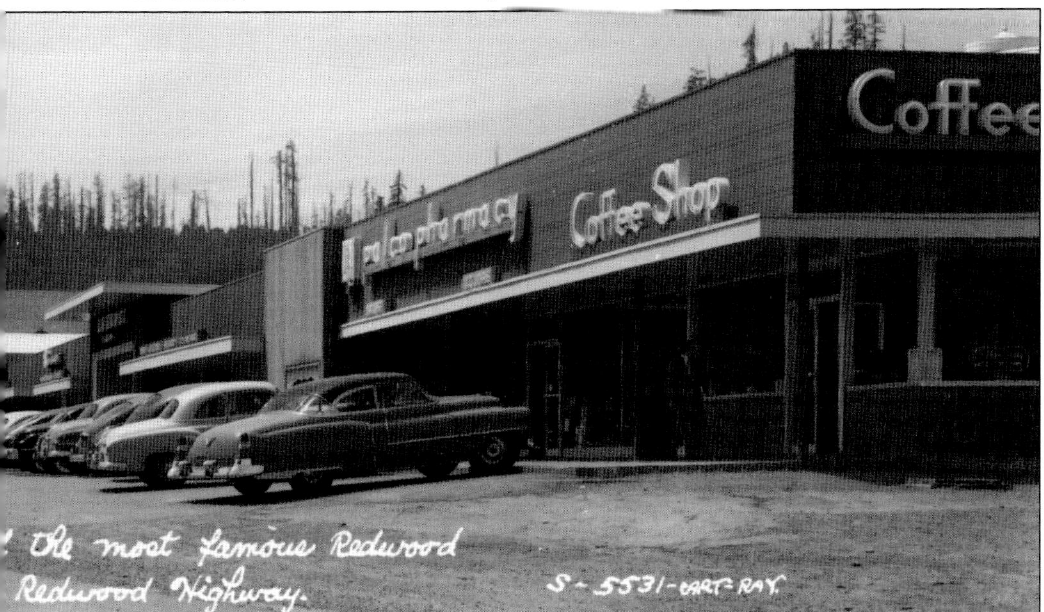

rented space for his grocery store from Pacific Lumber for many years, characterized the landlord-tenant relationship as something of a benevolent dictatorship, and pointed out that "PL's primary concern was for their workers," and storeowners were encouraged to be "team players." (Courtesy of the Humboldt County Office of Public Works, Tuttle Collection.)

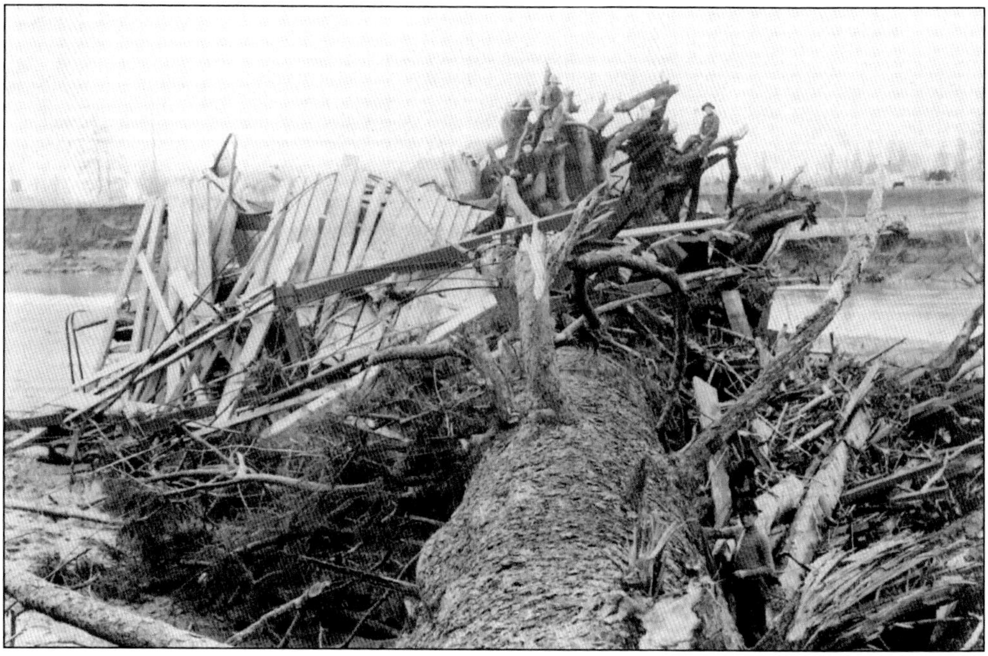

On Christmas Day 1955, the Eel surged over its banks once more. Torrential rain and a heavy snowpack combined to create the biggest flood in memory, and people in Rio Dell and Scotia watched helplessly as hundreds of houses, debris, and logs from towns and mills upstream were washed down the Eel before their eyes. While they had fared much better than many of their upstream neighbors, the flood knocked out power and water throughout the town. The Red Cross sent in disaster relief, and residents of Fortuna brought milk cans of water for the beleaguered community. (Courtesy of the Humboldt County Historical Society.)

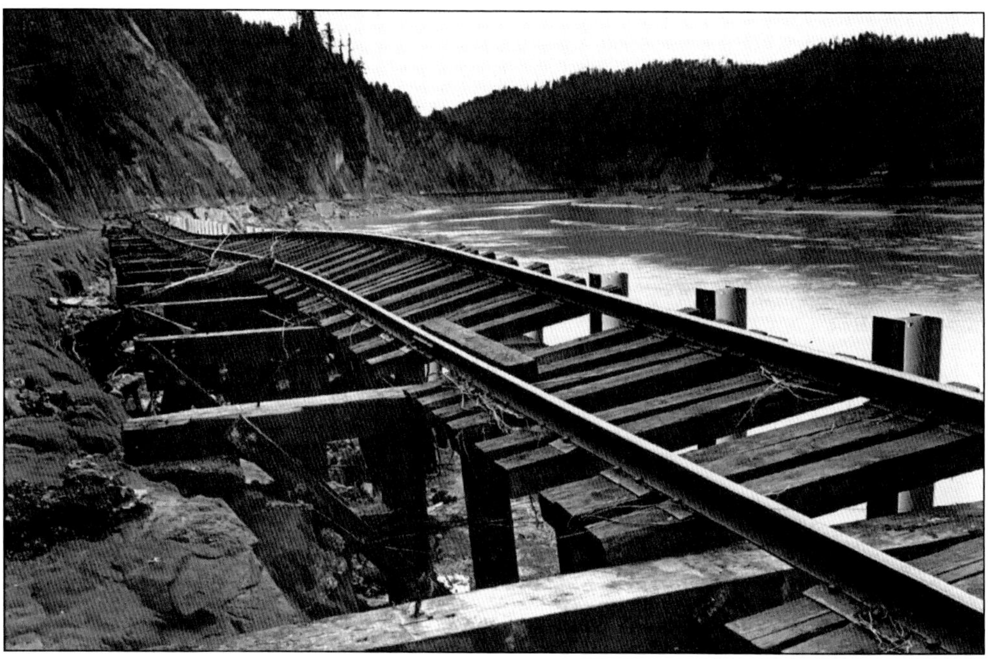

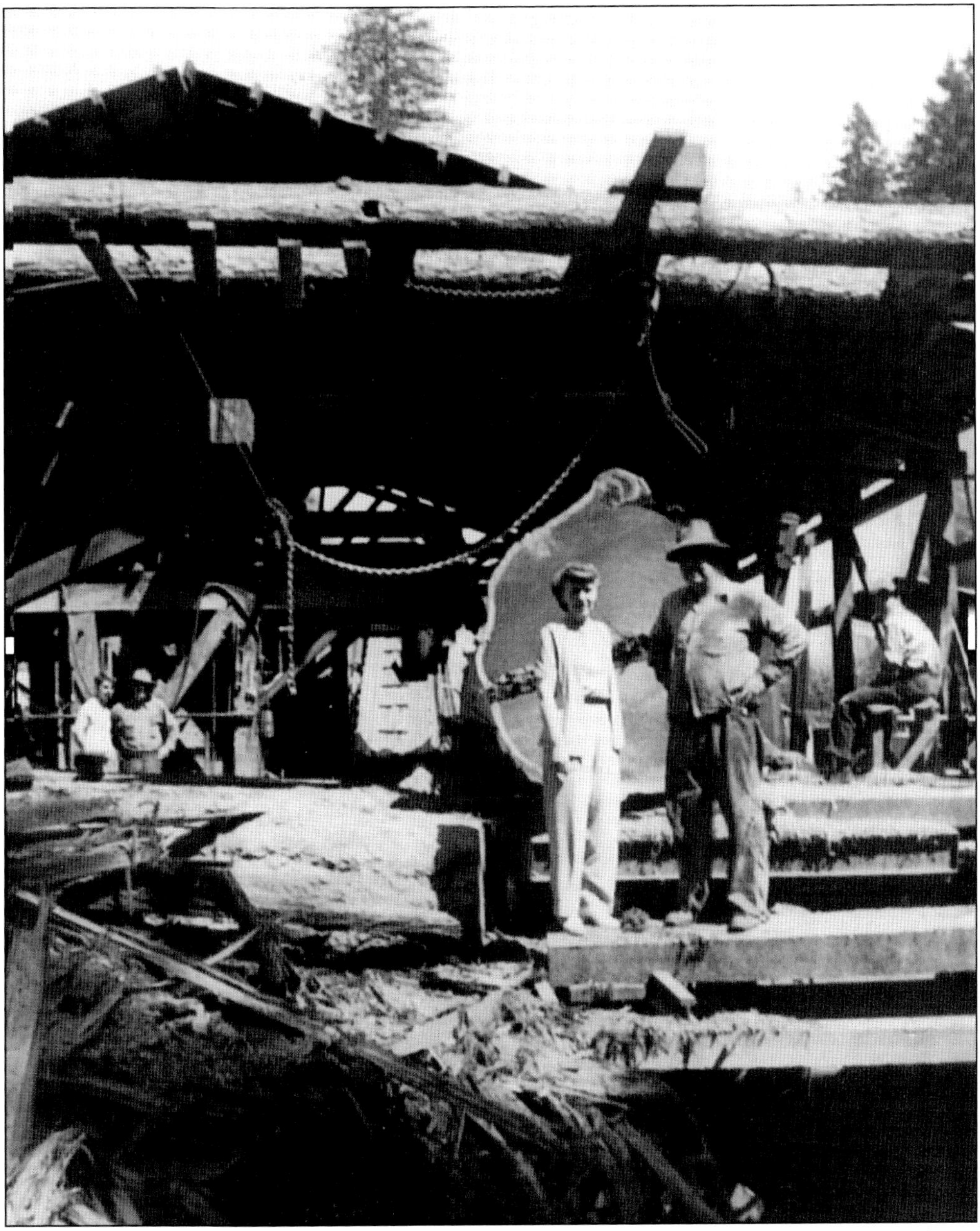

In 1958, Mel McLean and Stanley Shaffer purchased the Johnnie Voll sawmill at Metropolitan, near Rio Dell, and renamed it the Eel River Sawmill. McLean and Shaffer had previously operated a mill in McCann, logging the Perry, Wheat, and Whitlow properties in the southern part of the county. McLean's company was very successful, becoming one of the largest Douglas fir producers in the county. Expanding his operations in the early 1970s to include sawmills at Alton and Englewood, McLean's Eel River Sawmills provided jobs for many area residents. Eel River Sawmills endured as one of the biggest employers in the area until the beginning of the 21st century. McLean was deeply dedicated to the community and, with his wife, Grace, set up the Mel and Grace McLean foundation, a trust providing grants supporting charitable and community-related projects throughout the county. (Courtesy of the Mel and Grace McLean Foundation.)

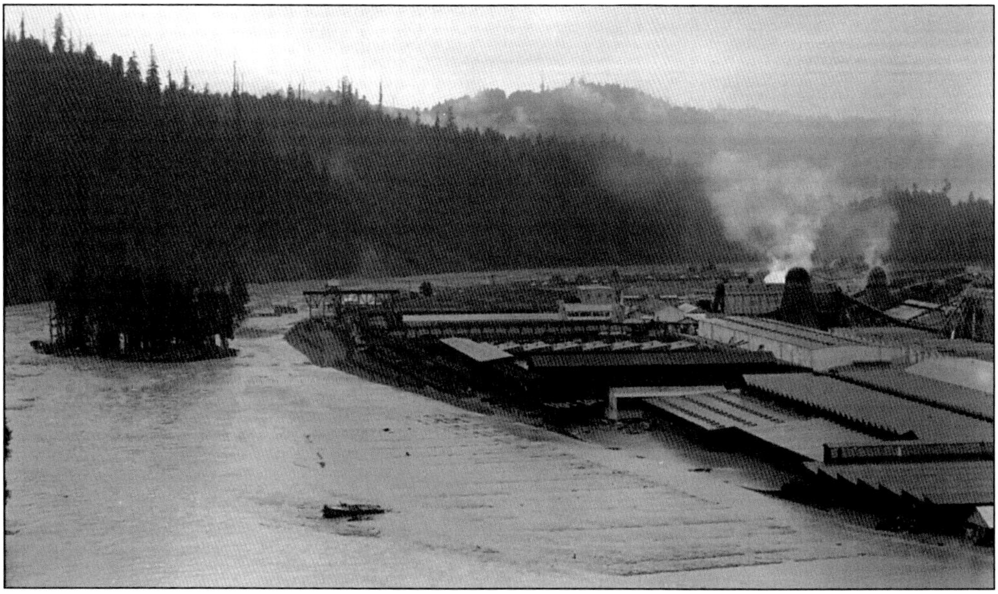

On Christmas Eve 1964, the Eel River rampaged once again, flooding its banks and destroying homes and whole communities along its course. This was the worst flood area residents had ever experienced, far surpassing the severity of the one less than a decade before. Houses were washed away in the low-lying parts of town next to the river, and the bridges were washed out at both ends of Rio Dell and south of Scotia, isolating the two communities. Again the town was without power, water, gas, or communication with the outside world. The community was shocked to learn that whole towns had been almost entirely wiped from the map, including Weott, Dyerville, Pepperwood, and Metropolitan. (Both, courtesy of Greg Rumney.)

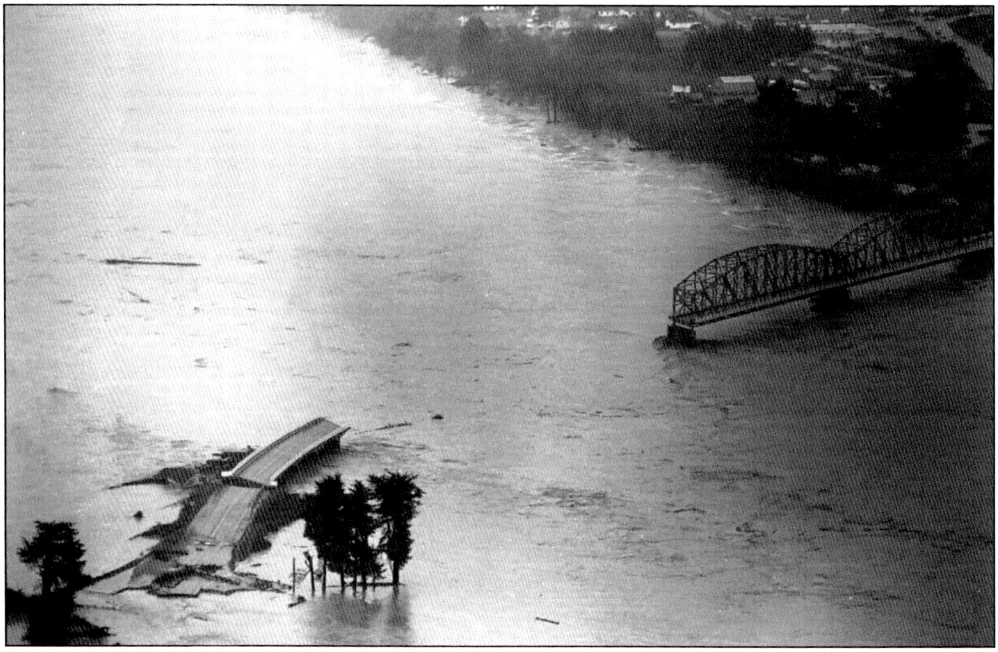

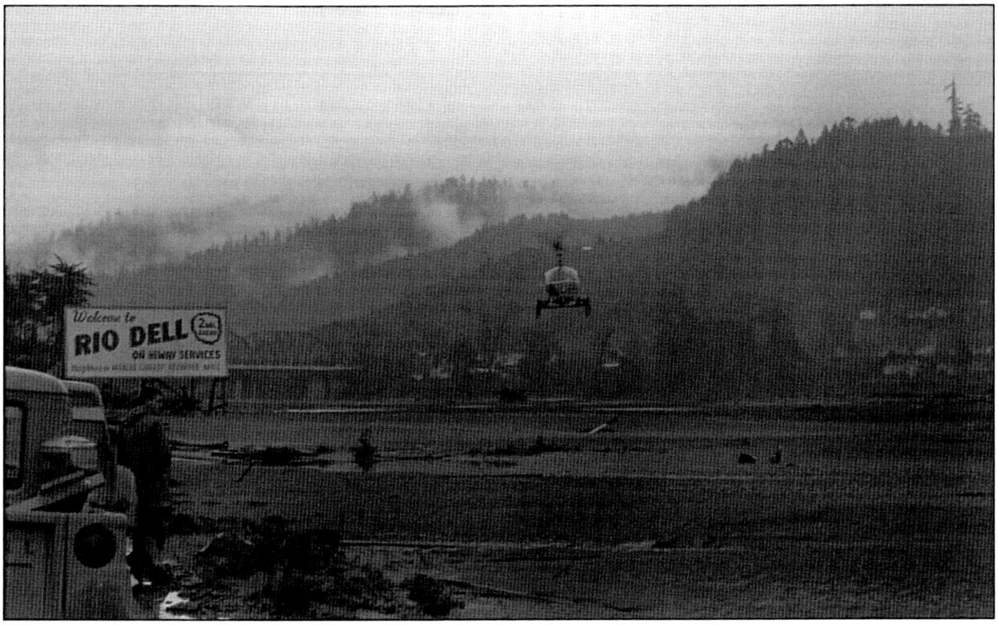

The community banded together, helping those who had been displaced by the raging waters of the Eel River. Families shared resources and used woodstoves for cooking and heating. Pacific Lumber evacuated homes near the river and converted mill buildings into temporary shelters for those displaced by the rising water. County and state services were quick to respond, and the National Guard was called out to provide emergency aid to the flood-ravaged county. Airplanes and helicopters flew constant rescue and aid missions to communities throughout the area. Private pilots in the county lent a hand with these efforts, using the highway at Rio Dell and Scotia as their runway. (Both, courtesy of Greg Rumney.)

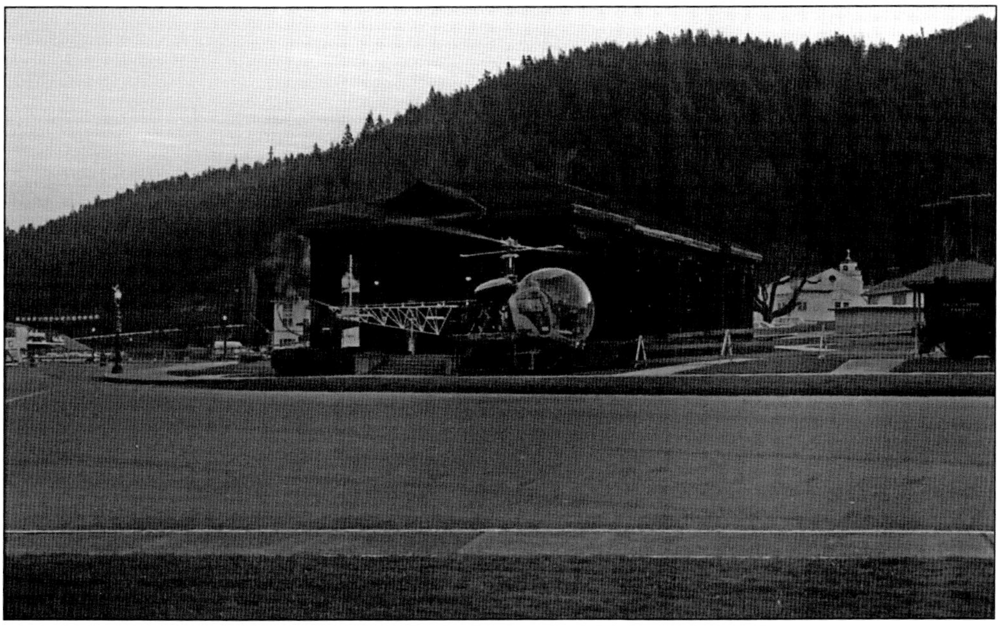

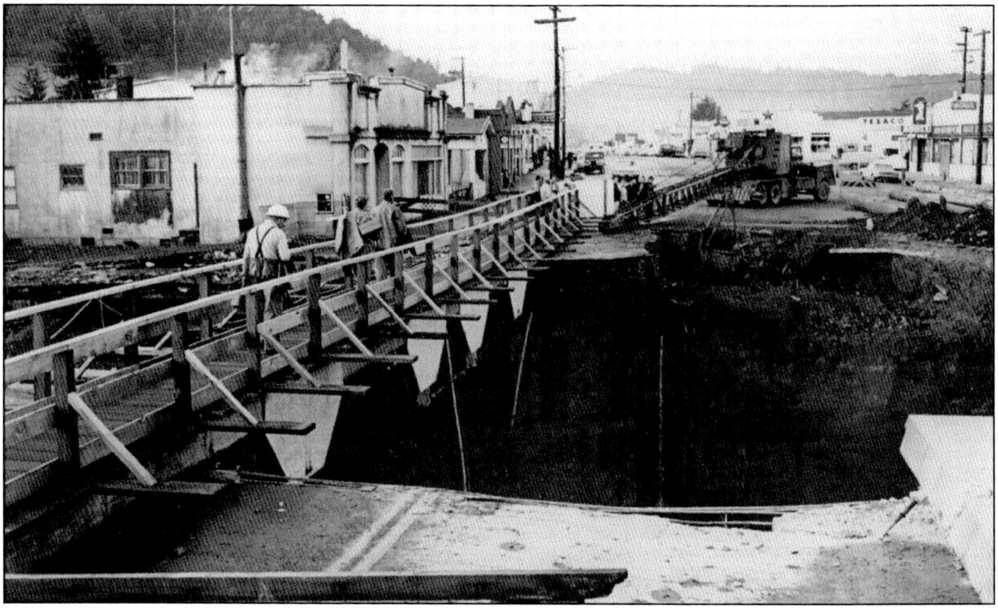

Utility workers and construction crews labored tirelessly through Christmas and into the new year to restore power and services. As the floodwaters receded, residents struggled to pick up the pieces. Many southern Humboldt families sought refuge in Scotia and Rio Dell after the disaster had swept away their homes upriver. The cleanup and rebuilding efforts began immediately, Pacific Lumber putting its crews to work clearing roads and removing debris from the stricken community. It was many months before area bridges were restored to their former glory. Miraculously, the Blue Slide Road from Rio Dell to Grizzly Bluff remained open. The road had been opened in February 1955 and, while it is still plagued with periodic slides and washouts, continues to be used today. (Both, courtesy of Greg Rumney.)

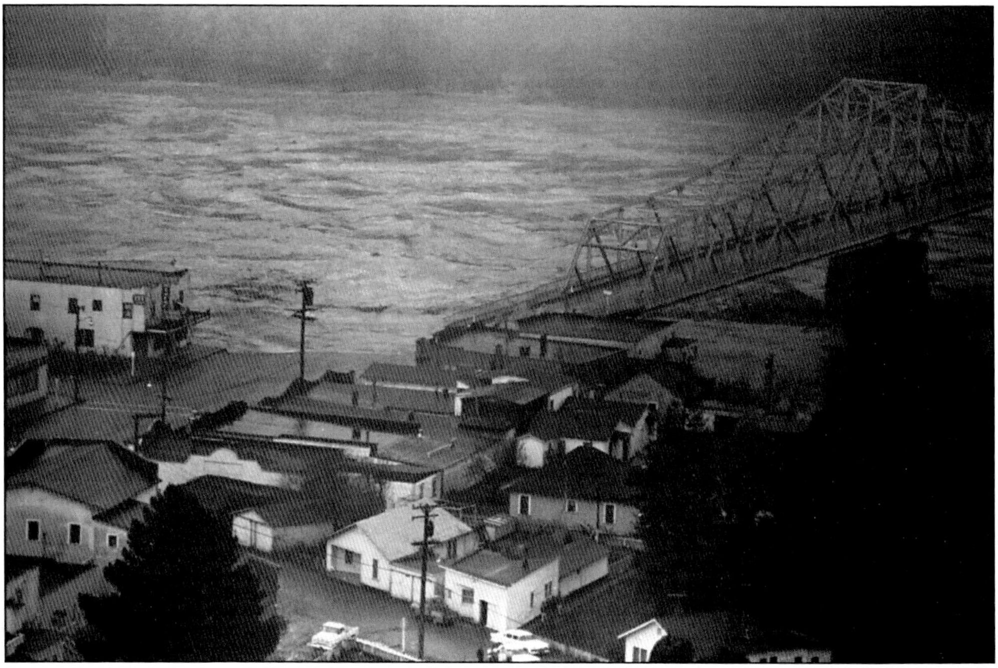

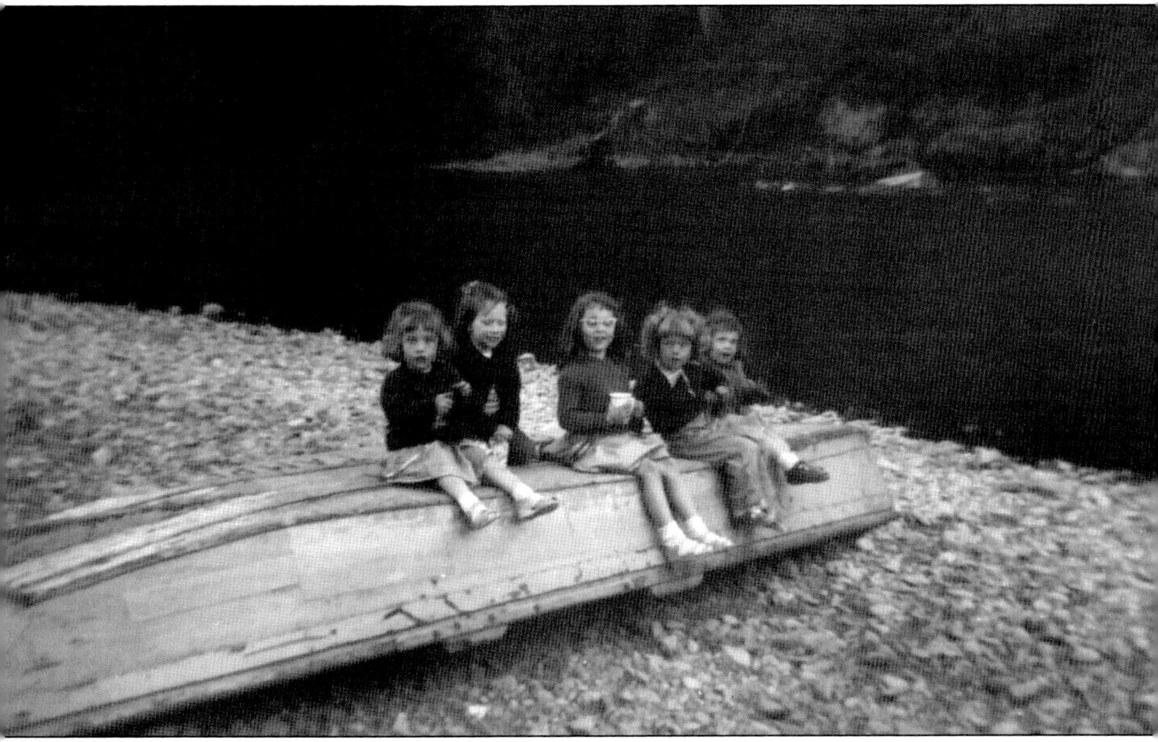

Today, few scars remain of the powerful floods that descended upon the area in 1955 and 1964. After weathering these storms together, the communities of Wildwood and Rio Dell officially came together under one banner, incorporated as the city of Rio Dell in February 1965. Lorenzo Painter's community had come a long way since its humble beginnings as a resort destination. (Courtesy of the Myers family.)

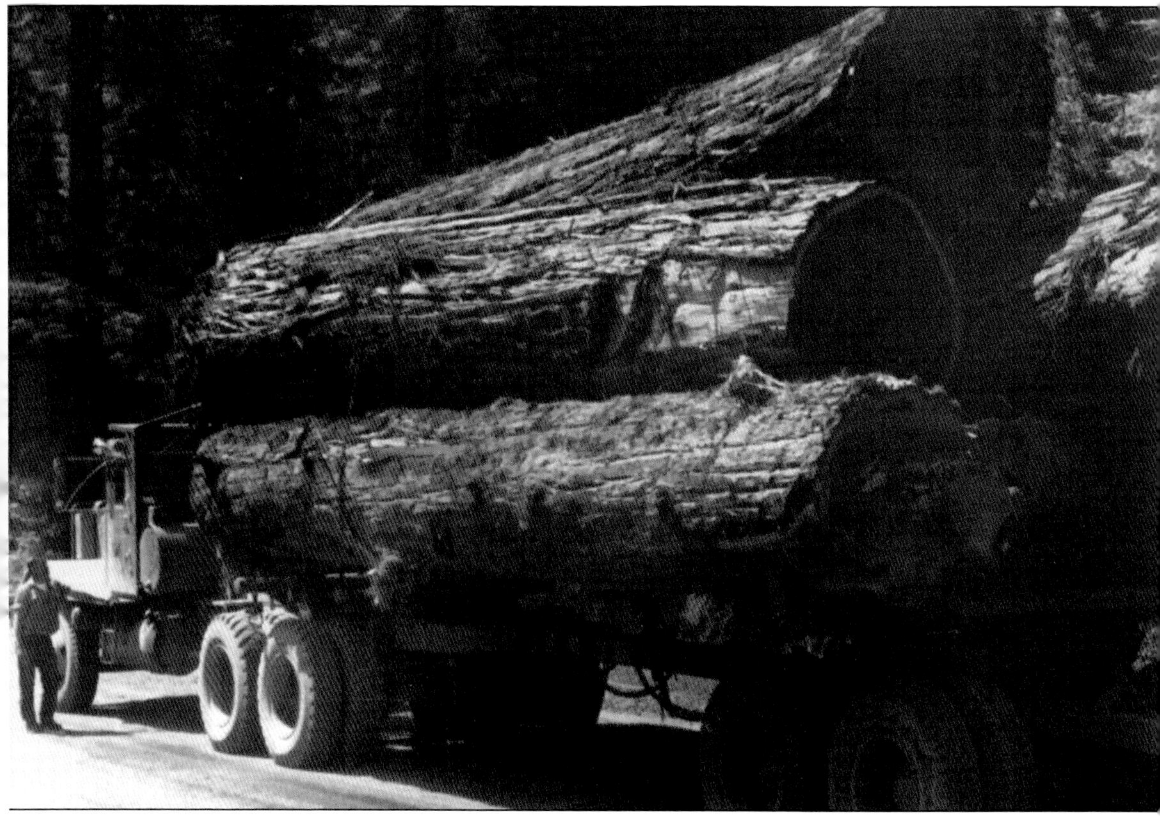

Scotia resumed business as usual in the post-flood years, harvesting its vast holdings and providing jobs for the people of the community. The Pacific Lumber Company would finally give up its trains and spur lines in the 1970s, transitioning to gravel roads and logging trucks. (Courtesy of the Town of Scotia Company.)

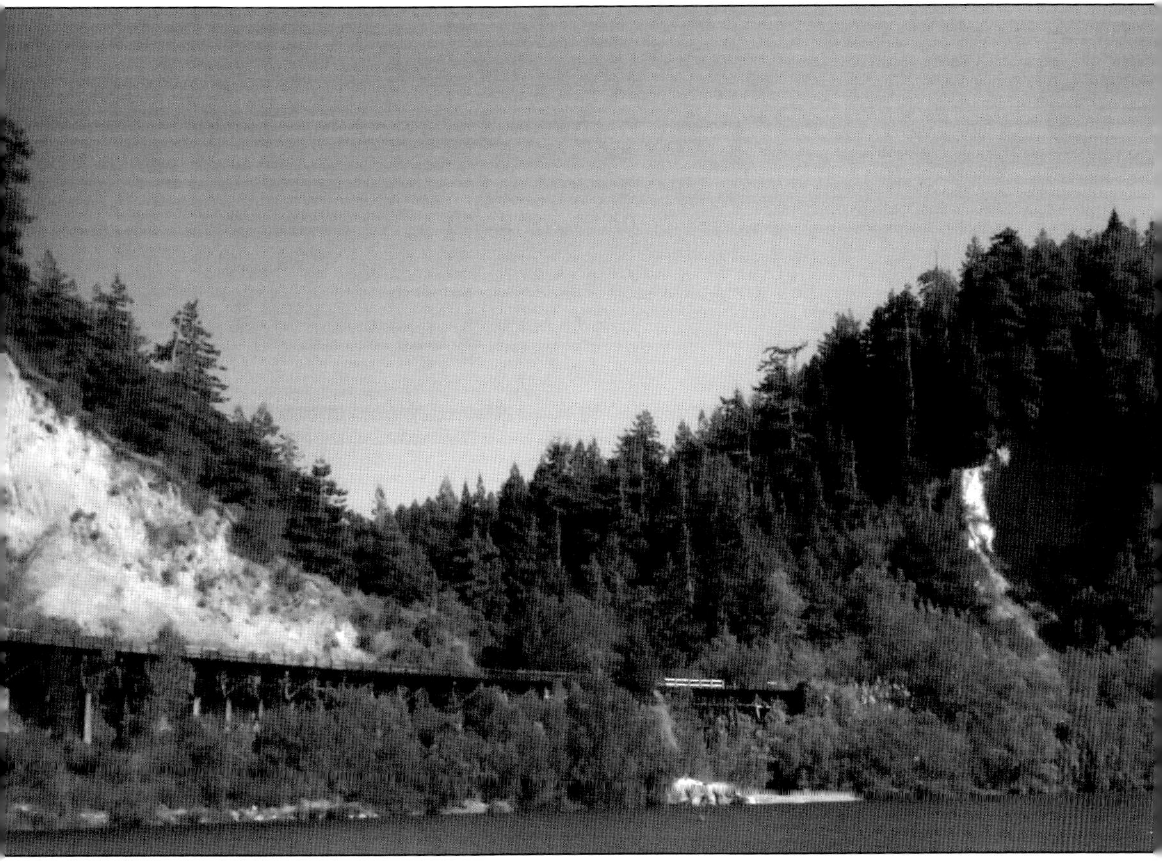

In 1978, a fire erupted in the Island Mountain Tunnel, stopping all trains along the rail line south, which had connected the county to the rest of the state in 1914. The resultant closure of the line south forced area timber companies to beginning using trucks to deliver their products to market and spelled the beginning of the end for the area's rail line. By 1980, the line was up and running again but was by now the most expensive piece of track to maintain in the country. The railroad changed hands several times in the following years before finally being abandoned after maintenance costs became unmanageable. Now blocked by dozens of slides and choked with impassable brush, the railroad lies neglected and nearly forgotten, a relic of a bygone era. (Author's collection.)

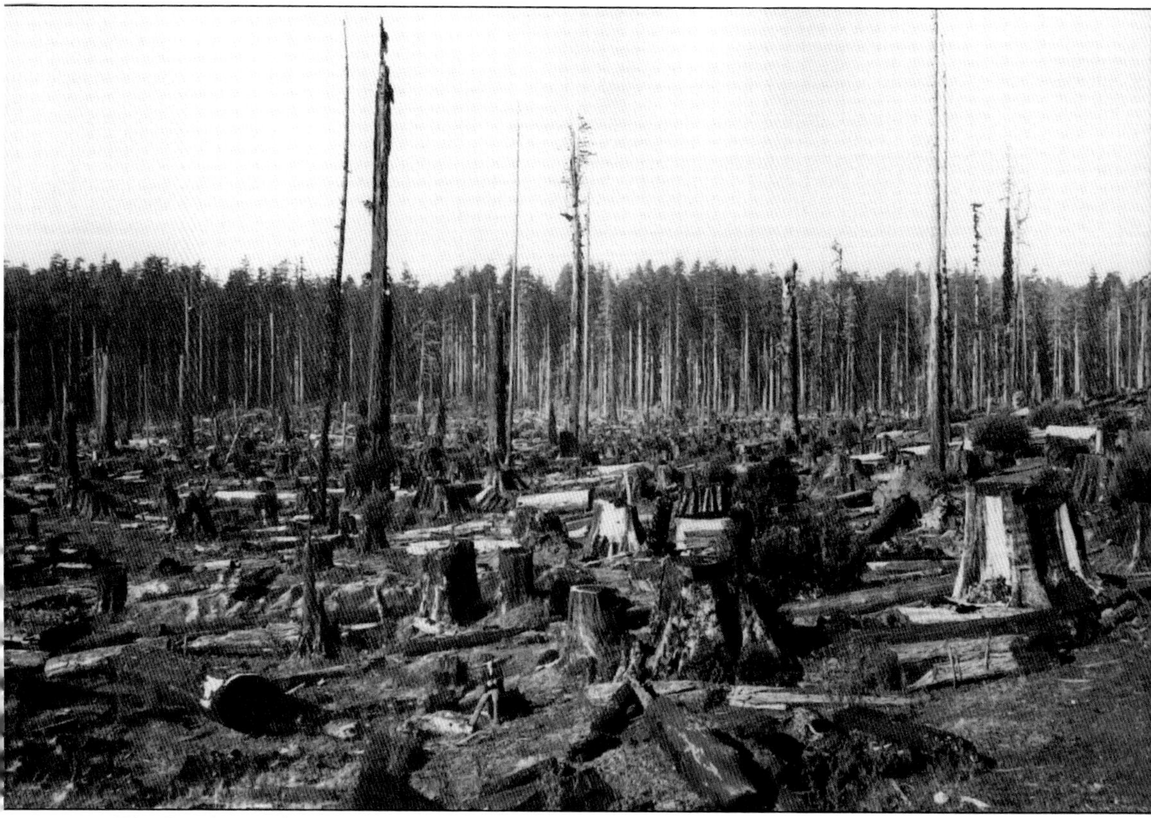

The Pacific Lumber Company and the communities it supported had endured whatever had come at them for a century. They had suffered through wars and depressions and weathered storms, floods, earthquakes, and powerful winds. Together, they created a community that thrived for generations. However, in 1985, they were completely unprepared for the storm that would descend upon their beloved company in the form of corporate raider Charles Hurwitz. Seizing control of the company in a hostile takeover, Hurwitz replaced the sustainable logging practices instituted by the Murphy family and began aggressively clear-cutting the company's holdings. His actions almost immediately drew the ire of environmental groups. Activists began protesting at the mill in Scotia, becoming a familiar sight in the small town. Years of protests, litigation, and strife ultimately resulted in the Pacific Lumber Company filing for bankruptcy in 2007. (Courtesy of the Humboldt State University Library, Humboldt Room, Palmquist Collection.)

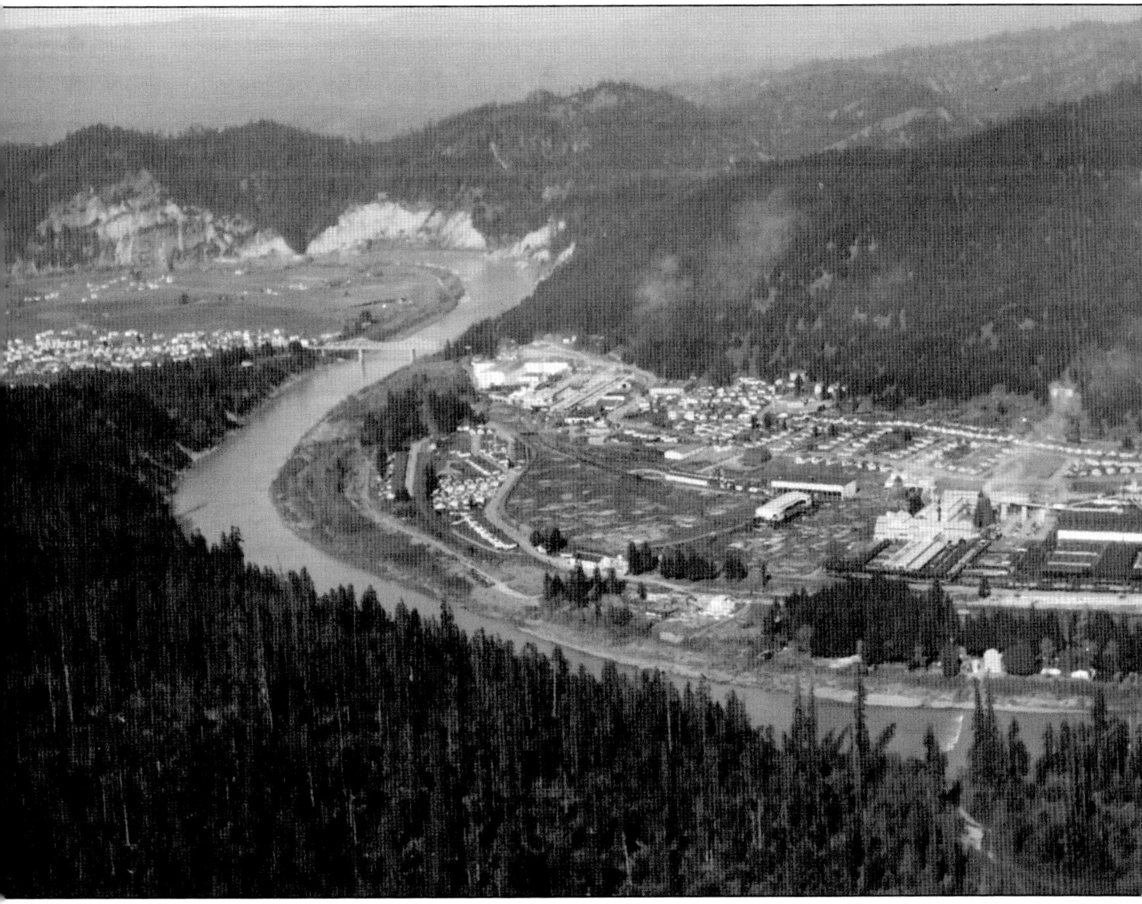

The sawmills in Scotia were purchased by the Mendocino Redwood Company and continue to operate, on a smaller scale, as the Humboldt Redwood Company. The houses and buildings that comprised the town of Scotia are now owned by the Town of Scotia Company, which continues to maintain the community. Rio Dell and Scotia remain close neighbors, helping each other out in times of need and trouble. Whether it be drought or flood, these sister cities, which started their continuing journey together, have maintained their close ties and friendships. Even with the loss of their major economic force with the downfall of Pacific Lumber, the father-figure company that cared so much for their communities, and the lack of the once-beloved morning whistle, the towns of Scotia and Rio Dell stand together, prepared to face whatever challenges the next 150 years may bring. (Courtesy of the Humboldt State University Library, Humboldt Room, Shuster Collection.)